Are You . . .

READY OR NOT
Here He Comes

G. EDWARD REID

Omega Productions
P.O. Box 600
Fulton, MD 20759

This book was
Edited by Lincoln E. Steed
Designed by Byron Steele
Cover design by Helcio Deslandes
Cover photo: PhotoDisc
Typeset: Times 11.5/13.5

PRINTED IN U.S.A

01 00 99 98 97   10 9 8 7 6 5 4 3 2

ISBN 1-878951-37-8

Introduction

With regard to the second coming of Christ, the emphasis in the New Testament is on **being** ready, with much information given on what that means and how to prepare. Jesus stated, "Therefore . . . be ready, for the Son of Man is coming at an hour you do not expect" (Matthew 24:44). But what does it mean to be ready? And are you ready for that day? Am I? Can one even know? Or do we just hope we are ready?

Many years ago, at a time when materialism, television, liberalism, and other concerns were hardly a factor, Ellen White wrote: "It is a solemn statement that I make to the church, that <u>not one in twenty whose names are registered upon the church books are prepared to close their earthly history, and would be as verily without God and without hope in the world as the common sinner</u>" *(Christian Service,* p. 41). Have things changed for the better? Have we as church members entered into a deeper relationship with our Saviour? Are we truly ready to meet our Maker?

As we study prophecy and current events we see a hand-in-glove match. It is clear to the serious Bible student that we are seeing the final events of earth's history taking place before our very eyes. What about those who are unconcerned and "too busy" to be bothered with what they term "sensationalism and doomism"? Many don't stop to realize that the invitation of our Lord to "be ready" does not have many options. In fact, when you really think about it, heaven has only one alternative—hell—eternal loss.

Let me illustrate from everyday life. Suppose someone invited you to the annual church picnic. You respond that you guess you won't go this year—that you will just stay home, relax, and watch TV. The invitation to heaven cannot be so lightly rejected because there are eternal consequences.

"Everything in the world is in agitation. The signs of the times are ominous. Coming events cast their shadows before. The Spirit of God is withdrawing from the earth, and calamity follows calamity by sea and by land. There are tempests, earthquakes, fires, floods, murders of every grade. Who can read the future? Where is security? There is assurance in nothing that is human or earthly. Rapidly are men ranging themselves under the banner they have chosen. Restlessly are they waiting and watching the movements of their leaders. There are those who are waiting and watching and working for our Lord's appearing. Another class are falling into line under the generalship of the first great apostate. **Few believe with heart and soul that we have a hell to shun and a heaven to win"** *(The Desire of Ages,* p. 636).

This book presents in a simple way the answers to two major concerns of last-day Christians. What does it mean to be ready? And, How can I be prepared for the very subtle deceptions of the devil that are hurled at the very elect in these last days? Jesus does not want to come and find us unprepared. He does not want us to be deceived by the devil. By carefully studying the inspired writings we can see clearly that not only is the Second Coming near at hand but that a way has been made for our rescue from this doomed planet. May this book strengthen your faith in God, your confidence in the prophetic revelations, and your resolve, if the Lord comes in our lifetime, to join Enoch and Elijah in being translated from this world to the heavenly kingdom.

Contents

CHAPTER 1

The Second Coming*

The battles with Satan will finally come to an end. There will be a mighty shaking and sifting. Many will be indifferent to important end-time events. Others will be led away from Scripture by "damnable" heresies. Many will reject the straight testimony of the True Witness. Vicious persecution will follow. But the battles with Satan <u>will</u> end. Then the church militant will become the church triumphant—at the second coming of Christ.

The Second Coming and the events surrounding it will be awesome—an unprecedented display of the majesty of God. It will be the most cataclysmic event on earth since the Creation. Everyone on earth will know that it's "over." There will be no more business, no more empty pleasure, no more traveling, no more crime, no more investments in the stock markets, no more Super Bowls, no more World Series, no more Nike commercials, no more "normal activities" of any kind. Everything stops!

God's faithful people have gone through a terrible trial. They have endured the time of persecution brought about by the Sunday law. They have been protected by God during the seven last plagues—"It shall not come nigh thee." Even as the skies brighten with Christ's coming the wicked are so filled with hatred for God's faithful that they throw aside the protection of life by human laws.

At that time God's people will not be found in plush homes in Adventist ghettos, condos at ski resorts, or beach houses on the coast. They will be found in prison cells or hidden in solitary retreats in the forests and mountains. They will not be watching television or videos or having vegeburger parties. They will be pleading with God for divine protection. He is their only hope for survival.

Apparently, the death decree, allowing God's people to be killed, is to go into effect at midnight on a certain day. In great anticipation of this hour the wicked shout taunts, announcing their evil intent. Crowds of evil men surround God's people. But the wicked do not understand that the very hour the death decree goes into effect is when God will deliver His people. The wicked will be prevented from carrying out their purpose. God will allow no martyrs after the close of probation.

Just as the wicked are about to totally annihilate God's people a series of supernatural events take place. First a dense blackness, deeper than the darkness of night, falls upon the earth. Then a massive and brilliant rainbow appears, spanning the entire heavens and seemingly encircling each praying company of God's people. The wicked freeze in their tracks and lose interest in killing God's people. Their only thought now is self-preservation.

The righteous, praying earnestly for deliverance, do not see the rainbow when the wicked do. But they hear a clear voice saying, "Look up." When they look up they see the rainbow and the heavens parting. The angry black clouds are moved back, and like Stephen, they can see all the way to heaven. There they see Jesus in the glory of God, seated upon His throne. Jesus assures them that they will be delivered. Losing all fear, they utter a shout of victory.

Signs and Wonders

Suddenly the sun appears in its full strength. Like a celestial light switch, the scene jolts from pitch-black midnight to high noon in an instant. Uncomprehending, the wicked are filled with terror and amazement. Nature which had appeared so orderly now seems to have gone berserk. The rivers stop flowing. Dark, heavy clouds roll in and crash against each other. Then God's voice, in tones like a mighty waterfall, proclaims, "It is done." His voice shakes the heavens and the earth. This shaking becomes a mighty earthquake. It is the "Big One." To use a modern expression: this is the mother of all earthquakes. The Bible says there has never been one so mighty and so great. Then it seems that every natural disaster known to man happens at the same time— tornadoes, hurricanes, tidal waves (tsunami), and hailstorms with fifty-pound stones! And these disasters truly are "acts of God."

The results of these great supernatural events are incredible. Mountain chains begin to sink into the earth. Inhabited islands disappear into the sea. Coastal cities are washed away. The hailstones crush the homes of the wealthy. And most significant, the prison walls are broken open and God's people are set free.

Those who are familiar with the Bible know that it tells of two major resurrections. The resurrection of life is experienced by the righteous dead at the second coming of Christ. The resurrection of damnation is when the wicked of all ages are raised at the end of the millennium. The wicked will see the righteous coming down to earth with Jesus in the Holy City. They will then suffer their final destruction—death by fire. The Bible also speaks of a special resurrection so that those who pierced Jesus can see Him coming in power and glory. Joining them in this resurrection will be some of the most violent opponents of truth down through the ages. And some of God's faithful people—those who have died in the faith of the third angel's message—are also raised to see the King in His beauty coming in the clouds of heaven.

The thick clouds that have rolled across the heavens open and shut, causing bursts of sun to shine through like the avenging eye of God. Lightning is so thick and constant that it seems as if the earth is covered in a sheet of flame. Mysterious voices declare the doom of the wicked. The wicked soldiers of fortune who were just about to destroy the people of God are now overwhelmed with fear. They cry for the rocks and the mountains to fall on them and to hide them from this great disaster.

The Righteous Raise Their Voices in Singing

But God's people—those who have sacrificed all for Him—are now forever secure, hidden "under His wings." They break into spontaneous Scripture songs, "The Lord is our refuge and strength. . . ." The clouds roll back, revealing the stars of heaven in awesome beauty. Glory streams earthward from the open gates of the heavenly city.

God's law on two huge tables of stone appears displayed in the heavens. The words are traced in fire much like the writing on the wall at Belshazzar's feast. Those who have violated God's law and mocked those who by God's grace kept the law are now filled with horror and despair. Too late they realize that they have been fighting against God.

Too late they realize that their religious leaders have led them to perdition while professing to guide them to the gates of paradise.

As the Ten Commandments fade from view in the heavens, the voice of God announces the day and hour of Christ's coming. His words surge throughout the earth like the loudest thunder. Then, as God's people stand listening with their faces turned upward, their glorification begins. "Their countenances are lighted up with His glory, and shine as did the face of Moses when he came down from Sinai. The wicked cannot look upon them." As this blessing settles upon God's people, there is a mighty shout of victory.

Jesus Returns as King of Kings

These events follow one another in rapid succession because "soon there appears in the east a small black cloud, about half the size of a man's hand." God's people recognize this as the literal second coming of Christ. As the cloud nears the earth it is apparent that it is made up of angels—millions of them. They are singing anthems of praise to Jesus. The heavens seem filled with angels. It is a picture that no one can adequately describe. As Jesus comes closer, the angels stop singing and there is an awful silence. The wicked are absolutely speechless. Raised to view this moment, those who condemned Jesus to death, mocked Him, spat on Him, whipped Him, and crucified Him are gripped with terror and remorse.

Aftershocks of the great earthquake are still causing the earth to tremble. The results of the quake are seen everywhere. There are deep caverns in the earth, and caves and overhanging rocks have appeared as parts of mountains have fallen away. The terror-stricken wicked run into these openings and cry out to the rocks to fall on them. These are their last words: "Fall on us, and hide us from the face of him that sitteth on the throne, and from the wrath of the Lamb: for the great day of his wrath is come; and who shall be able to stand?" (Revelation 6:16, 17, KJV).

The righteous, so recently blessed by the glory of God, also cry out. But their voices are full of joy and praise as they exclaim, "Lo, this is our God; we have waited for him, and he will save us" (Isaiah 25:9, KJV).

What a scene! Amid the cacophonous sounds of the natural disasters, the earthquake, the lightning, the thunder, the cries of the wicked, God's faithful cry out in praise. Then, louder than all, the voice of God is heard calling forth the sleeping saints. He does not make a specific call as He did in the case of the brother of Mary and Martha—"Lazarus, come forth." Now it's time for the general resurrection of the righteous—all who have been faithful since the days of Adam. God cries out, "Awake, Awake, Awake, ye that sleep in the dust, and arise!"

From all over the earth God's faithful people rise—those who have accepted God's great gift of forgiveness and regeneration. The prison house of death is broken open. The righteous come out of their graves with the same stature as they were at the time of their death. Adam, who is in the group, stands in great contrast to those who died in later generations. He is of lofty height and majestic form. But all arise with the freshness and vigor of eternal youth. Their bodies have been changed. No longer corrupted with disease and the scars of accidents and injuries, they are changed to beautiful immortal beings.

The Living Are Changed

The living righteous are also changed "in a moment, in the twinkling of an eye," as Paul puts it. When God announced the day and hour of His coming, they were glorified. Now they are made immortal. Significantly their change does not involve their character. That change has taken place during the hours of probation—accomplished by the indwelling Christ through the work of the Holy Spirit. Now an awesome reunion takes place. The angels gather the elect from throughout the globe. They bring little children to their mother's arms. Friends long separated by death are reunited, never to part again. As all the righteous who have ever lived stand together on the earth praising God, they begin to ascend together to meet the Lord in the air.

Ezekiel's description of God's chariot now becomes a reality. On each side of the cloudy chariot are wings, and beneath it are living wheels. As the chariot rolls upward, the wheels cry out, "Holy." The wings, as they move, cry, "Holy." The surrounding angels cry, "Holy, holy, holy, Lord God Almighty." And moving upward toward the New Jerusalem the redeemed cry out, "Alleluia!"

The trip to heaven takes seven days. On the way the saints are given an awesome view of the universe in its unpolluted splendor. The organizing committee of angels prepare the saints for the triumphal entrance into the Holy City. The saints are set in a hollow square around

Jesus. Jesus personally places the crown of victory on the head of each of the saints. Each crown bears the new name of the recipient. Each person is given a victor's palm and a shining harp.

With all these activities the travel time passes quickly, and soon they see the Holy City. As they approach the city Jesus opens wide the pearly gates. As the redeemed enter, they see the Paradise of God and the beautiful Garden of Eden.

Jesus Is Satisfied

Jesus sees the results of the travail or trial of His soul and is satisfied. His joy is in seeing the saints for whom He died now safe in the heavenly realms. The redeemed will also share the same joy as they see about them those for whom they have labored and prayed. The thrill is heightened by the realization that those won became evangelists themselves and have gained others.

In a dramatic moment amidst all the celebration, the two Adams are about to meet. Of course they met on the cloudy chariot, but now before the angels and the assembled throng, Jesus stands with outstretched arms ready to receive the father of our race. Adam is about to rush into the arms of Jesus, when he sees the nailprints in His hands. Instead of embracing Jesus, Adam falls at His feet and cries, "Worthy, worthy is the Lamb that was slain." Jesus gently lifts him up and points toward the Garden of Eden, Adam's former earthly home, from which he had been banished. For nearly 1,000 years Adam's life on earth had been filled with sorrow as he had witnessed the results of his sin—the dying leaf, the slain sacrifices, and the blight of sin. Faithfully he had repented of sin, trusting in the merits of the Saviour. He died in the hope of the resurrection. Now all is restored.

Adam runs to the garden, transported with joy. He sees the very trees that were once his delight—trees from which he had eaten in the days of his innocence and joy. He sees the vines that he had trained with his own hands. His mind begins to grasp the reality of what he is seeing. Jesus leads Adam to the tree of life, picks its special fruit, hands it to him, and tells him to eat. Adam looks about him at the great multitude of the saved—all standing in the Paradise of God. He casts his crown at the feet of Jesus and hugs Him in spontaneous gratitude. He picks up his harp and fills heaven with a triumphant solo, "Worthy,

worthy, worthy, is the Lamb that was slain, and lives again." All the faithful are so moved that they follow the example of Adam and lay their crowns at Jesus' feet and join him in praise to Jesus.

On the Sea of Glass

There they stand on the sea of glass—the ransomed of earth, those who have "gotten the victory over the beast, and over his image, and over his mark, and over the number of his name." They sing together a new song. It is the song of Moses and the Lamb—a song of deliverance. Down through the ages the faithful have been educated and disciplined in the school of trial. They have walked narrow paths and been purified in the furnace of affliction. They have endured opposition, hatred, and scorn. They went through terrible conflicts, practiced self-denial, and experienced bitter disappointments. By their own experience they learned the evil of sin and its power. These heirs of the kingdom have come from hovels, dungeons, scaffolds, the mountains, deserts, from the caves of the earth, and the depths of the sea. Millions went down to the grave in infamy because they refused to yield their faith. But now they stand on the sea of glass. The decisions of earth are reversed. They are no longer feeble, afflicted, scattered, and oppressed. They stand together in heaven clothed in robes far richer than those ever worn by the most honored of earth. Again they break forth in singing.

Reality begins to set in—a reality that will continue to unfold throughout eternity. Jesus is "the Man" in heaven. Every time an angel comes near Him, he covers his face and cries, "Holy, holy, holy." Everyone looks to Jesus as the reason for being—the source of all joy. Yet He is the one who humbled Himself to die on a cross to save to the uttermost any who would believe on Him. The people cannot hold back. Again and again they break forth in singing, "Worthy, worthy, is the Lamb." As they behold the beauty and joy of heaven they forget the past trials and struggles and exclaim together, "Heaven is cheap enough." Eternity is just beginning. Jesus looks again on the sight of the redeemed in heaven and, seeing the results of His great sacrifice, He is satisfied.

---

* No apologies for much of my source material for this chapter. Ellen White's description of these events in chapter 40 of *The Great Controversy* is a masterpiece of prophetic insight. Read it again sometime. It will give you goose bumps and an appreciation for the grandeur of the final events ahead.

CHAPTER 2

Ready or Not

We all know what it means to be ready. We've all had to be ready or get something ready many times in the past. Being ready makes one feel good, and not being ready is so frustrating. Pastors get sermons ready. Cooks get meals ready. Teachers get lesson plans ready. Builders get houses ready. Travelers get cars ready. And farmers get ready for harvest. And each of these people is frustrated and upset if they can't get ready.

Being ready generally requires some thought and action. Readiness presupposes some future event or activity. When one is ready there is a certain satisfaction—a lowered level of stress. Since I travel quite frequently by air, I have learned to prepare ahead of time for the appointment. This statement is axiomatic, of course, because it doesn't ever work to get ready after an event. Actually quite a lot of planning and preparation goes into getting ready for a trip. So I have a checklist of questions that I go through when "getting ready." What activities will I need to plan clothes for? What kind of group will I be speaking to? How many times will I speak? Do I have my notes for each presentation? When does the plane leave? Where are my tickets? How will I get to the airport? The list goes on!

Dictionary definitions of "ready" use the word "prepared" to define readiness. As in "prepared mentally or physically for some experience or action." The title of this book, *Ready or Not,* gives the impression—designed by the author and anticipated by the reader—that a great event is about to take place. And this event will require a state of readiness. In fact, it is the greatest event in terms of world impact since Creation. It goes without saying that we want to be ready.

14

The mission of John the Baptist and that of God's remnant messengers at the end of time is to go out in the spirit and power of Elijah "to make ready a people prepared for the Lord" (Luke 1:17).

It is a very sobering thought to realize, as the Bible indicates clearly in both the Old and New Testaments, that many who are looking for the coming of Christ will not be ready, and will as a consequence be lost. Those who are saved will be "ready." The purpose of this book is to discover what it means to be ready and how to get ready. No-one needs to be lost.

The Old Testament prophet Amos warned:

> "Woe to you who desire the day of the Lord!
> For what good is the day of the Lord to you?
> It will be darkness, and not light.
> It will be as though a man fled from a lion, and a bear met him!
> Or as though he went into the house, leaned his hand on the
>   wall, and a serpent bit him.
> Is not the day of the Lord darkness, and not light?
> Is it not very dark, with no brightness in it?" (Amos 5:18-20).

Jesus warned of the same danger in His sermon on the mount. And He wasn't just speaking of those who consciously choose the wrong road. In this case He is speaking about those who make a profession of Christianity.

"Not everyone who says to Me, 'Lord, Lord,' shall enter the kingdom of heaven, but he who does the will of My Father in heaven.

"Many will say to Me in that day, 'Lord, Lord, have we not prophesied in Your name, and done many wonders in Your name?'

"And then I will declare to them, 'I never knew you; depart from Me, you who practice lawlessness!'" (Matthew 7:21-23).

Many years ago, at a time when the materialism, television, liberalism, and other concerns of today were hardly a factor, Ellen White wrote: "It is a solemn statement that I make to the church, that not one in twenty whose names are registered upon the church books are prepared to close their earthly history, and would be as verily without God and without hope in the world as the common sinner" (Christian Service, p. 41). Ellen White wrote this statement while in Australia and sent it to America to be read before the General Conference in session on

February 4, 1893. She went on to say, "The end is near, stealing upon us so imperceptibly, so noiselessly, like the muffled tread of the thief in the night, <u>to surprise the sleepers</u> **off guard and unready**" *(ibid.).*

In answer to the question of His disciples, "What will be the sign of Your coming and the end of the world?" Jesus gave enough details to fill two chapters in our Bibles. He wanted us to know what it would be like in the end times. In Matthew 24 Jesus gives signs that one will find in our world just prior to His coming. Signs like wars, natural disasters, false prophets, etc. Then in chapter 25 He tells what it will be like in the church just before He comes. Jesus used three stories to emphasize: the importance of being ready, what to do while waiting, and the basis upon which the judgment is meted out. In each story only those who claim to be His followers are part of the picture. And yet in each story many of those who planned to go home with Him were left out.

In the first story the virgins—those who profess the truth—are divided into wise and foolish based on their reception of the Holy Spirit and His transforming power. The foolish are not ready for the coming of the bridegroom and end up missing the wedding. The wise, on the other hand, are described as "<u>those who were ready</u> went in with Him to the wedding; and the door was shut."

In the second story the Master's servants are each given talents, described as temporal means. (See *Testimonies,* vol. 1, p. 197.) Those who use this means wisely, investing it for the Master, are rewarded with the words "Well done." The unfaithful servant, on the other hand, buries his talent in the earth. He uses it for himself. He is cast into the outer darkness where there is weeping and gnashing of teeth.

In the third story those professing to believe in and follow God are divided into two groups, the sheep and the goats. The division is not based on belief, but on practice. The question is, Has your heart been transformed from selfishness to love? Have you spent time and money in support of those less fortunate—the least of these, My brethren?

With unquestionable urgency the words of Jesus call out to us today, "<u>Be ready</u>, for the Son of Man is coming at an hour you do not expect" (Matthew 24:44). Luke records a similar warning: "But take heed to yourselves, lest your hearts be weighed down with carousing, drunkenness, and <u>cares of this life</u>, and that Day come on you unexpectedly. For it will come as a snare on all those who dwell on the face of the whole earth. <u>Watch therefore</u>, and pray always that you may be counted worthy to escape all these things that will come to pass, and to stand before the Son of Man" (Luke 21:34-36). These words were given to the Christian community. There is a need for readiness, watching, and faithfulness on the part of God's children.

"Being ready" includes having a sanctified relationship with Jesus that will equip us to share the reasons for our faith. "But sanctify the Lord God in your hearts, and <u>always be ready</u> to give a defense to everyone who asks you a reason for the hope that is in you, with <u>meekness and fear</u>" (1 Peter 3:15). The attitude of the presenter has much to do with the reception.

Those who get to know God through the study of His Word realize that He is "good, and ready to forgive, and abundant in mercy to all those who call upon" Him (Psalm 86:5). As we contemplate God's plan for us we are confronted with a high and even unattainable standard in our own strength. But God has promised the power for success to all who believe. Whenever God points out the standard, He always shows the way and provides the power to reach it.

God's High Standard

Inside the Edmonton, Alberta, mall—one of the largest enclosed shopping areas in the world—there is a recreation and entertainment area that includes many exciting rides. I don't remember the name of this particular ride—this type of ride usually has a name like "mind bender" or "the snake ride" or some other creative name. Since there is a very significant danger factor, such as falling out while you are upside down, there are numerous safety devices. These things include harnesses and belts, etc. While observing those who were purchasing tickets I noted that there was a height requirement. If you weren't at least that tall you weren't allowed to ride. There were no exceptions. You couldn't say, "But my dad will sit right beside me and hold my hand," or "I promise to hold on tight." If you were not a certain height you didn't get on. There were no exceptions. In this case the standard was arbitrarily set as a certain height.

We must all understand that God has a standard for those who ride on the cloud to heaven. It is not arbitrary. There is a reason. Sin will not arise the second time. So no one will be allowed in who does not meet God's standard. It is a high standard and there are no exceptions. You meet the standard or you don't go.

Sometimes we are tempted to try to explain it away or change it, but God's standard is perfection and holiness. The Bible is clear regarding what God expects of us. "Therefore <u>you shall be **perfect**</u>, just as your Father in heaven is perfect" (Matthew 5:48). "Pursue peace with all men, and **holiness**, <u>without which no one will see the Lord</u>" (Hebrews 12:14). "<u>You shall be **holy**</u>, for I the Lord your God am holy" (Leviticus 19:2). "He chose us in Him before the foundation of the world, <u>that we should be **holy** and without blame before Him in love</u>" (Ephesians 1:4).

Wow! What a standard. Does God really expect us to be perfect and holy? We know that the answer is yes, because men and women who followed God in the past have been described as being perfect and holy. Peter talks about "holy women, who trusted God" (1 Peter 3:5). God describes His people as a "holy nation" (1 Peter 2:9). And we note from Peter's second sermon that "God has spoken by the mouth of all His holy prophets since the world began" (Acts 3:21).

The list could go on and on. The Shunammite couple who built an extra room for the prophet Elisha called him a "holy man of God" (2 Kings 4:9). The process of inspiration, by which God speaks to man, is described as "holy men of God speaking as they were moved by the Holy Ghost" (2 Peter 1:21). Job was described by God as "perfect and upright" (Job 1:8). And Noah is described as "just and perfect" (Genesis 6:9).

Another way that we know that God expects holiness of His people is by what He says when all is said and done. "He who is unjust, let him be unjust still; he who is filthy, let him be filthy still; he who is righteous, let him be righteous still; he who is holy, let him be holy still" (Revelation 22:11). There will be only two groups when Jesus completes His work of judgment: the saved and the lost, the good and the bad, the righteous and the wicked. Revelation presents on the one side the unjust and the filthy—obviously forever lost. On the other side are the righteous and the holy—obviously forever saved. We will study further how one attains to the state of righteousness and holiness; but it is clear to anyone who reads the Scriptures that God's standard has not changed. We need to address the topic of readiness in such a way that a reader can easily understand it and be able to explain to others this most important experience.

The Bible uses many interesting metaphors to describe readiness. Concepts such as the wedding garment, the robe of righteousness, oil in the lamps, and waiting and watching. By looking at these important illustrations we see what God expects and understand how to do it.

Ellen White explains the standard and how to reach it in a very straightforward and simple way. "The condition of eternal life is now just what it always has been,—just what it was in Paradise before the fall of our first parents,—perfect obedience to the law of God, perfect righteousness. If eternal life were granted on any condition short of this, then the happiness of the whole universe would be imperiled. The way would be open for sin, with all its train of woe and misery, to be immortalized" *(Steps to Christ,* p. 62). She follows this precise explanation with the "how" of justification and sanctification.

"Since we are sinful, unholy, we cannot perfectly obey the holy law. We have no righteousness of our own with which to meet the claims of the law of God. But Christ has made a way of escape for us. He lived on earth amid the trials and temptations such as we have to meet. He lived a sinless life. He died for us, and now He offers to take our sins and give us His righteousness. If you give yourself to Him, and accept Him as your Saviour, then, sinful as your life may have been, for His sake you are accounted righteous. Christ's character stands in the place of your character, and you are accepted before God just as if you had not sinned" *(ibid.).* This is called justification— God's substitutionary death for our sins.

"More than this, Christ changes the heart. He abides in your heart by faith. You are to maintain this connection with Christ by faith and the continual surrender of your will to Him; and so long as you do this, He will work in you to will and to do according to His good pleasure. . . . Then with Christ working in you, you will manifest the same spirit and do the same good works—works of righteousness, obedience" *(ibid.,* pp. 62, 63). This is called sanctification—God's regenerating power in our lives—effecting a change in attitude, character, and lifestyle.

Through justification we are forgiven and through sanctification we are changed into the likeness of God. Both aspects of our salvation come as a gift from God. But we respond with "obedience—the service and allegiance of love—the true sign of discipleship" *(ibid.,* p. 60). As the psalmist so aptly stated, "God is my strength and power, and He makes my way perfect" (2 Samuel 22:33). "So we have nothing in ourselves of which to boast. We have no ground for self-exaltation. <u>Our only ground of hope is in the righteousness of Christ imputed to us **and** in that wrought by His Spirit working in and through us</u>" *(ibid.,* p. 63).

We know that God has a standard we must meet for admittance to heaven. We know that others have met the standard. <u>We know that it is possible to meet the standard only by the power of God</u>. This is what it means to be ready. Just what is the holiness and perfection that God requires? "Higher than the highest human thought can reach is God's ideal for His children. Godliness—godlikeness—is the goal to be reached" *(Education,* p. 18).

My feelings right now, having finished the research and writing of *Even at the Door* and *Sunday's Coming,* are very much like those expressed by Ellen White at a tent meeting in Oakland, California, on July 2, 1869. She stated: "We have the deepest interest that this meeting, at this time, shall not be in vain. We want to see the work of God prospering. We know that it is a very important time. It is a solemn time. We feel the importance of our people's arousing and awaking, that they may understand the time in which we live. <u>The probation of all must soon close. And are we ready for the appearing of the Son of Man in the clouds of heaven</u>? Have we the wedding garment on? Or shall we be of that number that shall be left outside because unready? How anxious we are that every one of you should have the wedding garment on. Not the garment of your own righteousness, but the righteousness of Christ; that you should have this on, and so be prepared, that, when the examination of the guests shall take place, you many not be of those that shall be bound both hand and foot, and cast out, because unready. <u>It is readiness that we want</u>. <u>It is fitness that we want</u>. And who is ready? <u>To be unready will be an entire failure</u>. <u>To be unready will be an eternal loss</u>. But if we can, in this day of probation, see that we are unready; if we can here see our wretchedness, and our need, and now humble ourselves before God, He will be found of us, and He will work for us mightily. And now is the time for us to begin to work. You that have not entered, heart and soul and spirit, into this work, now is the time for you to engage in it with all your souls" *(Review and Herald,* August 17, 1869).

Of course this was written a long time ago, but the questions are still very relevant. What preparation have we made for the judgment? Have we made our peace with God? Are we concerned about those around us? Are we practicing what we preach? We all must realize that profession is worthless without a practice that enters into our daily lives. Are we getting ready to meet the King? Will we hear His words "Come up higher" when He comes?

Now is the time and here is the place where we are to make the preparation. "This world is a training school for the higher school, this life is a preparation for the life to come. Here we are to be prepared for entrance into the heavenly courts. <u>Here we are to **receive** and **believe** and **practice** the truth until we are made ready for a home with the saints in light</u>" *(Maranatha,* p. 57).

A few years ago I had a weekend speaking appointment in the Atlanta area. I made all the mental, physical, and spiritual preparations. I was ready. My son was taking me to the airport in Baltimore when he asked, "What airline are you taking today?" I reached into my pocket for my ticket to double-check. I knew I was flying Delta. And then I rechecked the departure time. My scheduled flight left an hour before we got to the airport! Apparently, the departure time of a flight I had taken earlier in the week had stuck in my mind, and I had failed to check again the night before when my current flight departed.

Fortunately for me, Delta had another flight with an available seat that left later that morning for Atlanta, and I was able to meet my appointment—albeit with very little time to spare. When Jesus comes back there is not a second trip for those who are unprepared to meet the first one. The first one is the last one. We all know that now. God does not want to surprise us. He wants us to be ready. We must be ready. And we can be ready in His power.

As I have done the research for this book I have described my findings to my friends as exciting and awesome. This is not a doom and gloom book. This is a book about the exciting activity of getting ready to meet the King of kings. This is no time for discouragement, because Jesus lives to make intercession for us. He is interested in our eternal welfare. And He will help all those who call upon Him.

CHAPTER 3

Not Just Somewhere in Time

Many stories begin "Once upon a time . . ." or "Long ago and far, far away . . ." The fables that follow such introductions are simply the imaginings of men. After all, life is far too important to base it on a fairy tale or a soap opera. We need to know that the words and story line of Scripture are very much of reality. They impact where we live—today. Many so-called Christians today dismiss the plain statement of Scripture, saying, "Oh sure, God is involved somehow, but since He is eternal, time does not enter in too much in His dealings with men." The theistic evolution concept, which seems to be spreading in its acceptance today, presents a picture of a God out there someplace, but things just happen in a rather random manner.

The truth outlined in His Word ("thy word is truth," John 17:17) is that God is very precise in His dealings with men. God has a plan and He is following it precisely. This was the central theme of my book *Even at the Door*. What's more, He wants us to know just where we are in time! God's prophetic time line can only add urgency to the question of readiness addressed in this book.

From the time of Adam on, mankind has looked for a Saviour. Enoch, the seventh from Adam, was even given a vision of the Second Coming. Abraham saw the heavenly home "afar off." But as salvation history progressed God wanted mankind to understand more precisely the parameters of the great controversy—the battle between good and evil and the final victory of good.

There are many time prophecies in the Scriptures. And it is evident when one studies these time prophecies that God is very trustworthy in His predictions. At just the appointed time the predicted event takes place. Apparently, God used the lifetime of Methuselah and the 120-year preaching of Noah to predict the year that the Flood would come. There was also the prediction and fulfillment of the 400 years of affliction in Egypt (see Gen. 15:13 and Ex. 12:41), the 70 years of Babylonian exile, and the 70-week prophecy that pinpointed the work of the Messiah. In these shorter time prophecies last-day Christians can understand how God works—He does what He says He will do, and He does it right on time.

Now we can reason as God asks us to. We can go from the known to the unknown—from the fulfilled prophecies to faith in those yet to be fulfilled. In the prophecies of Daniel and the Revelation the Christian church can understand not only the parameters of prophetic time, but they also contain a double-checking mechanism, by identifying the rise and fall of the world empires and showing their dealings with God's people. (These prophecies are explained in detail in the appendix of my book *Sunday's Coming!)*

Three great prophecies remained to be fulfilled for the Christian church: the 1260 years, the 2300 years, and God's great week of time. The 1260-year prophecy was first given in the time of the prophet Daniel, some 500 years before Christ's first advent. It spans the time between the fall of Rome and the beginning of the time of the end. As succeeding prophecies are progressive and give more details, Daniel 7 adds information on the little horn power that is not given in the image prophecy of Daniel 2. Protestant Bible scholars have identified this period as the 1260-year time span from A.D. 538 to 1798—the time of the papal domination of the Christian world.

Regarding the tremendous prophetic insights given by Daniel, we are told: "Honored by men with the responsibilities of state and with the secrets of kingdoms bearing universal sway, Daniel was honored by God as His ambassador, and was given many revelations of the mysteries of ages to come. His wonderful prophecies, as recorded by him in chapters 7 to 12 of the book bearing his name, were not fully understood even by the prophet himself; but before his life labors closed, he was given the blessed assurance that 'at the end of the days'—in the closing period of this world's history—he would again be permitted to stand in his lot and place. It was not given him to understand all that God had revealed of the divine purpose. 'Shut up the words, and seal the book,' he was directed concerning his prophetic writings; these were to be sealed 'even to the time of the end.' 'Go thy way, Daniel,' the angel once more directed the faithful messenger of Jehovah; 'for the words are closed up and sealed till the time of the end. . . . Go thou thy way till the end be: for thou shalt rest, and stand in thy lot at the end of the days.' Daniel 12:4, 9, 13.

"As we near the close of this world's history, the prophecies recorded by Daniel demand our special attention, as they relate to the very time in which we are living. With them should be linked the teachings of the last book of the New Testament Scriptures. Satan has led many to believe that the prophetic portions of the writings of Daniel and of John the revelator cannot be understood. But the promise is plain that special blessing will accompany the study of these prophecies. 'The wise shall understand' (verse 10), was spoken of the visions of Daniel that were to be unsealed in the latter days; and of the revelation that Christ gave to His servant John for the guidance of God's people all through the centuries, the promise is, 'Blessed is he that readeth, and they that hear the words of this prophecy, and keep those things which are written therein.' Revelation 1:3. . . . .

"A careful study of the working out of God's purpose in the history of nations and in the revelation of things to come, will help us to estimate at their true value things seen and things unseen, and to learn what is the true aim of life. Thus, viewing the things of time in the light of eternity, we may, like Daniel and his fellows, live for that which is true and noble and enduring. And learning in this life the principles of the kingdom of our Lord and Saviour, that blessed kingdom which is to endure for ever and ever, we may be prepared at His coming to enter with Him into its possession" *(Prophets and Kings,* pp. 547, 548).

Those who have studied these important prophecies have concluded that, after generations, centuries, and millenniums, the whole plan of salvation comes to its "time of the end" in 1798. The picture of Revelation 13 begins to come into clear focus with the wounding of the Papacy and the rise of the United States to a place of prominence in world history. That means we are now living in the time of the end!

The second long-time prophecy, referred to earlier, is the 2300-year prophecy. The establishment of the beginning and ending dates of this prophecy are firmly established because of a fixed interim event—

the ministry of the Messiah. The ending date is October 22, 1844. When those who first understood this time line established this date they had their math right but mistakenly thought that it would be the date for the second coming of Christ. Of course, it was actually the date for the beginning of the great pre-advent judgment. When Jesus comes the second time, His reward is with Him, so it is obvious that the judgment has already taken place—at least the guilt or innocence part of the judgment. The fact that the 2300-year prophecy is fulfilled underscores the reality that we are not only living in the time of the end, we are also living during the time of the great day of atonement—the time of the pre-advent judgment.

The third end-time time line is the great week of time. The early Adventist pioneers wrote and spoke about this time line. Some of the most notable were Hiram Edson, O.R.L. Crosier, F. B. Hahn, James White, Joseph Bates, J. N. Andrews (with six full articles on the topic printed in the *Review and Herald*—July 17 to August 21, 1883), and Ellen G. White. (For an in-depth study of this topic consult my book *Even at the Door.)* This time line is not given to set a day and hour for the Second Coming, but rather to give the general parameters for the probation and judgment of mankind. It is, however, significant to note that we are obviously very near the end of the sixth millennium and the beginning of the seventh millennium—the great Sabbath of the earth when it will rest in desolation. (See *Bible Readings for the Home,* current hardback edition, pp. 317, 321 or the chapter on the millennium in any edition.)

This review of grand and awful Bible prophecies should underscore the fact that we are not just somewhere in time—we are at the very end. The Creation, the Fall of man, the Flood, the Exodus, the Babylonian captivity, the birth of Christ, the fall of Rome, the period of papal dominance, the Reformation, the beginning of the time of the end, the beginning of the great pre-advent judgment—these events are all history. Today's reality is: We could well be the generation that sees the literal second coming of Christ and are either translated live from earth to heaven or are slain by the brightness of His coming. The relevant and most pressing question is Are we ready or do we even care?

CHAPTER 4

Signs Upon Signs

The great time lines of the Bible place us at the time of the end. The Bible also identifies the "signs" or conditions that will exist at the end—these are in abundant supply today. Natural disasters, calamities, and momentous events in the religio-political world quickly come to mind.

People are noticing the frequency and intensity of natural disasters, floods, tornadoes, and bitter cold winters that kill livestock and halt commerce. We know that sometime in the near future the devil himself will appear on earth in a masterful attempt to personate Christ, but "even now he is at work. In accidents and calamities by sea and by land, in great conflagrations, in fierce tornadoes and terrific hailstorms, in tempests, floods, cyclones, tidal waves, and earthquakes, in every place and in a thousand forms, Satan is exercising his power. He sweeps away the ripening harvest, and famine and distress follow. He imparts to the air a deadly taint, and thousands perish by the pestilence. These visitations are to become more and more frequent and disastrous. Destruction will be upon both man and beast. 'The earth mourneth and fadeth away,' 'the haughty people . . . do languish. The earth also is defiled under the inhabitants thereof; because they have transgressed the laws, changed the ordinance, broken the everlasting covenant.' Isaiah 24:4, 5" *(The Great Controversy,* pp. 589, 590).

Today there is such a frequency of calamities, accidents by land, sea, air, and rail that the authorities are hardly through with one investigation or cleanup before another event occurs. In fact, the financial losses for these disasters and calamities is so great that in early 1996 the news magazines reported that Lloyd's of London, the world's largest and most well-known casualty insurer, was at the point of insolvency.

Wars and political instability continue to cause death and displacement of millions. Things are not getting better! Rwanda's refugee crisis and the Chechneian struggle for independence are two prime examples.

The Pope Endorses Evolution

One of the major religious bombshells of 1996 was the news that Pope John Paul II had endorsed the theory of evolution as "more than a hypothesis" and a more likely explanation for the origins of man than the Genesis story. On October 23, 1996, the pope sent a message to members of the Pontifical Academy of Science meeting in plenary assembly. The text of his message is recorded in *Inside the Vatican,* January 1997, pp. 28, 29. Apparently, this was not "news" to many in the Catholic community, but to many Protestants and Bible-believing Catholics it was a real shocker.

All the major news services picked up the story. Reuter's, *Time, U.S. News, Christianity Today, World,* The Washington *Post,* The New York *Times,* and many more covered the story.

The *U.S. News* report was headlined **"The Pope and Darwin."**

Did God create mankind in His image, as the Bible says, or did humans evolve from animals, as Darwin theorized nearly 150 years ago? According to Pope John Paul II, evolution may be the better explanation. Weighing in on a debate that has divided Christians for decades, the pope declared that evolution is "more than just a theory" and is fully compatible with the Christian faith. But in a letter to the Pontifical Academy of Sciences, he also reaffirmed church teachings that while the human body may have evolved gradually, the soul "is immediately created by God" in each person.

"The pope's statement may rankle biblical fundamentalists, who take the Genesis creation story literally, but it is likely to have little impact on the Roman Catholic Church, which has long looked favorably on evolution. In 1950, Pope Pius XII called evolution a 'serious hypothesis' worthy of study. And as early as the fifth century, St. Augustine warned against a literal reading of the Genesis creation account. But John Paul II went further than previous popes in declaring that a 'convergence' of scientific evidence gathered in the past 50 years makes 'a significant argument in favor of this theory'" *(U.S. News & World* Report, November 4, 1996, p. 12).

In its coverage of the news the New York *Times* stated that the pope's statement "is unlikely to change significantly the teaching of evolution in the Catholic schools in the United States, where it is already a standard part of the curriculum." There has been quite a backlash from the Christian community. However, in an attempt to defend the pope's statement a writer in the Catholic newspaper *Our Sunday Visitor,* November 24, 1996, stated: "I can't understand the controversy about Pope John Paul II's statement on evolution. Apparently, the shock has to do with the public's ability to disassociate contradictory evidence. The rejection of evolution requires a special selectivity about modern information. In the century and a half since Charles Darwin first reported the news of his theory, investigations have never contradicted an apparent evolutionary trajectory of the species. <u>So why the consternation about the Pope saying that evolution seems to be the path that God's creation took</u>?"

The problem is very simple. How can one say that he accepts Christ as Saviour in the third chapter of John and at the same time reject Him as personal Creator in the first chapter of John? Even more significant is the rejection of God's six-day Creation account in the fourth commandment. Could this be another evidence that Sunday's coming? The Sabbath, as a memorial of Creation, is of great importance to Bible-believing Christians. However, another theological problem arises when one believes in evolution. What about the Resurrection? If God did not create me, why should I say that He will recreate me? To those who believe in fiat creation—ie., He spoke and it was done—the Resurrection is no problem. If one's life is ended in a fire or even if we simply return to dust in the grave, that is no problem with God. He has our complete DNA number in His mind and can recreate us in every detail—memory and all. With evolution the chances of my evolving again are nil!

The Associated Press Story

On August 11, 1996, Jan Cienski, an Associated Press writer from Richmond, Virginia, wrote an article that appeared in numerous papers across the United States. The article was headlined under several titles such as "Book Calls Pope the Devil's Ally," and "Adventist Book Denounced as Anti-Catholic." Cienski was referring to the book *God's*

Answers to Your Questions, an abridged version of the book *Bible Readings for the Home,* which has been in print for over 100 years, with millions of copies in circulation. This new edition, printed in the magabook format, is sold by student literature evangelists door-to-door. Cienski, a Roman Catholic, was offended to read in the prophecy section of the book that the seventh head of the beast of Revelation 13 is the papacy, or the antichrist.

He said that after deciding to write a story about the book he contacted both Roman Catholic and Protestant leaders and both told him the same story: "The book's conclusions have no biblical basis" and "It's outrageous and inflammatory and untrue biblically in any sense." Cienski quoted William Donohue of the Catholic League, who stated: "Linking the pope to the Antichrist springs from the days of the Reformation 500 years ago . . . but that has not been done in mainline Protestant churches for centuries." Sibley Towner, a Presbyterian theology professor, was quoted as saying, "Anti-Catholic language these days usually comes from small sectarian groups affiliated with right-wing political causes such as the Ku Klux Klan." In his conclusion Cienski states that much of his concern is that "this book comes at a time when relations between evangelical Christians and Catholics have been improving. In 1994, Southern Baptists, the country's largest Protestant denomination, and the Catholic Church endorsed a dialogue between the two denominations. The Christian Coalition also has been trying to build ties to socially conservative Catholics" (Richmond *Times-Dispatch,* August 11, 1996).

When one digests this material, several very important points are made:

1. It is stated that the Adventist interpretation is without biblical foundation.
2. No one believes that the papacy is the antichrist anymore—we are told.
3. Only right-wing political groups like the KKK use anti-Catholic language.
4. Protestants and Catholics are building ties now.

Yes, the cause for which many Protestant Reformers gave their lives has now been abandoned by most Protestant denominations. Though most of the Reformers, in their writings, took the position that the pope was the antichrist, many are backpeddling now to be more "politically correct." But we know that "now is the time for God's people to show themselves true to principle. When the religion of Christ is most held in contempt, when His law is most despised, then should our zeal be the warmest and our courage and firmness the most unflinching. To stand in defense of truth and righteousness when the majority forsake us, to fight the battles of the Lord when champions are few— this will be our test. At this time we must gather warmth from the coldness of others, courage from their cowardice, and loyalty from their treason" *(Testimonies for the Church,* vol. 5, p. 136).

Growing Marian Devotion

Perhaps the most well-known and most visited Marian shrine in the United States is the Fowler Farm in Conyers, Georgia. Nancy Fowler, "a 48-year-old housewife and mother of two teenaged sons, has attracted an estimated 2 million 'pilgrims' to her 180-acre farm in Conyers, Ga., where apparitions and other 'miraculous' phenomena are claimed to be taking place."

George Collins, "a retired civil engineer from Mississippi, transcribes and interprets the 'messages' Mary allegedly has been giving Fowler on the 13th of every month since 1990. He is one of many unpaid volunteers—calling themselves 'Our Loving Mother's Children'— who live here on Fowler's farm, which has become one of the most celebrated sites of alleged Marian apparitions in the world today."

"Though little is known about Fowler's background, literature printed by Our Loving Mother's Children gives some information on how the alleged visionary's experiences began. In 1983, Fowler was working as a registered nurse, but her well-paying and prestigious job left no time for her family or the practice of her faith. She began to be harassed by demons, she claims, and it was only after she quit her job and started attending Mass again that she found relief. But not for long. Collins explained that Fowler fell into a deep depression soon after, and in February 1987, when she was in 'a state of great personal despair,' Christ supposedly appeared to her in a silent apparition in her home. 'Jesus appeared to her and changed her life,' Collins said. 'But He had more in store for her than one glorious appearance.' In October of that same year, during a pilgrimage to Medjugorje, Bosnia-

Herzegovina, Fowler claims to have received a heavenly call to become a prophet. After she returned home, her alleged visions of Mary began sometime in 1988, and two years later, Mary supposedly told Fowler to go public with the 'messages.'"

Many individuals who have become part of the Our Loving Mother's Children group have moved to Georgia, where many actually live on the Fowler farm, from other states. In other words their entire lives have been modified as a result of this Marian phenomena. For example, "Mrs. Dale Peters moved from Florida to Atlanta to be near the site. 'I had always been a good Catholic, but I came to Conyers looking for something deeper because I knew there had to be something more than I had,' she explains. 'After my first visit, there were some questions. It was a lot to swallow. But then I kept feeling this call to return again and again.'"

"Out of all the Conyers devotees, however, perhaps none has contributed more to the cause than Robert Hughes, a wealthy Virginia wholesale tile distributor. It was Hughes who purchased the untilled farm Fowler and the others utilize at a sheriff's auction for $200,000. Hughes explained how he had learned that the neighbors were 'giving Nancy a hard time because people were parking on their land on apparition days. I learned the farm next to Nancy's house was up for sale, and I suggested to Nancy that I put up the money to buy it,' he said. 'As we sat at the kitchen table the day I made the offer, we all suddenly began to smell fresh roses, so I felt that was God's sign for me to buy the land.' Though they [Our Loving Mother's Children] would prefer that the 'miracles' weren't necessary for people to believe in the 'messages' from Mary, Hughes frankly admits that without the 'small signs,' he probably never would have committed so much to the cause. 'I agree that it would be better if we didn't need the signs,' he said. 'But people are human, and we need signs to deepen our faith. The signs helped me, encouraged me.'"

Supporters of the Conyers phenomena admit that "a large percentage of those who come to Conyers do so 'in genuine searches for answers to the riddle of life.' They go on to say, 'There is no question that the vast majority of those who visit [Conyers] willingly testify that her [Nancy Fowler's] claims are valid. However, it is no secret that many of these same pilgrims come to the site in search of something and decide not to leave empty-handed—even if it means convincing themselves that they witnessed miraculous signs.'"

The Catholic Church has not officially recognized the validity of the miracles or apparitions at the Fowler farm, but they did run a two-part series of articles totaling four pages in the Catholic weekly, *Our Sunday Visitor*. The quotes above were taken from the second article, printed on September 22, 1996. Both articles were prepared by Robert R. Holton, a senior correspondent for *Our Sunday Visitor*.

The December 1996 issue of *Life* magazine devoted the cover and 12 pages of pictures and text to Mary. The article begins, "You could copy on an eight-and-a-half-by-eleven sheet everything there is about Mary in the New Testament. . . . To get from such skimpy evidence to what she has become is an astonishing example of how an idea can develop out of small beginnings. . . . Why are two billion Hail Marys said daily? Why did five million people, many non-Christian, visit Lourdes this year to drink of the healing waters? Why did more than 10 million trek to Guadalupe to pray to Our Lady? Why is it thought that more girls have been named for Mary than for any other historical figure? Why the apparitions? Why the need to talk with *her?* What is it about Mary?" *(Life,* December 1996).

The article gives a brief history of the Marian phenomena. "The Mary of today started not with Christ's birth, nor with the gospels, but with a second-century document called *The Book of James*. The text filled in details of Mary's birth, marriage, Annunciation. It was not then—and never has been—accorded canonical authority, but it didn't prevent it from inspiring the tradition of devotion to Our Lady. But even with *James,* Mary was barely formed. In the second century the concept of Jesus' virgin birth was fiercely debated, and the notion that Mary remained a virgin her entire life wasn't on the table. By the fifth century, however, Mary's perpetual virginity was part of who she was. The Counsel of Ephesus in 431 accorded her, against much opposition, the title Mother of God. This boosted Mary toward being, as historian Karen Armstrong puts it, 'a major celebrity.'

"In medieval times a metaphysical concept attached itself to Mary, that of the Immaculate Conception—often confused with the virgin birth of Jesus—which held that she was free from Original Sin from her first moment in the womb of her mother, rendering her saintly even before birth. Mary herself is said to have confirmed the doctrine in a fourteenth-century visitation to St. Bridget of Sweden.

"To the degree that Catholicism departed from the simple biblical view of Mary and listed toward a more ethereal Mary, the Protestant Reformation begged to differ with Rome. The reformers—Luther, Calvin, others—saw a good, married, loving mother as an excellent role model. End of story. The Mary of the Immaculate Conception seemed to be claiming spiritual attributes properly reserved for Christ. The Vatican turned a deaf ear to the Reformers, boosting Marian devotion at the Council of Trent (1545-63) and instituting the Feast of the Holy Rosary in 1573. Hail Marys fell like rain, and new prayers to Our Lady were written every day.

"During the past 150 years, the Vatican has issued [only] three new dogmas, and two have concerned Mary; first, absolute belief in the Immaculate Conception, and second [in 1950], in the Assumption—Mary's bodily rise to heaven. Both upset the Protestants mightily, but what could they do?

"In 1969 Pope Paul VI lifted a canonical requirement that religious books, including ones on apparitions, be approved." This opened the door to the unofficial acceptance of the nearly 200 apparition sites around the world and the books written about them.

"Pope John Paul II [the current pope] has been the leader of the world's Catholics since 1978. He has also been the standard-bearer for the world's classical Marians. . . . His motto is *Totus tuus* (All yours—referring to Mary). When he survived the would-be assassin Mehmet Ali Agca's bullets on May 13, 1981, he noted that the attack occurred on the anniversary of the 1917 Church-approved apparition at Fatima, Portugal, and he credited his survival to intercession by the Blessed Virgin. When godless Communism fell in the Eastern bloc, which included his beleaguered homeland, the pope said this, too, was thanks to Mary."

The *Life* article concludes, "One of the intriguing aspects of the latest rise of Mary is this: The emotional need for her is so irresistible to a troubled world that people without an obvious link to the Virgin are being drawn to her. It's not news that Muslims revere Mary as a pure and holy saint—she's mentioned 34 times in the Koran, which upholds her virginal conception of Jesus—but to see large numbers of Muslims making pilgrimages to Christian Marian shrines is a remarkable thing. Interdenominational Marian prayer groups are springing up throughout the world. Many Protestants, even some who still reject notions of a supernatural Virgin, miss Mary. 'I envy Catholicism's Mary,' says Forrest Church, raised a Catholic but now a Unitarian minister. 'Protestantism has nothing that can replace the part that she could or might play in their churches.'

"Forrest Church has a dream—of a middle-ground Mary, an Everymary who can transcend ideologies and give this tumultuous world the mother it needs. '<u>I would like to think that she could be a bridge between religions,</u>' he says, '. . . <u>someday . . . I think we can come together through Mary</u>.'" The article's authors themselves conclude, "Mary, in a world we cannot see, might lead to an ecumenical reunion of Christian churches."

With these thoughts in mind there are two other significant phenomena associated with the current rise of Marian interest. The first is a book recently written by Dr. Charles Dickson, a Lutheran pastor who is currently serving as the pastor of St. John's church in Taylorsville, North Carolina. The book, titled *A Protestant Pastor Looks at Mary,* is being advertised in full-page ads in the Catholic weekly, *Our Sunday Visitor,* and is available from Our Sunday Visitor Press. The ad blurb includes the wording "Now Lutheran pastor Charles Dickson provides a voice of reason in the centuries-old controversy. By bridging the gap between the Protestant and Catholic views, Dr. Dickson brings all Christians—Catholics and Protestants—to a greater understanding of Mary of Nazareth, the unique woman chosen to be the Mother of the Saviour. Dr. Dickson . . . is active in ecumenical work" *(Our Sunday Visitor,* September 8, 1996, p. 14).

Second, *Inside the Vatican* is now reporting that study groups and others are planning for and urging the pope to issue a "new Marian Dogma" which would define Mary as "Coredemptrix, Mediatrix of all Graces, and Advocate of the People of God." The article "Toward a New Marian Dogma" goes on to state that "there is serious consideration being given within the Vatican to the proclamation of a Marian dogma in conjunction with the celebrations of the Great Jubilee of the Year 2000." The report states that Vincenzo Cardinal Fagiolo, the pope's highest-ranking advisor on canon law, has already prepared a statement urging the pope to issue the dogma. It states, "May God grant to the Church the joy of opening the Third Millennium of the Christian era with the dogmatic proclamation of Mary Mediatrix. Have courage, Holy Father, the Christian people will follow you and you will not lack the support of good theologians, who are numerous. What a happy, glorious, immortal crown for the Holy year 2000."

The article concludes, "Would it not be appropriate to honour her at the end of this century of crimes against life and innocence by defining her as Coredemptrix, Mediatrix and Advocate of Life? That final Marian Mystery of the Coronations seems to us to provide the perfect context. Assumed into heaven, crowned by her Son, ruling with him on the highest throne of humility, Mary is the perfect flower of our race. In her, by grace, 'nothing is impossible to God' " *(Inside the Vatican,* August-September 1996, pp. 56-59).

The Scott Hahn Story

In 1993 Ignatius Press printed a book titled *Rome Sweet Home— Our Journey to Catholicism,* by Scott and Kimberly Hahn. The book tells the story of a young Presbyterian couple who converted to Catholicism. Cardinal John O'Connor wrote these words for the back cover of the book: "For the last few years, Scott and Kimberly Hahn have been speaking around the country—and making tapes that circulate around the globe—sharing with thousands all about their conversion to the Catholic Church and the truth and splendor of the Catholic faith. Now this outstanding Catholic couple has finally put their story into print as they recount their incredible spiritual journey 'back home' into God's worldwide family, the Catholic Church."

In the historic document "Evangelicals and Catholics Together" the Catholics urged Protestants not to "steal their sheep" but to work together with them to reach the unconverted in the world. Now, as you have just read, letters are being sent out to thousands (including me!) from New Hope, Kentucky, where *Inside the Vatican* is printed in the United States, and from St. Joseph Communications, in West Covina, California, urging folks to buy Hahn's book *Rome Sweet Home* and order his tapes, "Protestant Minister Becomes Catholic," which they claim have sold over 200,000 copies. In ads for the tape set it is stated that "he has almost single-handedly led thousands of fallen-away

Catholics and Protestants back to the Faith—in an age where thousands are leaving the church."

In early 1996 I received a complimentary copy of *Sursum Corda,* a new magazine of the Catholic Revival movement. The cover headline reads: "The Best-kept Secret in the Church—Protestant Seminary Manufactures Catholic Converts." The article inside is headed "Protestant Pastors on the Road to Rome," with the subtitle comment "In the past ten years at least fifty Protestant pastors have resigned their posts and found their way to Rome. Most had been raised to despise the Catholic Church. All have sacrificed comfort and security. How did they find the truth? How have they fared as Catholics? How do they enrich the Church?" The article goes on to state that many of the recent graduates of Gordon-Conwell Theological Seminary, a Protestant institution, have converted to Catholicism and that they have led nearly 150 of their fellow Protestant pastors into the church. Of course the article does not mention that in Latin America alone more than 8,000 members leave the Catholic Church every day of the year. The point is well taken, however, that many are making decisions in the great controversy right now!

It is not my purpose in this book to write another book about eschatology, but rather to underscore the fact that the Second Coming is near and to share inspired counsel on how we can be ready for this grand event. However, this chapter will help one to see that what Jesus said in John 14:29 is important for today: "And now I have told you before it comes, that when it does come to pass, you may believe." An interesting point is made in the publication *Vatican Watch,* a supplement to the August-September 1996 issue of *Inside the Vatican.* Author Robert Moynihan asks the question "Why Watch the Vatican?" And then he gives the following answer: "Because when Rome speaks, people still listen, more than ever before. Because in religious matters more roads than ever lead to, and come from, Rome. Because the Vatican, as the spiritual and administrative center of Roman Catholicism, directly influences the lives of nearly 1 billion Catholics and indirectly influences events throughout the world."

Is Sunday Coming?
On February 6, 1997, the Adventist News Network released the

following bulletin: "British Adventist Church Opposes European Parliament Resolution Backing Sunday. London, United Kingdom . . . [ANN] Seventh-day Adventists in Britain are voicing their objection to the December 1996 resolution by the European Parliament which called for member states to respect Sunday as the day of rest.

"Speaking on the issue on behalf of the Adventist Church in Britain, Dr. Jonathan Gallagher, Religious Liberty Director, expressed opposition to such a move. He said, 'To try to legislate religion is dangerous. Just look back in history and you see what happened when states try to enforce religious observance. To make Sunday the official day of rest for the whole European community discriminates against many other minorities and will not solve society's problems.'

"However, Gallagher also pointed out that the resolution itself called for a recognition that in Europe's multicultural society there are other groups whose alternative days of rest need to be respected.

"Promoted by David Hallam, member of the European Parliament, the so-called 'resolution of urgency' states that 'the traditions and the cultural, social, religious and family needs of its citizens' should be upheld by identifying Sunday as a special day.

"This action comes after the European Court of Justice ruled that Sunday did not have any special significance in a case regarding work practices. The court's view that no specific importance should be attached to Sunday as a day of rest and that anyone working on Sunday should not be discriminated against has angered supporters of 'Sunday specialness.'

"The UK-based Keep Sunday Special Campaign (KSS) has welcomed the vote of the European Parliament, stating that it shows the desire of Europe's politicians to support Sundaykeeping. They cite the ruling as endorsing the view that Sunday observance is a way of maintaining the structure of society and upholding family values. Director of the KSS, Dr. Michael Schluter, commented that the vote showed how Europe was united on the importance of Sunday. 'Strong personal relationships in the family and community are a crucial factor in the health of the individual employer or employee. . . . The clear statement by the European Parliament puts the Sunday issue back on the political agenda.' " [Jonathan Gallagher]

In another report from London the "Loss of the Sabbath" is blamed for the falling church attendance there. "Leaders of Britain's Anglican

Church have blamed the commercialisation of Sunday for the cata-strophic decline in the numbers attending church. Publication of offi-cial statistics earlier this month revealed that the total average attendance in 1995 was down a massive 36,000 from the previous year to 1,045,000. It had been hoped that the figures would show a slow-down in church decline, but this latest announcement confirms 'that church-going had suffered its biggest haemorrhage for 20 years,'" reports Britain's *Sunday Telegraph.*

"Former Archbishop Dr. Robert Runcie complained that falling congregations were associated with much greater entertainment op-portunities on Sunday, while vocal vicar The Rev. Tony Higton says that 'Sunday used to be very quiet and people would stay home or go for a walk. But now it's the same as Saturday. We have become so ma-terialistic. We seem to worship Mammon rather than God.' Although numbers attending church have been falling for many years, he blames the commercialisation of Sunday for accelerating the fall.

"One vicar, who did not want to be named, has spoken favourably of the days when Sunday church attendance was required by law. The Sunday Observance Act of 1625 and others made it a crime not to be in church, with a massive fine (for the time) of one shilling for those who refused to obey.

"While expressing regret for the falling numbers of church-goers, spokesperson for the Seventh-day Adventist Church in Britain, Pastor John Surridge, said that he hoped no legislation would be used to sup-port Sunday observance. 'Besides Sunday is not the Sabbath anyway, as the Bible itself makes clear. The Sabbath is the seventh day of the week. Most importantly it would be sad to see concern over Sunday-keeping being used as a way of legalizing religion.' Noting the recent European Parliament backing for laws to make Sunday a special day, he expressed concern that such actions could pave the way for real lim-itations on religious liberty." (This story was reported by Jonathan Gallagher in the *Adventist News Network,* February 28, 1997.)

This report, like the many others cited in *Sunday's Coming,* points out that there is presently an increased agitation for Sunday from many quarters. We must watch these developments and entities as they press their agenda. This movement for increase in Sunday sacredness is a clear sign of the times—a marker for the imminent return of Jesus.

CHAPTER 5

The Invitation

During His earthly ministry Jesus frequently spoke in parables or stories to teach important lessons regarding His kingdom. At least three of His stories tell of a great supper planned for the culmination of the great controversy.

These stories are central to the theme of this book because, taken together, they outline what it means to be ready for the Second Coming. It is no mystery: these simple stories lay it all out.

The story of the great supper is recorded in Luke 14:1, 12-24 and *Christ's Object Lessons,* p. 219 ff. This story was told in the home of a Pharisee who had invited Jesus to Sabbath dinner.

The story of the wedding garment is recorded in Matthew 22:1-14 and *Christ's Object Lessons,* p. 307 ff. Jesus told this story at the Temple in Jerusalem to a large number of people, including many of the chief priests and Pharisees.

The story of the wedding feast is recorded in Matthew 25:1-13 and *Christ's Object Lessons,* p. 405 ff. Jesus told this story in a private meeting with His disciples on the Mount of Olives. As they watched the sunset together they observed in the distance a home that was brilliantly lighted for wedding festivities.

These three stories all tell of the special banquet planned at the end of time, but they each give different details or unique perspectives regarding who is invited, their response to the invitation, and the preparation needed to attend the banquet. The stories also point out that many of those planning to attend will grow weary of waiting and be unprepared when the time finally arrives to enter the banquet hall.

This great banquet celebration is also prefigured in the Old

Testament sanctuary service and the yearly round of festivals or feast days. The last one, the only one left to be fulfilled in antitype, is the Feast of Tabernacles. This feast prefigured the great banquet in heaven when the saints are taken there at the Second Coming. Ellen White was shown the banquet setting and wrote of it in *Early Writings,* pp. 19, 20. She told of a tour of heaven and the great temple and of that first great celebration in heaven. "After we beheld the glory of the temple, we went out, and Jesus left us and went to the city. Soon we heard His lovely voice again, saying, 'Come, My people, you have come out of great tribulation, and done My will; suffered for Me; come in to supper, for I will gird Myself, and serve you.' We shouted, 'Alleluia! Glory!' and entered into the city. And I saw a table of pure silver; it was many miles in length, yet our eyes could extend over it. I saw the fruit of the tree of life, the manna, almonds, figs, pomegranates, grapes, and many other kinds of fruit. I asked Jesus to let me eat of the fruit. He said, 'Not now. Those who eat of the fruit of this land go back to earth no more. But in a little while, if faithful, you shall both eat of the fruit of the tree of life and drink of the water of the fountain.'"

It sounds like an awesome banquet, doesn't it? Not just silver setting, but even the table is made of silver and it's many miles in length! Jesus wants to have a place there for you and me—for every one of us. This is one invitation that I have accepted and don't plan to miss.

The Great Supper

Upon review of these three stories many important factors are evident. Factors that will spell the difference between success and failure in the game of life. In the first story a man gave a great supper and invited many. At suppertime he sent his servant to tell those who were invited, "Come, for all things are now ready." But the Bible says, "They all with one accord began to make excuses" (Luke 14:18). This is incredible. It sounds much like Lot's wife hating to leave Sodom when the angels came to deliver them. So here those who had been invited and for whom the feast was prepared decided at the last minute that they had more pressing matters to attend to. One invitee said, "I have bought a piece of ground, and I must go and see it. I ask you to have me excused." Another said, "I have bought five yoke of oxen, and I am going to test them. I ask you to have me excused." Still another said, "I have married a wife, and therefore I cannot come." This man didn't even bother to ask to be excused. He just said, "I cannot come."

Obviously, none of the excuses were founded on real necessity. The man who wanted to go see his new property had already purchased it. But it was now the focus of his attention—to the detriment of all other interests. The man who had purchased the oxen—his business interests—had already tried them out before the purchase, but he just wanted to savor his purchase and play with his new equipment. The man who married a wife knew that if he had really wanted to attend the supper, his new wife was welcome too. But he represents those who allow others to distract them from the object which should be their primary focus.

And so the pretense of "I cannot come" really meant "I do not care to come." Their minds were preoccupied with other interests.

By this story of the great supper Jesus represents the blessings offered through the gospel. It reveals that many will choose the world above Himself, and will, as the result of that choice, lose heaven. In the reality of the story Jesus had been to the trouble and expense of making a great preparation at an immense personal sacrifice; but when He gave the final call to the meal, it was met with excuses.

It is an unusual paradox that for many people the very blessings that they have received from God become a barrier to separate their souls from their Creator and Redeemer.

The man who said, "I have married a wife, and therefore I cannot come," represents a very large group of people. There are many today who allow their husbands, wives, or friends to prevent them from heeding the gospel call. Those who refuse the call of Jesus because they fear division in the family, supposing that in refusing to obey God they are ensuring peace and prosperity in their home, are under a fatal delusion. In rejecting the love of Christ they are rejecting the only thing that can bring real purity and steadfastness to human love. So in rejecting the offer of mercy they not only lose heaven, but also the opportunity for a truly happy home life here as well.

The Bible states that in the last days men will be absorbed in worldly pursuits, in pleasure-seeking and money-getting. They will be blind to eternal realities. A look at the cross section of any community will let us know that this is just the way it is today. Men and women are rushing on in the chase for gain and selfish indulgence <u>as if there</u>

were no God, no heaven, and no hereafter. We cannot forget that we have heaven to win and hell to shun. Only the foolish live for this life only. "The fool has said in his heart, 'There is no God'" (Psalm 14:1).

"In Noah's day the warning of the flood was sent to startle men in their wickedness and to call them to repentance. So the message of Christ's soon coming is designed to arouse men from their absorption in worldly things. It is intended to awaken them to a sense of eternal realities, that they may give heed to the invitation to the Lord's table" *(Christ's Object Lessons,* p. 228).

When the excuses were relayed to the one who had prepared the banquet the command was given to go into the streets and lanes, the highways and hedges, and compel them to come. This tells us in no uncertain terms that the gospel invitation is open to everyone. Whosoever will may come. **The entire human family has been invited.** The invitation is open to each of us. And you can tell anyone you meet—anyone—that they are invited. Jesus is waiting to welcome them.

The Wedding Garment

Just as Daniel 7 adds details to the basic story of Daniel 2, the story of the wedding garment adds details to the great supper story. Both illustrate the gospel invitation. But in the wedding garment story of Matthew 22, those who refuse the invitation are destroyed! One other unique factor is added. In both parables the feast is provided with guests, but the Matthew 22 account emphasizes that there is a preparation to be made by all who attend the feast. In this story every guest was provided a wedding garment. It was a gift from the king. By wearing it the guests showed their respect for the giver of the feast. When the king came in to see the guests, one man was seated there in his regular clothes. Asked why he was not wearing a wedding garment, he was speechless. Why? Because there was no excuse! He couldn't say, "I couldn't afford one," or "They didn't have my size." There simply was no excuse! He was self-condemned.

"The guests at the wedding [gospel] feast are those who profess to serve God, those whose names are written in the book of life. But not all who profess to be Christians are true disciples. Before the final reward is given, it must be decided [from among those whose names are written in the book of life] who are fitted to share the inheritance of the righteous. This decision must be made prior to the second coming of Christ in the clouds of heaven; for when He comes, His reward is with Him" *(Christ's Object Lessons,* p. 310). This is the work of the investigative judgment.

"The lives of all His professed followers pass in review before God. All are examined according to the record of the books of heaven, and according to his deeds the destiny of each is forever fixed" *(ibid.).* "And there shall in no wise enter into it [the New Jerusalem] any thing that defiles, or causes an abomination or a lie, but only those who are written in the Lamb's Book of Life" (Revelation 21:27). Here is presented a most significant detail. Those who enter heaven are not just forgiven, they are also transformed. They are changed from their old sinful ways—transformed into the likeness of Christ. They are fit for the heavenly home. They are ready to live in the company of holy beings, for they are without fault before God.

The idea that God wants to prepare me for heaven has just recently sunk into my consciousness in a way that brings real joy to my heart. I have taken it as a sign that Jesus really is coming soon and in His great unbounded love and mercy, He wants me to be ready to meet Him in peace. Now it seems that everywhere I go in the Scriptures God is saying things that encourage me to want to be like Him. And He cautions me that if I am not, I won't be with Him in heaven.

What I want to share with you in this chapter and throughout the entire book is that the good news of the gospel is surely better than we have yet experienced or understood. It is great news that though we are sinners, and therefore subject to death, that Jesus' death on Calvary paid the price for our sin. He took my place on the cross. He died the second death—for me. Now I can live with a peace that passes understanding and in the hope of the Second Coming.

"'The wages of sin is death; but the gift of God is eternal life through Jesus Christ our Lord.' Romans 6:23. While life is the inheritance of the righteous, death is the portion of the wicked. Moses declared to Israel: 'I have set before thee this day life and good, and death and evil.' Deuteronomy 30:15. The death referred to in these Scriptures is not that pronounced upon Adam, for all mankind suffer the penalty of his transgression. It is 'the second death' that is placed in contrast with everlasting life" *(The Great Controversy,* p. 544).

But the good news gets even better. Not only has Jesus promised and made provision for my forgiveness, He also wants to transform me from my old sinful ways and character into a new being in the image of God. And just as with my forgiveness, this work of transformation is all a gift from Him. But I do have a part to play—I must accept the gift. I must surrender my will. So many of the Bible stories tell of this experience. As we share these throughout this book it will certainly increase our realization of the necessity for transformation and how it is brought about.

This has been such good news to me that every time I sat down at the computer in the evenings to work on this book I prayed that somehow God would give me the words to say. I prayed for His words to make it interesting enough to motivate each reader. I prayed for grace to present the material in such a way as to inspire others to make this awesome experience a part of their lives. The material in *Even at the Door* and *Sunday's Coming!* gave detailed and documented evidence that the Second Coming is right on schedule and is in fact imminent. But it is one thing to know about end-time events, and, as the stories of Jesus present so clearly, it is quite another to be ready. We would all have to agree that being ready is much more important than knowing precisely when Jesus will return, even though I believe that God does want us to know when His coming is near.

Have you ever traveled a certain route—like to and from work for several months or years—and then one day noticed a house or some object that you have never seen before? It's been there all the time, but somehow you just hadn't seen it before? Or who hasn't been around when some funny experience has been told and you finally figure out the funny part—long after everyone else "got it"? Or have you ever just understood some concept and excitedly shared it with others just to find out that they already knew what is just "dawning on you"? I must confess that I feel a little funny getting excited about this topic and sharing it with you because no doubt you already know it. (Then why didn't you tell me!) But really, just maybe it is something that we can learn about and experience together. And besides, if some of you don't change from your grouchy old natures I am not sure that I want to spend eternity with you as my neighbor. And you'd want me a little more companionable if we are to live as neighbors for eternity—I am serious!

Part of my professional education includes a master's degree in Public Health from Loma Linda University. My training in Community Health Education taught me the interesting fact that nutrition plays a very vital and major role in total health. But I learned that there is not a separate diet that is just for ideal weight management, or another for reducing the risk of heart disease, or another for reducing the risk of cancer, and still another for reducing the risk of, or management of, maturity onset diabetes. A truly good diet—one that includes a wide variety of fruits, grains, nuts, and vegetables, prepared in a simple and unrefined manner, eaten with sufficient quantity to maintain ideal weight, with the very minimal use of sugar, salt, and fats—works best for all of the above! The same thing is true for spiritual nutrition. All the recipes in the Bible are really designed to produce the same dish—readiness for heaven.

Let me illustrate this. All of the following really mean the same thing. The list could even be much longer than this.

- Create in me a new heart and put a right spirit within me.
- I will take out the stony heart and put a heart of flesh within you.
- I will write My laws in your heart.
- Elijah will "make ready a people prepared for the coming of the Lord."
- He shall save His people from their sins.
- You must be born again.
- Unless you are baptized with the Spirit you will not see the kingdom of heaven.
- And there shall in no wise enter in anything that defileth.
- Blessed are the peacemakers, for they shall see God.
- Seek ye first the kingdom of God and His righteousness.
- To him that overcomes I will grant to sit with Me on My throne.
- The narrow way leads to life eternal.
- He who does these sayings of Mine is like the wise man who built on the rock.
- If you know these things, happy are ye if you do them.
- How could I do this great wickedness and sin against God?
- The counsel of the True Witness to the Laodiceans.
- He restoreth my soul.
- Now unto Him that is able to keep you from falling and to present you faultless.

- His wife has made herself ready.
- Arrayed in fine linen, clean and bright—the righteous acts of the saints.

The list could literally go on and on. The bottom line, however, for each of the above phrases is the same. <u>Those who have entered into a saving relationship with Jesus are changed</u>. They are not the same as they used to be. They are not self-righteous. They have the righteousness of Jesus. They are fit to live in the company of holy beings. And here is the most amazing part: They are changed while on earth during the hours of probation. The character change does not take place "in a moment, in the twinkling of an eye" on the way to heaven. Only those will be on the way to heaven who have been changed by the power of God down here. We must find out more about this change and how it comes about.

As we saw in *Sunday's Coming,* prophecy is simple and God wants us to understand it. One must study as for hidden treasure, but the truth will be found. The same thing is true regarding the concept we are now considering. Salvation is simple. God has made provision for us to escape the penalty of death and to change us from sinning beings to obedient followers. But what is the wedding garment and how does one put it on? Putting on the wedding garment is actually the same as all the points mentioned in the list above. It means that we trade our old natures (characters) for the nature and character of Christ.

"<u>By the wedding garment in the parable is represented the pure, spotless character which Christ's true followers will possess</u>. . . . It is the righteousness of Christ, His own unblemished character, that through faith is imparted to all who receive Him as their personal Saviour." . . .

"<u>Only the covering which Christ Himself has provided can make us meet [ready] to appear in God's presence</u>" *(Christ's Object Lessons,* pp. 310, 311).

The wedding garment does not hide our sins; it transforms us. "If we confess our sins, He is faithful and just to forgive our sins <u>and to cleanse us from all unrighteousness</u>" (1 John 1:9). It is God who does the work, but it is our characters that are changed! While explaining the family relationship between husbands and wives, Paul compared God's love for His church. "Christ also loved the church, and gave Himself for it, that He might sanctify and cleanse it with the washing of water by the word, that He might present it to Himself a glorious church, not having spot or wrinkle or any such thing, but that it should be holy and without blemish" (Ephesians 5:25-27).

In fact we are told that "this robe, woven in the loom of heaven, has in it not one thread of human devising. Christ in His humanity wrought out a perfect character, and this character He offers to impart to us" *(Christ's Object Lessons,* p. 311). We cannot repeat often enough and in too many ways that what God requires and how we satisfy Him is clear and simple.

Looking at the finished product from many perspectives, we get an overall picture.

"By His perfect obedience He [Christ] has made it possible for every human being to obey God's commandments.

"When we submit ourselves to Christ,

> the heart is united with His heart,
>
> the will is merged with His will,
>
> the mind becomes one with His mind,
>
> the thoughts are brought into captivity to Him; we live His life.

"This is what it means to be clothed with the garment of His righteousness" *(ibid.,* p. 312). We can digest this for starters, but the counsel becomes even more understandable and practical. In the parable, the guests at the wedding feast were inspected by the king. The only guests admitted to the feast were those who had obeyed the king's requirements and put on the wedding garment. "So it is with the guests at the gospel feast. All must pass the scrutiny of the great King, and only those are received who have put on the robe of Christ's righteousness. Righteousness is right doing, and it is by their deeds that all will be judged. Our characters are revealed by what we do. The works show whether the faith is genuine" *(ibid.).*

We shall see, as we examine this material, that in the biblical sense and repeated so clearly in the Spirit of Prophecy, righteousness by faith goes beyond my acceptance of God's forgiveness. It also includes my acceptance by faith of Christ into my heart by His Spirit. This acceptance brings about a transformation in my life. I become a new person. A miracle takes place. I begin to grow in grace and in the knowledge of my Lord and Saviour.

I can believe that Jesus is the Messiah, that the prophecies are true, that Jesus is coming soon, and that there is no other name under heaven whereby man can be saved. I can make a profession of Christianity, be baptized and have my name registered in the books of the remnant church; but unless I am transformed by the indwelling Spirit of God my profession is worthless!

The Bible makes this point very clearly in the story of the two builders. Luke records: "But why do you call Me 'Lord, Lord,' and do not the things which I say" (Luke 6:46)? Matthew's account is even more specific. "Not everyone who says to Me, 'Lord, Lord,' shall enter the kingdom of heaven, but he who does the will of My Father in heaven. Many will say to Me in that day, 'Lord, Lord, have we not prophesied in Your name, cast out demons in Your name, and done many wonders in Your name?' And then I will declare to them, 'I never knew you; depart from Me, you who practice lawlessness!'" (Matthew 7:21-23). If I am lawless I am disobedient. It's just that simple.

The Bible is very plain about this idea that obedience is evidence of our faith and that Christ is living in us. Another very explicit text states: "Now by this we know that we know Him, if we keep His commandments. He who says, 'I know Him,' and does not keep His commandments, is a liar, and the truth is not in him. But whoever keeps His word, truly the love of God is perfected in him. By this we know that we are in Him. He who says he abides in Him ought himself also to walk just as He walked" (1 John 2:3-6). When commenting on these verses, Ellen White draws this conclusion: "This [obedience to the commandments] is the genuine evidence of conversion. Whatever our profession, it amounts to nothing unless Christ is revealed in works of righteousness" (Christ's Object Lessons, p. 313). It should be obvious to anyone familiar with the gospel that these works of righteousness are not meritorious in regard to salvation but that they are the evidence of a saving relationship with Christ and a response of love to Him.

Nicodemus

The most well-known verse in the New Testament and perhaps in all the Bible is John 3:16: "For God so loved the world that He gave His only begotten Son, that whoever believes in Him should not perish but have everlasting life." These words were originally spoken to Nicodemus in a secret night meeting with Jesus. The story of

Nicodemus is critical here because in this instance Christ was dealing with a man who outwardly was a model "Christian"—one who had a reputation for good works. So also did the rich young ruler, for that matter. If works of righteousness are a sign of conversion and commitment, then what did Nicodemus lack? The amazing story gives a clue. Regarding this story, so important for understanding salvation, Ellen White says: "Jesus not only tells Nicodemus that he must have a new heart in order to see the kingdom of heaven, but tells him how to obtain a new heart. . . . This lesson is one of the greatest importance to every soul that lives; for the terms of salvation are here laid out in distinct lines. If one had no other text in the Bible, this alone would be a guide for the soul" *(Testimonies to Ministers,* p. 370).

Nicodemus was a leader in the Jewish nation. He was rich, well-educated, and honored. He was a member of the Sanhedrin, the Jewish court of justice. He had apparently supported Jesus before the court on at least one occasion (see John 7:50). He had observed Jesus at work in Jerusalem and was attracted to Him. He wanted to talk with Jesus and learn more about Him, but he feared that it would be humiliating for him as a ruler of the Jews to have an open meeting with a lowly Galilean.

By asking around, Nicodemus found out that Jesus frequently retired to the Mount of Olives at night. So waiting until the city was asleep, he went looking for Jesus. But what could he say under the circumstances? This highly educated civil and religious leader meets the "unlearned" teacher from Galilee. Nicodemus feels a strange timidity. He begins the conversation by trying to acknowledge the extraordinary gifts that Jesus had exhibited. "Rabbi," he says, "we know that You are a teacher come from God; for no one can do these signs that You do unless God is with him" (John 3:2). Jesus did not recognize this greeting but rather, looking right into his eyes, and reading the real question of his heart, he said, "Most assuredly, I say to you, unless one is born again, he cannot see the kingdom of God" (John 3:3).

"Nicodemus had come to the Lord thinking to enter into a discussion with Him, but Jesus laid bare the foundation principles of truth. He said to Nicodemus, It is not theoretical knowledge you need so much as spiritual regeneration. You need not have your curiosity satisfied, but to have a new heart. You must receive a new life from above before you can appreciate heavenly things. Until this change takes place, making all things new, it will result in no saving good for you to discuss with Me My authority or My mission" *(The Desire of Ages,* p. 171).

If we brought this story down to the 1990s Nicodemus would have been a member of the General Conference Committee and maybe a college president—a rich one! "He was startled at the thought of a kingdom too pure for him to see in his present state" *(ibid.).* He was rather caught off guard and blurted out, "How can a man be born when he is old?" Jesus came back with the same answer as before, but with a few more details. "Most assuredly, I say to you, unless one is born of water and the Spirit, he cannot enter the kingdom of God" (John 3:5). "Nicodemus knew that Christ here referred to water baptism and the renewing of the heart by the Spirit of God" *(ibid.,* p. 172). Being "baptized by the Spirit" is not synonymous with speaking in tongues or finding your spiritual gift. It is receiving the Holy Spirit into your heart so that He can begin His work of renewing your heart. Scripture also calls it the renewing of your mind: "And do not be conformed to this world, but be transformed by the renewing of your mind, that you may prove what is that good and acceptable and perfect will of God" (Romans 12:2).

"The Christian's life is not a modification or improvement of the old, but a transformation of nature. There is a death to self and sin, and a new life altogether. This change can be brought about only by the effectual working of the Holy Spirit" *(ibid.).* Nicodemus looked perplexed, so Jesus used the illustration of the wind to help him understand.

"The wind blows where it wishes, and you hear the sound of it, but cannot tell where it comes from and where it goes. So is everyone that is born of the Spirit" (John 3:8). The wind cannot be seen, but its effects are very striking. Having been involved in the logging business in my early years, I know of two situations that are very definitely impacted by the wind. The first is forest fires. When there is no wind it is much easier to contain the fire. The wind can push a fire up an entire canyon is just a few seconds. You can't see the wind, but you can see and hear the power. My personal involvement in logging was in the actual cutting of timber. The falling and bucking of trees—as we called it. When falling a tall tree, the wind was a factor as to whether or not we could place the tree where we wanted it to go. Frequently a faller would stop his saw after notching the tree, and to check for adverse winds he would grab a handful of sawdust and throw it into the air. You couldn't see the wind, but you could tell if there was a wind by the direction in which the sawdust was blown.

So, "Patiently Jesus unfolded the plan of salvation to Nicodemus, showing him how <u>the Holy Spirit brings light and transforming power to every soul that is born of the Spirit</u>. Like the wind, which is invisible—yet the effects of which are plainly seen and felt—is the baptism of the Spirit of God upon the heart, revealing itself in every action of him who experiences its saving power" *(The Spirit of Prophecy,* vol. 2, p. 130).

In the chapter "The Test of Discipleship," the book *Steps to Christ* contains a very relevant statement: "A person may not be able to tell the exact time or place, or trace all the chain of circumstances in the process of conversion; but this does not prove him to be unconverted. Christ said to Nicodemus, 'The wind bloweth where it listeth, and thou hearest the sound thereof, but canst not tell whence it cometh, and whither it goeth: so is everyone that is born of the Spirit.' John 3:8. Like the wind, which is invisible, yet the effects of which are plainly seen and felt, is the Spirit of God in its work upon the human heart. <u>That regenerating power, which no human eye can see, begets a new life in the soul; it creates a new being in the image of God</u>. While the work of the Spirit is silent and imperceptible, its effects are manifest. <u>If the heart has been renewed by the Spirit of God, the life will bear witness to the fact</u>. While we cannot do anything to change our hearts or to bring ourselves into harmony with God; while we must not trust at all to ourselves or our good works, <u>our lives will reveal whether the grace of God is dwelling within us</u>. A change will be seen in the character, the habits, the pursuits. <u>The contrast will be clear and decided between what they have been and what they are</u>. The character is revealed, not by occasional good deeds and occasional misdeeds, but by the tendency of the habitual words and acts" (pp. 57, 58).

This distinction between one who is converted and one who has not experienced conversion is like day and night. "Light and darkness are not more distinct than are the state of the converted and the unconverted" *(Signs of the Times,* May 18, 1882). In other words, you can tell if you or someone else has been converted. Because it is the work of the Spirit, and the fruit of the Spirit is seen in their lives. Note the day and night difference between those who are unconverted and the converted as recorded in Scripture.

"Now the works of the flesh are evident, which are: adultery, fornication, uncleanness, licentiousness, idolatry, sorcery, hatred, contentions, jealousies, outbursts of wrath, selfish ambitions, dissensions, heresies, envy, murders, drunkenness, revelries, and the like; of which I tell you beforehand, just as I also told you in time past, that those who practice such things will not inherit the kingdom of God" (Galatians 5:19-21).

In contrast is the character of one who has been born again through the working of the Spirit. Notice that the word "fruit" is in the singular. This is not an either/or situation. When you have the Spirit in your heart all of the manifestations of the fruit are in your life.

"But the fruit of the Spirit is love, joy, peace, longsuffering, kindness, goodness, faithfulness, gentleness, self-control. Against such there is no law. And those who are Christ's have crucified the flesh with its passions and desires. If we live in the Spirit, let us also walk in the Spirit" (Galatians 5:22-25).

"While the wind is itself invisible, it produces effects that are seen and felt. So the work of the Spirit upon the soul will reveal itself in every act of him who has felt its saving power. When the Spirit of God takes possession of the heart, it transforms the life. Sinful thoughts are put away, evil deeds are renounced; love, humility, and peace take the place of anger, envy, and strife. Joy takes the place of sadness, and the countenance reflects the light of heaven. No one sees the hand that lifts the burden, or beholds the light descend from the courts above. The blessing comes when by faith the soul surrenders itself to God. Then that power which no human eye can see creates a new being in the image of God.

"It is impossible for finite minds to comprehend the work of redemption. Its mystery exceeds human knowledge; yet he who passes from death to life realizes that it is a divine reality" *(The Desire of Ages,* p. 173).

Nicodemus couldn't believe his ears. He had read all the texts about a new heart, a right spirit, and so on, before—but he had never understood them in the way Jesus explained them to him. In the eyes of his fellow men, his life had been just and honorable. But now, standing in the presence of Jesus, he suddenly felt unclean and unholy. He responded to Jesus, "How can these things be?" Jesus then reminded him of the experience in the wilderness when the snakes had bitten the Israelites and God asked Moses to prepare a brass serpent and hang it on a pole for all to see. All those who looked would be healed and their lives spared.

Many have wondered why it was a serpent that was raised up. We now know that Jesus was made "in the likeness of sinful flesh" (Romans 8:3) and He became sin for us. There was no healing power in the serpent, of course, but it pointed forward to the work of Christ.

"In the interview with Nicodemus, Jesus unfolded the plan of salvation and His mission to the world. In none of His subsequent discourses did He explain so fully, step by step, the work necessary to be done in the hearts of all who would inherit the kingdom of heaven" *(ibid.,* p. 176).

The kind of obedience that Jesus is looking for is not the feeble struggling attempts that we give in trying hard to live up to the standard that God has set. It is an obedience that springs from a transformed heart and it is performed in the power of God. It is the service and allegiance of love.

You will no doubt remember hearing someone say, "Well, nobody's perfect. It's not possible to obey God perfectly. He knows my heart and He loves me. I will just trust Him to save me." Having studied this topic in depth, it now seems that this is just a cop-out. Because "Satan had claimed that it was impossible for man to obey God's commandments; and in our own strength it is true that we cannot obey them. But Christ came in the form of humanity, and by His perfect obedience He proved that humanity and divinity combined can obey every one of God's precepts.

" 'As many as received Him, to them gave He power to become the sons of God, even to them that believe on His name.' John 1:12. This power is not in the human agent. It is the power of God. When a soul receives Christ, he receives power to live the life of Christ" *(Christ's Object Lessons,* p. 314).

God's High Standard

Because God's standard is so high ("Be ye therefore perfect") and man's power to obey is so weak, we have a tendency in our own minds to lower the standard so we can reach it. Or we say that it is not possible and God will make up the difference. God's plan, however, is not to lower the standard, but rather to empower man through the indwelling Spirit to reach the standard. "<u>God requires perfection of His children</u>. His law is a transcript of His own character, and it is the standard of all character. <u>This infinite standard is presented to all that there may be no mistake in regard to the kind of people whom God will have to compose His kingdom</u>. The life of Christ on earth was a perfect expression of God's law, and when those who claim to be children of God become Christlike in character, they will be obedient to God's commandments. <u>Then the Lord can trust them to be of the number who shall compose the family in heaven</u>. Clothed with the glorious apparel of Christ's righteousness, they have a place at the King's feast. They have a right to join the blood-washed throng" *(ibid., p. 315).*

We can see that God's standard is perfection of character and we are not to make a mistake about the kind of people who will populate heaven. It is those who obey from a transformed heart. They are safe to save for eternity. The wedding garment is the robe of Christ's righteousness!

"The man who came to the feast without a wedding garment represents the condition of many in our world today.

"They profess to be Christians, and lay claim to the blessings and privileges of the gospel:

> Yet they feel no need of a transformation of character.
>
> They have never felt true repentance for sin.
>
> They do not realize their need of Christ or exercise faith in Him.
>
> They have not overcome their hereditary and cultivated tendencies to wrongdoing.
>
> Yet they think that they are good enough in themselves, and they rest upon their own merits instead of trusting in Christ.

"Hearers of the word, they come to the banquet, but they have not put on the robe of Christ's righteousness" *(ibid.).*

Why would anyone be found seeking entrance to the wedding feast without the required wedding garment? The answer is: "<u>They have refused the gift</u> which alone could enable them to honor Christ by representing Him to the world. The work of the Holy Spirit is to them a strange work" *(ibid.)*. "Those who reject the **gift** of Christ's righteousness are rejecting the attributes of character which would constitute them the sons and daughters of God. They are rejecting that which alone could give them a fitness for a place at the marriage feast" *(ibid., pp. 316, 317)*.

Some may be thinking, *You are going way beyond the gospel here.* "All you have to do is believe," they say. "God is love. He loves me too much to destroy me." "But the love of God does not lead Him to excuse sin. He did not excuse it in Satan; He did not excuse it in Adam or in Cain [or in Moses, Achan, Lot's wife, the rich young ruler, etc., etc.]; nor will He excuse it in any other of the children of men. He will not connive at our sins or overlook our defects of character. He expects us to overcome in His name" *(ibid., p. 316)*.

But does this overcoming business have to happen now? Ellen White concludes her comments about the wedding garment by saying, "There will be no future probation in which to prepare for eternity. It is in this life that we are to put on the robe of Christ's righteousness. **This is our only opportunity to form characters for the home which Christ has made ready for those who obey His commandments.**

"The days of our probation are fast closing. The end is near. To us the warning is given, 'Take heed to yourselves, lest at any time your hearts be overcharged with surfeiting, and drunkenness, and cares of this life, and so that day come upon you unawares.' Luke 21:34. Beware lest it find you unready. Take heed lest you be found at the King's feast without a wedding garment" *(ibid., p. 319)*.

The Wedding Feast

The third story about the great supper is found in Matthew 25:1-13. It is commonly known as the parable of the ten virgins.

This story has an interesting setting. It was evening and Jesus and His disciples were alone on the Mount of Olives. We know some of the details of this evening because it was as they watched the setting sun glistening on the dome of the Temple that Jesus told them of the coming destruction of Jerusalem and its Temple. The disciples were also aware that Jesus would be leaving them soon, although He had told them that He would come back again to take them to heaven. It was with these thoughts in mind in this private time with Jesus that they asked Him a two-part question: "When will these things be?" (the destruction of Jerusalem) and "What will be the sign of Your coming and the end of the world?" (the Second Coming).

The Bible devotes two entire chapters to the answer Jesus gave to these urgent questions. (Matthew 24 and 25). In Matthew 24 Jesus gives "signs" in the world that warn that the Second Coming and the end of the world are near. These signs are things that we read about in the newspaper—wars, famines, pestilences, earthquakes, false prophets, etc. In Matthew 25, however, the focus is not on the world "out there" but on what it will be like in the church just before the Second Coming. This chapter contains three stories or parables:

The ten virgins—with the emphasis on being ready.

The talents—telling us what to do while waiting.

The sheep and the goats—outlining the basis upon which judgment is meted out.

As Jesus begins to answer the questions, the sun has just set and lights are beginning to come on in the homes below. People are beginning to light their lamps. The disciples see one home where there are many lights and a group is gathering to form a marriage procession.

In many parts of the East, wedding festivities are held in the evening. The groom goes to meet the bride at her home and then brings her back to his home. By torch or lamplight the bridal party goes from her father's house to the groom's home, where there is a feast prepared for the invited guests. As the disciples watch the preparations for a wedding procession, Jesus tells them the story of the ten virgins "by their experience illustrating the experience of the church that shall live just before His second coming" *(Christ's Object Lessons,* p. 406).

At first glance the girls appear to be all alike:

They are all young unmarried girls.

They are all waiting for the arrival of the bridegroom.

They all have lamps.

And when the bridegroom is delayed they "all slumbered and slept."

Those waiting for the bridegroom are called virgins because they profess a pure faith. Their lamps represent the word of God. "Thy word is a lamp unto my feet" (Psalm 119:105). We know that the oil is the

Holy Spirit (see Zechariah 4:1-14). While the virgins are waiting for the delayed bridegroom there doesn't seem to be any difference among them. But when the cry goes out, "He is coming," the foolish virgins find that they are destitute of the oil of the Holy Spirit. What makes half of the virgins foolish is that they failed to prepare—they are not ready.

"Without the Spirit of God a knowledge of His word is of no avail. The theory of truth, unaccompanied by the Holy Spirit, cannot quicken the soul or sanctify the heart. One may be familiar with the commands and promises of the Bible; but unless the Spirit of God sets the truth home, the character will not be transformed. Without the enlightenment of the Spirit, men will not be able to distinguish truth from error, and they will fall under the masterful temptations of Satan" *(ibid.,* pp. 410, 411).

It is most intriguing to realize that the lack of the Holy Spirit in this story has the same results as the failure to have on the wedding garment in the other story. And both stories talk about the transformation of the heart—the character. This was the only difference between the wise and the foolish. "The class represented by the foolish virgins are not hypocrites. They have a regard for the truth, they have advocated the truth, they are attracted to those who believe the truth; but they have not yielded themselves to the Holy Spirit's working. . . . The Spirit works upon man's heart, according to his desire and consent implanting in him a new nature; but the class represented by the foolish virgins have been content with a superficial work. They do not know God" *(ibid.,* p. 411). This superficial work of not knowing God is apparently what Paul was referring to when he stated that "in the last days perilous times will come: For men will be lovers of themselves . . . having a form of godliness but denying its power" (2 Timothy 3:1, 5). Many last-day Christians deny the power of God by not allowing that power to transform their lives. "Through the Holy Spirit, God's word is a light as it becomes a transforming power in the life of the receiver. By implanting in their hearts the principles of His word, the Holy Spirit develops in men the attributes of God" *(ibid.,* p. 414).

As we saw earlier, the gospel means more than just believing. Ellen White concludes her comments on the ten virgins by saying, "The religion of Christ means more than the forgiveness of sin; it means taking away our sins, and filling the vacuum with the graces of the Holy Spirit" *(ibid.,* p. 420). In the story of the ten virgins there is an interesting paradox. Why can't the wise virgins share a little of their oil with the foolish ones? It would seem the "Christian thing to do." The Spirit's working in our hearts develops character. And character is not transferable. No one can believe for another. No one can receive the Spirit for another. No one can be transformed for another. No one can share with another the character which is the fruit of the Spirit's working. Perhaps the most interesting point in this story is when Jesus said, "And those who were <u>ready</u> went in with him to the wedding; and the door was shut" (Matthew 25:10). That's the point of this entire book—being ready.

Remember we have a heaven to win and a hell to shun. No doubt the saddest words of all Scripture are those spoken to the foolish virgins, "I know you not."

From these three stories of the great supper we learn that:

1. Everyone is invited—everyone! But some become so engrossed in the things of this world that they finally refuse the invitation to the supper and say, "Have me excused."
2. There is a preparation to be made. The guests must have on the wedding garment. It's a free gift, but you must have one. It is the transforming power of God provided by His indwelling Spirit that brings forth obedience to God's law.
3. The waiting time is longer than expected. We might get weary, but we will be ready if we have been filled with and transformed by the Holy Spirit.
4. The time to make preparation is now—not when the cry goes out, "He's here!"

Many professional people today have sophisticated time-management systems to keep them organized and "focused" on what is important in the press of life. To name a few there are the Day Timer, the Franklin Quest System, special computer programs, and large notebook calendars. In most systems the individual user is encouraged to note in a special order the projects or appointments that are planned for the future. Those that are most important are placed at the top of each day's list. Being ready for the great supper should be at the top of every day's list, and be transferred to the top of every succeeding day, week, month, and year.

Do you ever make a written list when you are getting ready for a special appointment? I do. Our family has always enjoyed camping in the fall. Camping is fun—if you are prepared. Fun—unless you forget something important like matches. So I make a list: food, clothes, flashlight with extra batteries, stove, fuel, water, ax, dry wood, sleeping bag and pad, tent, bug spray, and of course, matches. Wouldn't it be terrible to have a very special appointment planned and then miss it? We can't let that happen in regard to the great supper. Have you told the Lord that you are planning to be there? Are you getting ready?

A couple of years ago I was in Colorado Springs for an appointment. On my return trip, I arrived at the airport a couple of hours early, checked my luggage, and got my seat assignment. Then I went to the gate designated for the flight to Denver and on to Baltimore. Since I was so early, there was another flight that left from that same gate to another destination before my scheduled flight. I watched as passengers came to the gate area in preparation for the earlier flight. Some family members and friends came to greet those on the arriving flight. The plane came and unloaded and all the waiting passengers got on. The plane door was shut and the jetway pulled back. Then the powerful little tractor pushed the plane back away from the gate area. Finally it began to move under its own power down the taxiway.

Colorado Springs is not a busy airport as airports go, so for just a few short seconds I was left alone. Only the ticket agent remained, doing the final paperwork for the flight that had just left. Just then a man came rushing into the gate area shouting, "Stop that plane! That's my plane!" The ticket agent quickly explained that once the plane was under its own power and moving away from the gate area, it could not be called back. The man then became very discourteous. He lost his temper. He stated that they knew that he was going to be on that plane since he had purchased his ticket "more than a month ago." The agent explained that frequently folks with tickets do not show up for a particular flight because their circumstances have changed. And so if passengers are not there on time the plane must leave on schedule to make its later connections. It cannot wait for someone who might never show up. The agent pointed out to the man that since he had had his ticket for over a month, he had known for at least that long when the flight would leave. It was up to him to make the necessary arrangements to be at the airport on time. The application to our spiritual destination—our meeting with a soon-coming Lord—seems quite clear.

CHAPTER 6

The Robe of Righteousness

As a general rule of etiquette we are told to "dress for the occasion." If I am going waterskiing I would wear a bathing suit and life vest. The same outfit would be quite ridiculous for snow skiing, however. When I see someone dressed in a full suit of insulated clothes, gloves, and face mask, I think they are probably going for a snowmobile ride. If I see someone in comfortable shorts, colorful T-shirt, white socks, and "tennis shoes," I get the impression that person is going walking or jogging.

When you see a man dressed in tough pants, leather boots, leather gloves, and a hard hat you would likely think him a construction worker. If you see a person dressed with a helmet, shoulder pads, a jersey with numbers, tight pants with a stripe down the side, and shoes with spikes on them you are probably looking at a football player. If you see a family leaving their home on Sabbath morning all dressed up, with shoes shined and Bibles under their arms you could well be seeing some Seventh-day Adventists going to church. It is quite appropriate to dress for the occasion. In addition, our dress and mannerisms tell a story about who we are and where we are going.

What would you expect to see a person wearing if he or she is on their way to heaven to live with Jesus and the angels? Would any of the outfits I have described above be appropriate? If they are really serious about going to live with Jesus they will be wearing the robe of Christ's righteousness—the wedding garment. Though you might not be able to see the actual weave of the white robe, you could tell they had one on. By their very mannerisms—you could tell.

The Robe of Righteousness

There are numerous references in the Bible to the robe that must be worn by those who are saved and taken to the eternal kingdom. This robe of righteousness is the same as the wedding garment we discussed in the last chapter. We look at it now in this chapter as the robe of righteousness. The new perspectives here will add to our understanding of what it is and how to get one. One quickly sees that the garments that we have devised are not what God had in mind. Adam and Eve tried to form garments of fig leaves to take the place of the covering of light that God had given them at Creation. In fact, even when we have on real clothes instead of leaves they are described as "filthy rags" (Isaiah 64:6). But God has something much better in mind. It is an expensive, spotless robe, woven in the loom of heaven. It is provided to the repenting, believing sinner.

Isaiah described his delight in having received such a garment. "I will greatly rejoice in the Lord. My soul shall be joyful in my God. For He has clothed me with the garments of salvation, He has covered me with the robe of righteousness, as a bridegroom decks himself with ornaments, and as a bride adorns herself with her jewels" (Isaiah 61:10). When the lost (prodigal) son comes to himself and returns home, his father says to his servants, "Bring out the best robe and put it on him" (Luke 15:22).

Ellen White makes the application this way: "He [Jesus] bids you exchange your poverty for the riches of His grace. We are not worthy of God's love, but Christ, our surety, is worthy, and is abundantly able to save all who shall come unto Him. Whatever may have been your past experience, however discouraging your present circumstances, if you will come to Jesus just as you are, weak, helpless, and despairing, our compassionate Saviour will meet you a great way off, and will throw about you His arms of love and His robe of righteousness. He presents us to the Father clothed in the white raiment of His own character" *(Thoughts From the Mount of Blessing,* pp. 8, 9). As a financial counselor and teacher I find this a very intriguing statement. Christ is my "surety." He "co-signs" for me. This is something that I counsel folks never to do for anyone else, because so often the co-signer ends up paying the debt. And Christ does so in this case as well! I am not credit-worthy. But He becomes my surety. I am worthy of death for my sins. He died for ME! He has already paid my debt!

Conversion Is a Big Deal

Conversion is not just acknowledging our sinfulness. It also involves our sorrow for sin and turning away from it. It is a state of surrender to God that invites Him to do the work of cleansing—of regeneration and restoration. After King David's tragic encounter with Bathsheba he responded to God in a way that has been used as a model for all sinners down through time. Again and again he pleads with God, "Forgive me, change me, give me strength for victory." In his own words he says, "Hide Your face from my sins, and blot out all my iniquities [forgive me]. Create in me a clean heart, O God, and renew a steadfast spirit within me [change me]. Do not cast me away from Your presence [forgive me], and do not take Your Holy Spirit from me [I need His cleansing power]. Restore to me the joy of Your salvation, and uphold me with Your generous Spirit [give me strength]" (Psalm 51:9-12).

In his second sermon, Peter outlines this same experience. "Repent therefore and be converted, that your sins may be blotted out, so that times of refreshing may come from the presence of the Lord" (Acts 3: 19). We all need to understand the process of conversion. It is a big deal because it is a miracle when it happens. People don't change of themselves. We all know that. We are the victims of our inherited and cultivated tendencies to evil. "The conversion of the human soul is of no little consequence. It is the greatest miracle performed by divine power. Actual results are to be reached through a belief in Christ as personal Saviour. Purified by obedience to the law of God, sanctified by a perfect observance of His holy Sabbath, trusting, believing, patiently waiting, and earnestly working out our own salvation with fear and trembling, we shall learn that it is God that worketh in us to will and to do of His good pleasure" *(Evangelism,* p. 289).

I found two very explicit statements that describe the change that takes place in the life of one who is converted. Do they describe your experience? The first is in *The Faith I Live By,* page 139.

"Conversion is a work that most do not appreciate. It is not a small matter to transform an earthly, sin-loving mind and bring it to understand the unspeakable love of Christ, the charms of His grace, and the excellency of God, so that the soul shall be imbued with divine love and captivated with the heavenly mysteries. When he understands these things, his former life appears disgusting and hateful. He hates sin, and, breaking his heart before God, he embraces Christ as the life and joy of the soul. He renounces his former pleasures. He has a new mind, new affections, new interest, new will; his sorrows, and desires, and love are all new. . . . <u>Heaven, which once possessed no charms, is now viewed in its riches and glory; and he contemplates it as his future home</u>, where he shall see, love, and praise the One who hath redeemed him by His precious blood. The works of holiness, which appeared wearisome, are now his delight. The Word of God, which was dull and uninteresting, is now chosen as his study, the man of his counsel. It is a letter written to him from God, bearing the inscription of the Eternal. His thoughts, his words, and his deeds are brought to this rule and tested. He trembles at the commands and threatenings which it contains, while he firmly grasps its promises and strengthens his soul by appropriating them to himself."

The second statement is presented as a definition of conversion. "Conversion is a change of heart, a turning from unrighteousness to righteousness. Relying on the merits of Christ, exercising true faith in Him, the repentant sinner receives pardon for sin. As he ceases to do evil and learns to do well, he grows in grace and in the knowledge of God. He sees that in order to follow Jesus he must separate from the world, and after counting the cost, he looks upon all as loss if he may but win Christ. He enlists in His army and bravely and cheerfully engages in the warfare, fighting against natural inclinations and selfish desires and bringing the will into subjection to the will of Christ. Daily he seeks the Lord for grace, and he is strengthened and helped. Now self is dethroned, and God reigns supreme. His life reveals the fruit of righteousness. The sins he once lived he now hates. Firmly and resolutely he follows in the path of holiness. <u>This is genuine conversion</u>" *(In Heavenly Places,* p. 20).

When Paul described conditions in the last days he described our day to the "T." Think about the current state of society when you read his words. "But know this, that in the last days perilous times will come: For men will be lovers of themselves, lovers of money, boasters, proud, blasphemers, disobedient to parents, unthankful, unholy, unloving, unforgiving, slanderers, without self-control, brutal, despisers of good, traitors, headstrong, haughty, lovers of pleasure rather than lovers of God, <u>having a form of godliness, but denying its power</u>. And from such people turn away" (2 Timothy 3:1-5)!

A form of godliness with no power. Another name for it would be nominal Christianity. Profession without practice. But what is the power that is lacking? Is this description given because the volume is too low on the music? Hardly. The power is the grace of God that provides not only pardon, but also the power of transformation. It is the miracle-working power of God. It is also power for witnessing that will eventually lighten the whole earth. The powerless Christians Paul identifies are those who are not really experiencing the conversion experience. They don't enjoy Bible study, are not in love with their Saviour, and they have not accepted heaven as their real home.

I Die Daily

What did Paul indicate was his remedy for this powerless religion? The experience of dying daily contains the secret of Paul's victorious experience. Throughout his life of faithful service for the Saviour he had met on the Damascus road, Paul found that his old, unregenerate nature struggled for recognition and had to be constantly repressed. He well knew that the life of the Christian must be one of self-denial at every step of the road. A number of Bible writers apparently engaged in a daily recommitment of their lives to God. David cried out, "Be merciful unto me, O Lord: for I cry unto thee daily" (Psalm 86:3). Daniel, about whom no sin is ever mentioned, had the custom of planned prayer sessions three times each day (see Daniel 6:10). What did he pray about then? When you study his prayers you see that he prayed for wisdom and he prayed for others. No doubt his faithful prayer life was a major factor in his holy life.

Jesus, when commenting on the cost of discipleship, stated, "If anyone desires to come after Me, let him deny himself, and take up his cross daily, and follow Me" (Luke 9:23). The Scriptures record that the Bereans were "more noble than those in Thessalonia, in that they received the word with all readiness, and searched the Scriptures daily to find out whether these things were so" (Acts 17:11). Again, Jesus instructed that our prayers to the Father should include "Give us this day our daily bread" (Matthew 6:11).

This daily experience is encouraged for obvious reasons. "Genuine conversion is needed, <u>not once in years, but daily</u>. This conversion brings man into a new relation with God. Old things, his natural passions and hereditary and cultivated tendencies to wrong, pass away, and he is renewed and sanctified. But this work must be continual; for as long as Satan exists, he will make an effort to carry on his work. He who strives to serve God will encounter a strong undercurrent of wrong. His heart needs to be barricaded by constant watchfulness and prayer, or else the embankment will give way; and like a millstream, the undercurrent of wrong will sweep away the safeguard. No renewed heart can be kept in a condition of sweetness without the daily application of the salt of the Word. Divine grace must be received daily, or no man will stay converted" *(Our High Calling,* p. 215).

A daily spiritual exercise is spelled out in the book *Steps to Christ.* "Consecrate yourself to God in the morning; make this your very first work. Let your prayer be, 'Take me, O Lord, as wholly Thine. I lay all my plans at Thy feet. Use me today in Thy service. Abide with me, and let all my work be wrought in Thee.' This is a daily matter. Each morning consecrate yourself to God for that day. Surrender all your plans to Him, to be carried out or given up as His providence shall indicate. Thus day by day you may be giving your life into the hands of God, and thus your life will be molded more and more after the life of Christ" *(Steps to Christ,* p. 70).

This is not a mystery book. You don't have to read all the way to the last few pages to see "who done it?" We already know the stakes. God has a high unchangeable standard. We fall way short in our own efforts. But He met the standard and offers to help us meet it too. This book is about salvation. I do not claim to be a theologian, and I'm glad I don't need to be to understand and experience salvation. I have, however, spent many hours reading hundreds of Bible texts and statements from Ellen White's counsels on the topic of salvation and readiness for the Second Coming. What I have found are thrilling calls for surrender and regeneration. Some of this we have already shared—but it gets even better.

The Experience of Salvation

In the book *Seventh-day Adventists Believe,* the experience of salvation is described as follows: "In infinite love and mercy God made Christ, who knew no sin, to be sin for us, so that in Him we might be made the righteousness of God. Led by the Holy Spirit we sense our need, acknowledge our sinfulness, repent of our transgressions, and exercise faith in Jesus as Lord and Christ, as Substitute and Example. This faith which receives salvation comes through the divine power of the Word and is the gift of God's grace. Through Christ we are justified, adopted as God's sons and daughters, and delivered from the lordship of sin. Through the Spirit we are born again and sanctified; the Spirit renews our minds, writes God's laws of love in our hearts, and we are given power to live a holy life. Abiding in Him we become partakers of the divine nature and have the assurance of salvation now and in the judgment" (p. 118).

When we experience justification we are forgiven. When we experience sanctification we are changed into the likeness of Christ. "True repentance and justification lead to sanctification. Justification and sanctification are closely related, distinct but never separate. They designate two phases of salvation: Justification is what God does *for* us, while sanctification is what God does *in* us.

"Neither justification nor sanctification is the result of meritorious works. Both are solely due to Christ's grace and righteousness. 'The righteousness by which we are justified is imputed; the righteousness by which we are sanctified is imparted. The first is our title to heaven, the second is our fitness for heaven'" *(Review and Herald,* June 4, 1895).

"The three phases of sanctification the Bible presents are: (1) an accomplished act in the believer's past [justification]; (2) a process in the believer's present experience [regeneration]; and (3) the final result that the believer experiences at Christ's return [glorification]" *(ibid.,* p. 123).

If we have accepted Christ as our Saviour we have been justified. Our names have been recorded in the book of life. We have accomplished phase one of sanctification. Phase three of sanctification is the work of God alone on those who have accomplished phases one and two by accepting the free gifts of justification and regeneration. Phase two, regeneration, is perhaps the most critical for our attention now because faithfulness here keeps our names in the book of life in the judgment. "He who overcomes shall be clothed in white garments, and I will not blot out his name from the Book of Life, but I will confess his name before My Father and before His angels" (Revelation 3:5).

If you have not accepted Christ as your Saviour from sin and entered into the justified experience, I encourage you to do so now. In this experience we acknowledge our sinful condition and our need of

Christ, we confess our sins in repentance—a sorrow for sin and a turning away from it—and we thank God for His great gift to us. At the same time we ask God to "create in us a new heart and renew a right spirit within us." If you have accepted Christ as your Saviour from sin, you have been justified. The pressing need now, in the light of the nearness of Christ's second coming, is preparing for heaven—phase two of the sanctification process. This is the focus of the book—getting fit for heaven. It is a miraculous work, a gift from God, but it takes our personal involvement.

Only the Creator can accomplish the creative work of transforming our lives. He is willing and able to do this, as Paul explained. "Now may the God of peace Himself sanctify you completely; and may your whole spirit, soul, and body be preserved blameless at the coming of our Lord Jesus Christ. He who calls you is faithful, **who also will do it**" (1 Thessalonians 5:23, 24). Our sanctification is the work of God. However, He does not do so without our participation. We must place ourselves in the channel of the Spirit's working, which we can do by beholding Christ. As we meditate on Christ's life, study His Word, and share what God has done for us with others, the Holy Spirit restores the physical, mental, and spiritual faculties. "According to His mercy He saved us, through the washing of regeneration and renewing of the Holy Spirit" (Titus 3:5).

God desires to live within His people. It was because He had promised "I will dwell in them" (2 Cor. 6:16; cf. 1 John 3:24; 4:12) that Paul could say: "Christ lives in me" (Gal. 2:20; cf. John 14:23). This is why healthful living is so important. Our bodies are the temple of God! The Creator's indwelling daily revives the believers inwardly (2 Cor. 4:16), renewing their minds (Rom. 12:2; see also Phil. 2:5).

Partaking of the Divine Nature

In the first chapter of His second letter Peter explains how we can partake of the divine nature. "Grace and peace be multiplied to you in the knowledge of God and of Jesus our Lord, as His divine power has given to us all things that pertain to life and godliness, through the knowledge of Him who called us by glory and virtue, by which have been given to us **exceedingly great and precious promises,** that through these **you may be partakers of the divine nature,** having escaped the corruption that is in the world through lust" (2 Peter 2:2-4).

Then after giving God the credit for "all things that pertain to life and godliness," Peter outlines the part that man is to play in the sanctification process. "Giving all diligence, add to your faith virtue, to virtue knowledge, to knowledge self-control, to self-control perseverance, to perseverance godliness, to godliness brotherly kindness, and to brotherly kindness love." Peter starts his ladder to sanctification by saying, "Giving all diligence." Now he goes on to say, "Therefore, brethren, be even more diligent to make your call and election sure, for if you do these things you will never stumble; for so an entrance will be supplied to you abundantly into the everlasting kingdom of our Lord and Savior Jesus Christ" (2 Peter 1:5-11).

" 'Partakers of the divine nature.' Is this possible? Of ourselves we can do no good thing. How, then, can we be partakers of the divine nature?—By coming to Christ just as we are, needy, helpless, dependent. He died to make it possible for us to be partakers of the divine nature. He took humanity upon Himself that He might reach humanity. With the golden chain of His matchless love He has bound us to the throne of God. We are to have power to overcome as He overcame" *(Review and Herald,* April 14, 1904). Another statement makes the point even stronger. "By Christ's wonderful union of divinity with humanity, we are assured that even in this world we may be partakers of the divine nature, overcoming the corruption that is in the world through lust" *(Review and Herald,* May 13, 1909).

The transformation that takes place in the life and character of the Christian as he submits to the regenerating power of God is a mystery similar to that of the incarnation of the Son of God. "As the Holy Spirit enabled the divine Christ to partake of human nature, so that Spirit enables us to partake of the divine character traits. This appropriation of the divine nature renews the inner person, making us Christlike, though on a different level: Whereas Christ became human, believers do not become divine. Rather, they become Godlike in character" *(Seventh-day Adventists Believe,* p. 126).

A Total Lifestyle Change

There is no point in being "born again" if we are just going to go on living as we did before we accepted Christ. In the new-birth process brought about by the Holy Spirit a real transformation takes place. If we will cooperate with Him, God will change us as fallen beings into His image by transforming our wills, minds, desires, and characters.

"We are to comply with the terms of salvation, or we are lost. At the hour when we leave the service of Satan for the service of Christ, when true conversion takes place, and by faith we turn from transgression to obedience, the severest of the heart struggles takes place. But many accept the theory of truth, and compromise with the world, the flesh, and the devil. The soul that has truly experienced the transforming grace of Christ has chosen Christ for its portion; it yields to the gracious influence of His Holy Spirit, and thus the character is formed according to the divine pattern. We are to feel, to act, as one with Christ" *(Review and Herald,* January 31, 1893).

The Holy Spirit brings to believers a decided change. Instead of the "works of the flesh"—things like adultery, hatred, contentions, temper tantrums, selfishness, and intemperance (see Galatians 5:19-21)—the fruit of the Spirit is now starting to grow in the life of the believer. The fruit is manifested in its various forms: love, joy, peace, longsuffering, kindness, goodness, faithfulness, gentleness, and self-control (see Galatians 5:22, 23).

Our concern as we contemplate the soon return of Christ is the same concern that He expressed, "Will He find faith on the earth?" (Luke 18:8). Many "have nominally accepted the truth but they do not practice it" *(Testimonies,* vol. 6, p. 295). How can we really feel that we are ready to meet our Saviour when half of us don't even bother to attend church on Sabbath and an even larger number rob Him with impunity by withholding tithes and offerings? We are a privileged generation. We can stand on the shoulders of the apostles, the Reformers, our pioneers, Ellen White, and see much more than they saw. We have not only all the light that God gave them; we have also the ability to see the amazing fulfillment of world conditions which tell us that the end is near.

What Is Man's Part?

With just a little thought one can see that man has a part to play in his own salvation. For example, we all know that Jesus died for every man, woman, and child who have ever lived and all who will ever live. But will all be saved? No! Unfortunately, the Scriptures indicate that many take the broad road to destruction. What makes the difference then between those who are saved and those who are lost? It is the very thing we are talking about in this chapter. Those who are saved will make a conscious decision to accept the gift of God and then invite His Spirit to transform them.

Nature provides a good illustration of man's part in salvation. "God has given man land to be cultivated. But in order that the harvest may be reaped, there must be harmonious action between the divine and human agencies. The plow and other implements of labor must be used at the right time. The seed must be sown in its season. Man is not to fail of doing his part. If he is careless and negligent, his unfaithfulness testifies against him. The harvest is proportionate to the energy he has expended.

"So it is in spiritual things. We are to be laborers together with God. Man is to work out his salvation with fear and trembling, for it is God that worketh in him, both to will and to do of his good pleasure. There is to be co-partnership, a divine relation, between the Son of God and the repentant sinner. We are made sons and daughters of God. 'As many as received Him, to them gave He power to become the sons of God.' Christ provides the mercy and grace so abundantly given to all who believe in Him. He fulfills the terms upon which salvation rests. But we must act our part by accepting the blessing in faith. God works and man works. **Resistance of temptation must come from man, who must draw his power from God.** Thus he becomes a co-partner with Christ" *(Review and Herald,* May 28, 1908).

This point of man's involvement in his salvation has been a point of considerable interest to Christians. It is a point where one's opinions are interesting but on which I prefer to check out the inspired counsel. Here is another insight: "In one way we are thrown upon our own energies; we are to strive earnestly to be zealous and to repent, to cleanse our hands and purify our hearts from every defilement; we are to reach the highest standard, believing that God will help us in our efforts. We must seek if we would find, and seek in faith; we must knock, that the door may be opened unto us. The Bible teaches that everything regarding our salvation depends upon our own course of action. If we perish, the responsibility will rest wholly upon ourselves. If provision has been made, and if we accept God's terms, we may lay hold on eternal life. We must come to Christ in faith, we must be diligent to make our calling and election sure" *(Faith and Works,* p. 48).

This is a relationship between the individual and God. We need not concern ourselves with others unless we are interceding on their behalf. There was a time when some members were criticizing the work of Elder Haskell. Ellen White wrote a letter to one such person and said, "Weed diligently your own plot of ground, and let the gardens of others alone. The work is between God and your own soul. Do not delay" *(Manuscript Releases,* vol. 19, p. 52).

Again to the criticizers she wrote, "Let them remember that, while they are watching and criticizing others, they are neglecting to put on the robe of Christ's righteousness" (PH151, *Selections From the Testimonies for the Church,* p. 47).

So as intelligent beings it is time for us to focus on our own relationship with Christ. It is time to think soberly and candidly whether or not we desire to put forth the effort necessary to obtain the Christian hope. We must come to the place where nothing has a higher priority. For nothing else truly matters this much.

The Test of Discipleship

As we have already noted and will continue to see as we contemplate the terms of salvation, the oil in the lamps, the wedding garment, the robe of righteousness, and the answering of the door where Jesus stands knocking all point to the same experience—the conversion experience. The Bible says, "If anyone is in Christ, he is a new creation; old things have passed away; behold, all things have become new" (2 Corinthians 5:17). There is no question—if we are "in Christ," "born again," "converted," it will be evident—we will be different. A disciple is a follower. In the case of a Christian disciple—a follower of Christ. We live the life of Christ by His indwelling Spirit. This seems to be a mystery to so many, but the terms of discipleship are not complicated.

When discussing discipleship Ellen White noted, "If the heart has been renewed by the Spirit of God, the life will bear witness to the fact. While we cannot do anything to change our hearts or to bring ourselves into harmony with God; while we must not trust at all to ourselves or our good works, our lives will reveal whether the grace of God is dwelling within us. A change will be seen in the character, the habits, the pursuits. <u>The contrast will be clear and decided between what they have been and what they are</u>" *(Steps to Christ,* p. 57).

If the change is evident, what could one observe in the life of another who has been born again? "<u>The character is revealed</u>, not by occasional good deeds or occasional misdeeds, but <u>by the tendency of the habitual words and acts</u>" *(ibid.).* One short paragraph describes what change takes place when one is born again—converted, in Christ, wearing the robe of righteousness.

"Those who become new creatures in Christ Jesus will bring forth the fruits of the Spirit, 'love, joy, peace, long-suffering, gentleness, goodness, faith, meekness, temperance.' Galatians 5:22, 23. They will no longer fashion themselves according to the former lusts, but by the faith of the Son of God they will follow in His steps, reflect His character, and purify themselves even as He is pure. <u>The things they once hated they now love, and the things they once loved they hate</u>. The proud and self-assertive become meek and lowly in heart. The vain and supercilious become serious and unobtrusive. The drunken become sober, and the profligate pure. The vain customs and fashions of the world are laid aside. Christians will seek not the 'outward adorning' but 'the hidden man of the heart, in that which is not corruptible, even the ornament of a meek and quiet spirit.' 1 Peter 3:3, 4" *(ibid.,* pp. 58, 59).

When one has come to Christ he no longer tries to "just get by." He actually enjoys being obedient! "I delight to do Your will, O my God, and Your law is within my heart" (Psalm 40:8). No more does he question "What is wrong with this or that?" or "Just a little won't hurt, will it? God is love, He is not picky." "When, as erring, sinful beings, we come to Christ and become partakers of His pardoning grace, love springs up in the heart. Every burden is light, for the yoke that Christ imposes is easy. <u>Duty becomes a delight, and sacrifice a pleasure</u>. The path that before seemed shrouded in darkness, becomes bright with beams from the Sun of Righteousness" *(ibid.,* p. 59).

Can I know that I have passed from death to life? The answer is "Yes." <u>I can tell *if* my life has been changed</u>. "There is no evidence of genuine repentance unless it works reformation. If he restores the pledge, give again that he had robbed, confess his sins, and love God and his fellow men, <u>the sinner **may be sure** that he has passed from death unto life</u>" *(ibid.).*

A Readiness Test

The following test is designed to be administered by the individual being tested. It is quite personal and deals with matters of the heart. It is very accurate. It is not to be confused with the fruits test that God asked us to use when determining the difference between true and false prophets. Here is the test:

"No man stumbles into heaven. No one goes there blindfolded. If he will take time to consider, every man may know whether he is in the straight and narrow path, or on the broad road that leads to death and hell. Let every soul inquire,

(1) Is my heart renewed by the grace of Christ?

(2) Is it transformed by the Holy Spirit?

(3) Have I repented of my sins and confessed them?

(4) Are my sins forgiven?

(5) Am I a new creature in Christ Jesus?

(6) Do I count all things but loss for the excellency of the knowledge of Christ Jesus?

(7) Am I willing to make an entire consecration of every hour that remains to do service for the Saviour?

He gave His life for me; He is risen from the dead, and has brought life and immortality to light, that I might be a partaker of the divine nature.

(8) Will I purify my soul by obeying the truth, and becoming complete in Him?"

This self-test was printed by Ellen White in the *Signs of the Times,* January 25, 1897. If I can answer yes to the eight questions, I can be confident I am traveling the straight and narrow road that leads to life.

Pliable's Conversation With Christian

Any questions about going to heaven? Listen in on a unique conversation that John Bunyan, author of *The Pilgrim's Progress,* wrote for Christian and Pliable. He gives some interesting insights.

Pli. Come, neighbor Christian, since there are none but us two here, tell me now further, what the things are, and how to be enjoyed, whither we are going.

Chr. I can better conceive of them with my mind than speak of them with my tongue: but yet, since you are desirous to know, I will read of them in my book.

Pli. And do you think that the words of your book are certainly true?

Chr. Yes, verily; for it was made by Him that cannot lie.

Pli. Well said; what things are they?

Chr. There is an endless kingdom to be inhabited, and everlasting life to be given us, that we may inhabit that kingdom for ever.

Pli. Well said; and what else:

Chr. There are crowns of glory to be given us; and garments that will make us shine like the sun in the firmament of heaven.

Pli. This is excellent; and what else?

Chr. There shall be no more crying, nor sorrow: for He that is owner of the place will wipe all tears from our eyes.

Pli. And what company shall we have there?

Chr. There we shall be with seraphims and cherubims; creatures that will dazzle your eyes to look on them. There also you shall meet with thousands and ten thousands [that have lived before and will join us in the resurrection]; none of them are hurtful, but loving and holy; every one walking in the sight of God, and standing in His presence with acceptance for ever. In a word, there we shall see the elders with their golden crowns; there we shall see the holy virgins with their golden harps; there we shall see men, that by the world were cut in pieces, burnt in flames, eaten of beasts, drowned in the seas, for the love they bare to the Lord of the place; all well and clothed with im-mortality as with a garment.

Pli. The hearing of this is enough to ravish one's heart. But are these things to be enjoyed? How shall we get to be sharers hereof?

Chr. The Lord, the governor of the country, hath recorded that in this book; the substance of which is, If we be truly willing to have it, He will bestow it upon us freely.

[And now comes Pliable's awesome response.]

Pli. Well my good companion, glad am I to hear of these things: come on, let us mend our pace" (John Bunyan, *Pilgrim's Progress,* pp. 21, 22).

That's the way I feel too, don't you? Since God has described in His unerring Word what He has planned for those who love Him; and since we know we are so close to the end of the road, Let's hurry on!

With the goal in sight and the strength of the Lord let's move forward in faith and obedience. This is not a time for fear and timidity. "There is before the church the dawn of a bright, glorious day, if she will put on the robe of Christ's righteousness, withdrawing from all allegiance to the world. . . . From Christ is flowing the living stream of salvation. . . . When in faith we take hold of His strength, He will change, wonderfully change, the most hopeless, discouraging outlook. He will do this for the glory of His name" *(Sons and Daughters of God,* p. 218).

An Awesome Promise

This is a book about urgency and about hope. We can be ready. Jesus provides the terms of salvation and the power to meet them. Note this next tremendous promise—every sentence is power-packed.

"All who have put on the robe of Christ's righteousness will stand before Him as chosen and faithful and true. Satan has no power to pluck them out of the hand of the Saviour. Not one soul who in penitence and faith has claimed His protection will Christ permit to pass under the enemy's power. His word is pledged: 'Let him take hold of my strength, that he may make peace with Me; and he shall make peace with Me' (Isaiah 27:5). The promise given to Joshua is given to all: 'If thou wilt keep my charge, . . . I will give thee places to walk among these that stand by' (Zechariah 3:7). Angels of God will walk on either side of them, even in this world, and they will stand at last among the angels that surround the throne of God" *(God's Amazing Grace,* p. 316).

CHAPTER 7

Be Not Deceived

God's love for each one of us is beyond our comprehension. Why the Creator would stoop to become man and then suffer and die for us is a great mystery. However, as we accept this as fact by faith we have peace with God. And we will want to respond in loving obedience. It has occurred to me, while researching and writing this book, that this information about the new birth experience and the power of God to transform us is straight from heaven. God wants us to be ready for His coming! This is yet another indication that the Second Coming is soon. The harvest of earth is ripening.

We have now come to realize that no one just stumbles into heaven. Getting there will require choosing the narrow, less traveled road. It means making a decision to trust God fully and put our readiness for heaven as first priority. It means inviting the Spirit of God into our lives and asking God to transform us from the inside out. We in effect become transparent. What you see is what we are: sinners being transformed into beings fit to live in the company of those who are holy—the company of heaven. It's simple. We can't make excuses. We just need to recognize that we must change our hearts and our citizenship, and we can't do either alone. We need the power of God. He is waiting to give it. He wants to transform us. He died to make it possible! Surely this is the time to fully accept His offer!

Now comes a very significant reality. Once we are fitted with the robe of Christ's righteousness, once we have been made ready by the power of God, then along comes Satan. The Bible describes him as a roaring lion seeking whom he may devour. The devil's major tool is deception. From the time he deceived Eve in the Garden of Eden he has used this as his most effective tool.

Jesus warned us again and again to beware of deception. Just in Matthew 24 He waves the red flag warning of danger four times.

1. "Take heed that no one deceives you" (v. 4).

2. "For many will come in My name, saying, 'I am Christ,' and will deceive many" (v. 5).

3. "Then many false prophets will rise up and deceive many" (v. 11).

4. "For false christs and false prophets will arise and show great signs and wonders, so as to deceive, if possible, even the elect" (v. 24).

Let's consider ourselves warned!

The Emperor's New Clothes

Hans Christian Andersen, Denmark's most famous author, wrote many children's stories. But many of his tales have serious meanings intended for adult readers. One such story, "The Emperor's New Clothes," makes a very focused point to illustrate what we have talked about thus far.

It concerns an Emperor who was very clothes-conscious. One day two swindlers came to his city. They claimed that they could weave the finest cloth imaginable. Clothes made of this beautiful material had the magical quality of being invisible to any man who was unfit for his office, or anyone who was hopelessly stupid.

This appealed to the Emperor. So he advanced money to the swindlers and asked them to begin work at once.

They set up two looms and pretended to be weaving cloth. They asked for the silk and gold, which they put into their own bags, and continued to work at the empty looms.

The Emperor was curious to see the progress on his clothes. But he remembered that whoever was not fit for his office could not see it. He was confident of his own ability, but to be safe he decided to send his honest old minister to check it out.

"He can judge best how the stuff looks, for he is intelligent, and nobody is better fitted for his office than he," said the Emperor.

The good old minister was shocked to see only empty looms. But he dared not reveal his inability to see anything.

"'Oh, it is very pretty—quite enchanting!' said the old minister, peering through his glasses. 'What a pattern, and what colour! I shall tell the Emperor that I am very much pleased with it.'. . . .

"Soon afterwards the Emperor sent another honest official to the weavers to see how they were getting on, and if the cloth was nearly finished. Like the old minister, he looked and looked, but could see nothing, as there was nothing to be seen. . . .

" 'I am not stupid,' thought the man, 'so it must be that I am unfit for my post. It is ludicrous, but I must not let anyone know it.' So he praised the cloth, which he did not see, and expressed his pleasure at the beautiful colours and the fine pattern. 'Yes, it is quite enchanting,' he said to the Emperor.

"Everybody in the whole town was talking about the beautiful cloth. At last the Emperor wished to see it himself while it was still on the loom. With a whole company of chosen courtiers, including the two honest councillors who had already been there, he went to the two clever swindlers, who were now weaving away as hard as they could, but without using any thread.

" 'Is it not magnificent?' said both the honest statesmen. 'Look, your Majesty, what a pattern! What colours!' And they pointed to the empty looms, for they imagined the others could see the cloth.

" 'What is this?' thought the Emperor. 'I do not see anything at all. This is terrible! Am I stupid? Am I unfit to be Emperor? That would indeed be the most dreadful thing that could happen to me!'

" 'Yes, it is very beautiful,' said the Emperor. 'It has our highest approval,' and nodding contentedly, he gazed at the empty loom, for he did not want to say that he could see nothing. All the attendants who were with him looked and looked, and, although they could not see anything more than the others, they said, just like the Emperor, 'Yes, it is very fine.' They all advised him to wear the new magnificent clothes at a great procession that was soon to take place. 'It is magnificent! beautiful, excellent!' went from mouth to mouth, and everybody seemed delighted. . . .

"And so the Emperor marched in the procession under the beautiful canopy, and all who saw him in the street and out of the windows exclaimed: 'How marvelous the Emperor's new suit is! What a long train he has! How well it fits him!' Nobody would let the others know that he saw nothing, for then he would have been shown to be unfit for his office or too stupid. None of the Emperor's clothes had ever been such a success.

"'But he has nothing on at all,' said a little child.

"'Good heaven! Hear what the innocent child says!' said the father, and then each whispered to the other what the child said. 'He has nothing on at all,' cried the people at last. And the Emperor too was feeling very worried, for it seemed to him that they were right, but he thought to himself, 'All the same, I must go through with the procession.' And he held himself stiffer than ever, and the chamberlains walked on, holding up the train which was not there at all."

Jesus warns, "Behold, I am coming as a thief. Blessed is he who watches, and keeps his garments, lest he walk naked and they see his shame" (Revelation 16:15). It is a great deception of Satan to think that we don't need the wedding garment—the robe of Christ's righteousness. But any who do not have it will stand naked before the judgment bar of God. As far as God and spiritual things are concerned we are either clothed with Christ's righteousness or we stand naked and attempt to cover ourselves with fig leaves (see Genesis 3:7). Like the emperor in the story we think that we are rich, and increased with goods, and have need of nothing; but we don't realize that really we are wretched, and miserable, and poor, and blind, and naked (see Revelation 3:17). The most unfortunate position to be in is to actually recognize that we are naked as the emperor did and yet still go on more stiffly than ever.

Why don't our fig-leaf clothes account for anything? "This is the covering that the transgressors of the law of God have used since the days of Adam and Eve's disobedience. They have sewed together fig leaves to cover their nakedness, cause by transgression. The fig leaves represent the arguments used to cover disobedience" *(Review and Herald,* November 15, 1989).

Self-deception

Because a belief is sincerely held does not make it true. It makes the deception all the more subtle. Self-deception is very difficult to overcome. Some have convinced themselves that since man is not capable of changing himself we will continue living in known sin and then be changed at the Second Coming. This is self-deception! "Many are deceiving themselves by thinking that the character will be transformed at the coming of Christ, but there will be no conversion of heart at His appearing. Our defects of character must here be repented of, and through the grace of Christ we must overcome them while probation shall last. This is the place for fitting up for the family above" *(The Adventist Home,* p. 319).

"You will hear the cry 'Only believe.' Satan believed and trembled. We must have a faith that works by love and purifies the heart. The idea prevails that Christ has done all for us, and that we can go on transgressing the commandments and will not be held accountable for it. **This is the greatest deception that the enemy ever devised.** We must take our position that we will not violate the commandments at any cost, and be in that spiritual condition that we can educate others in spiritual things" *(Selected Messages,* vol. 3, p. 153).

Another aspect of the self-deception scheme is comparing ourselves with others or using our own standards instead of God's. There is much sexual impurity today in the Christian church. Many have rationalized that they are no worse than others that they know, or that God is love and He wants them to be happy and He surely wouldn't want them in a dead-end relationship. But the Bible is clear that those who are sexually impure, unless they repent and reform, are deceiving themselves and will not inherit the kingdom of God (1 Corinthians 6:9); they will receive the second death—death by fire (Revelation 21:8); and that they will end up outside the Holy City at the end with the murderers, sorcerers, idolaters, and liars (Revelation 22:15).

The Power of Deception

The devil's power of deception is so great that he induced a third of the heavenly angels to believe him and separate from God. He has since had 6,000 years of additional experience. He now comes as a wolf in sheep's clothing. He comes now in the form of ministers and teachers—so it is imperative for us to carefully weigh what we read and hear to make sure that it squares with the Bible.

Many today substitute membership in a religious organization for conversion. In Jesus' day many felt that since they were Jews and descendants of Abraham they were saved. Today some say, "I am a Catholic with roots all the way back to St. Peter. I am a part of the one holy Catholic Church." Others say (perhaps to themselves), "I am an

Adventist. I am a part of the remnant church." Or "I am a minister or teacher in the remnant church." "Accepting new theories, and uniting with a church, do not bring new life to anyone, <u>even though the church with which he unites may be established on the true foundation</u>. Connection with a church does not take the place of conversion. To subscribe the name to a church creed is not of the least value to anyone if the heart is not truly changed" *(Evangelism,* p. 290).

When Jesus told Peter that a time of trial and suffering was coming for Him, Peter replied with words that meant "No way, Lord. This will never happen to You!" Jesus responded with a command, "Get thee behind me, Satan." Satan was speaking through Peter, making him act the part of the tempter. Peter did not suspect that Satan was present, but Jesus could detect the presence of the deceiver, and in His rebuke to Peter He addressed the real foe.

Ministers Deceived and Deceiving

Ellen White warned that "there are men who profess to be ministers of the gospel who are teaching heresy, and deceiving many, and leading thousands in the way of apostasy" *(The Youth's Instructor,* September 27, 1894). Yes, the wheat and tares grow together until the harvest. But in the testing time, which surely is not far off, each person will have to make their stand for God or abandon His cause. Unfortunately, "many a star that we have admired for its brilliance will then go out in darkness. Those who have assumed the ornaments of the sanctuary, but are not clothed with Christ's righteousness, will then appear in the shame of their own nakedness" *(Prophets and Kings,* p. 188).

Feelings or Tradition Don't Make Truth

Satan has so deluded men that many believe that they are doing right when they oppose the law of God. Satan has led them to look upon God's law as an arbitrary requirement. Without this standard of truth many are left to depend on their feelings for their religious experience. But "feelings are often deceiving, emotions are no sure safeguard; for they are variable and subject to external circumstances. Many are deluded by relying on sensational impressions. <u>The test is</u>:

- What are you doing for Christ?
- What sacrifices are you making?

- What victories are you gaining?
- A selfish spirit overcome, a temptation to neglect duty resisted, passion subdued, and willing, cheerful obedience rendered to the will of Christ are far greater evidences that you are a child of God than spasmodic piety and emotional religion" *(Testimonies for the Church,* vol. 4, p. 188).

Frequently folks ask me, "What's wrong with this movement [or this book, etc.] because it seems so good. Why can't we join in the unity movement?" One of most insidious things about deception is that it needs some good and some truth to exist. In fact, the more truth the more subtle the deception. The following statement illustrates how and why error is believed by many to be truth. "Error cannot stand alone, and would soon become extinct if it did not fasten itself like a parasite upon the tree of truth. Error draws its life from the truth of God. The traditions of men, like floating germs, attach themselves to the truth of God, and men regard them as a part of the truth. Through false doctrines, Satan gains a foothold, and captivates the minds of men, causing them to hold theories that have no foundation in truth. Men boldly teach for doctrines the commandments of men; and as traditions pass on, from age to age, they acquire a power of the human mind. But age does not make error truth, neither does its burdensome weight cause the plant of truth to become a parasite. The tree of truth bears its own genuine fruit, showing its true origin and nature. The parasite of error also bears its own fruit, and makes manifest that its character is diverse from the plant of heavenly origin" *(Evangelism,* p. 589).

We know that Satan will make direct attacks on many of the truths that we have discovered in the Bible. Some of the areas include the Bible, the Spirit of Prophecy, the sanctuary, the state of the dead, Creation, miracles, tithing, and much more. It is foolish to think that we can find a better Guide than God, a wiser Counselor in any emergency, or a stronger Defense in trouble.

The Deceitfulness of Riches

One of the greatest hindrances to spiritual growth is affluence. Today we have good jobs, comfortable homes, nice cars, retirement plans, credit cards, and vacations. Things are really not that bad for many people. Why do we need God? Because we can't love both God and riches. "The love of money is the root of all kinds of evil, for which some have strayed from the faith in their greediness, and pierced themselves through with many sorrows" (1 Timothy 6:10). John counseled, "Do not love the world or the things in the world. If anyone loves the world the love of the Father is not in him" (1 John 2:15). But in spite of these warnings we still get tangled up in the web of materialism.

Ellen White described the mechanism this way: "I was shown that the love of the world was to a great extent taking the place of love to God. You are situated in a pleasant country, one that is favorable to worldly prosperity. This places you where you are in constant danger of having your interests swallowed up in the world, in laying up treasure upon the earth. **Your hearts will be where your treasure is.** You are situated where there are temptations to be plunging deeper and deeper into the world, to be continually accumulating; and while you are thus engaged, the mind becomes engrossed with the cares of this life to such an extent as to shut out true godliness. But few realize the deceitfulness of riches. Those who are anxious to acquire means are so bent upon this one object as to make the religion of Christ a secondary matter. Spiritual things are not valued and are not sought after, for the love of gain has eclipsed the heavenly treasure. **If the prize of eternal life were to be valued by the zeal, perseverance, and earnestness exhibited by those who profess to be Christians, it would not be half as valuable as earthly possessions.** Compare the earnest effort made to obtain the things of this earth with the languid, weak, and inefficient effort to gain spirituality and a heavenly treasure. No wonder that we experience so little of the illuminating influence from the heavenly sanctuary. Our desires are not in that direction; they are mostly confined to earthly pursuits, seeking for worldly things and neglecting the eternal. Prosperity is blinding the eyes and deceiving the soul. God may speak, but the rubbish of earth prevents His voice from being heard" *(Testimonies for the Church,* vol. 2, p. 183).

In another area one can see the deceitfulness of riches. It is the area of faithfulness in tithing. Many are willing to return one dollar out of ten or ten dollars out of a hundred. But when large amounts are made, for some reason, tithing becomes more difficult. Satan tells people that they would be better off keeping all "their money," using it as they see fit. God says that we will be blessed if we are honest with our tithes and liberal with our offerings. Now who are you going to believe? Who is lying and who is telling the truth? Many don't realize until they are overtaken by problems, that when they rob God of His portion they are really robbing themselves of heavenly blessings and the peace that comes with doing God's will and maintaining the covenant relation with Him.

Guarding Against Deception

There is hope. The devil is crafty, but God has his number. If we stay close to Jesus He will be our protection against the temptations and the deceptions of Satan. "The arrows of the destroyer are about to be hurled against the faithful ones, and no earthly power can turn aside the shaft. But could our eyes be opened we could see angels of God encircling the righteous, that no harm may come upon them" *(Our High Calling,* p. 362).

The Lord has provided abundantly for our warfare against deception. "The Bible is the armory where we may equip for the struggle" *(Review and Herald,* September 15, 1910). The word of truth must be our standard. But we can't just drift along with brief looks at the Sabbath School lesson on Friday night. "Do not think you can safely drift with the current; you must stem the tide, or you will surely become a helpless prey to Satan's power. You are not safe in placing your feet on the ground of the enemy, but should direct your path in the way cast up for the ransomed of the Lord to walk in. Even in the path of holiness you will be tried; your faith, your love, your patience, your constancy, will be tested. **By diligent searching of the Scriptures, by earnest prayer for divine help, prepare the soul to resist temptation.** The Lord will hear the sincere prayer of the contrite soul, and will lift up a standard for you against the enemy" *(The Bible Echo and Signs of the Times,* January 1, 1893).

CHAPTER 8

The Ultimate Authority

L ife is a journey. And the Christian life is described that way in
Bunyan's *Pilgrim's Progress*. Following the King's highway on
the way to heaven means that the problems of life are really just
encounters along the way. To understand the journey and to accurately
find the way, we need a map. The Bible is that map. An unknown
author described the guidebook this way:

"This book contains the mind of God, the state of man, the way of
salvation, the doom of sinners and the happiness of believers. Its doctrines are holy, its precepts are binding, its histories are true, and its decisions are immutable. Read it to be wise, believe it to be safe, and
practice it to be holy. It contains light to direct you, food to support
you, and comfort to cheer you. It is the traveler's map, the pilgrim's
staff, the pilot's compass, the soldier's sword and the Christian's char-
ter. Here paradise is restored, heaven opened, and the gates of hell dis-
closed. Christ is its grand object, our good its design, and the glory of
God its end. It should fill the memory, rule the heart, and guide the
feet. Read it slowly, frequently, and prayerfully. It is a mine of wealth,
a paradise of glory, and a river of pleasure. It is given to you in life,
will be opened in the judgment, and will be remembered forever. It involves the highest responsibility, will reward the greatest labor, and
will condemn all who trifle with its sacred contents."

These are grand statements about the Bible—the Book of books.
The Bible continues to be spread around the world by the millions of
copies. Yet how few are led to a study of its message and transformed
by the power of God to obey its precepts. In preparation for this chapter I collected over 1,000 pages of information on the Bible: there are

85

the statements of others, Bible texts, Spirit of Prophecy quotations, Bible studies, etc. An entire book could be written on this subject. And thousands have been. There are entire chapters in the writings of Ellen White on the topic of the Bible—chapters in *The Great Controversy, Education, Ministry of Healing,* and several other books as well. But in order to stay within the parameters of a single chapter in a book, I have decided just to share my own testimony and encourage you to find your own 1,000 pages of information. It will bless your soul. In Bible study the joy is in the journey **and** the destination!

Why I Believe the Bible Is God's Word

There are many questions in life. How do we know for sure what life is all about? How can we know what truth is? How do we really know which philosophy of life to believe and practice? I believe the Bible has an answer to all these questions. But how can we know that the Bible is true—that it is really the Word of God? After all, life is too short and serious to take the wrong road.

In my study I have found seven reasons why I believe the Bible is the Word of God. Once you can read it as God's authoritative Word you have a true standard upon which to function, to believe, to plan, to hope. You won't just take the word of others. You won't just believe the Bible out of a lack of options—an easy way out. You can use your reason—your God-given reason—to prove its claims. But taken together, the cumulative evidence is unmatched by any other philosophy, book, or way of life. All other options leave so much unanswered.

1. The Bible answers life's basic questions. This is not just philosophy; it is the basics of existence. It is reasonable to ask things like "Is there a God? What is truth? Where did I come from? Why am I here? Where am I going? What is it like after here?"

If there is a God He will reveal Himself. I believe that the cumulative evidence of these points proves that there is a God and that He has revealed Himself in many ways. We can understand that God exists through the study of nature and science, His providential leadings, the inspiration of His Word, answered prayers, fulfilled promises, fulfilled prophecies, etc.

In addition, there should be some normative standard somewhere to find the answers to basic questions. I ask the question

Where did I come from? I get the answer "In the beginning God created. . . ." God is my Creator. Why am I here, I ask? Because God created me, loved me, has a plan for my life. He wants me to live with Him—now and forever. And where am I going? I am going home! He has prepared a place for those who believe in Him and trust Him. It will be heaven for a while and then He will create a new heaven and a new earth to be our final home. Many ask and wonder if there is consciousness beyond this life. Life is a journey, and when it is over men rest in their graves in a state of unconsciousness until there is a great resurrection when all who have followed God's way of salvation will be restored to life. They will then join with the faithful who are alive at the end of earth's history. The two groups will go together to be with the Lord. There they are freed from sorrow, pain, and death. These are the answers my Bible gives to life's basic questions.

2. The Bible presents history in an unbiased manner. We all have our biases. We see our own lives, for example, in the best possible light. Most of us understand that it is in general true that when a person writes an autobiography he tends to remember and record mostly positive things. Or when a friend writes a biography the result again is quite positive. On the other hand, if a politician were to write a biography of his opponent the result would be quite different.

The Bible seems to present men in an unbiased manner. Even the stars of the Bible—its main characters—are portrayed warts and all. The stories of Adam, Noah, Moses, Abraham, David, the disciples, and Paul all tell of their frailties as well as their strong points. In fact, their faults are more fully presented than their virtues. This has been a subject of wonder to many, and has given infidels occasion to scoff at the Bible. But it is one of the strongest evidences of the truth of Scripture that the facts are not glossed over, nor are the sins of its chief characters suppressed. We are more likely to be getting the truth this way.

3. The Bible has an inner consistency. The Bible claims to have been written over a 1,600-year period. This time period extends from about 1,500 years before Christ, the time of Moses, and extends to the time of the disciple John, near A.D. 100. It was written in different ages—centuries—by men who differed widely in rank and occupation, in mental and spiritual endowments, and levels of education. Yet, taken as a whole, it presents a perfect harmony. The truths that it presents unite to present a perfect whole that is adapted to meet the wants of men in all circumstances and experiences of life.

4. The Bible has been preserved over a 3,500-year period essentially unchanged. When one considers all that could have happened to the Bible over a period of 3,500 years it is obviously only by divine intervention that the Word was kept intact. Consider, for example, that for nearly 3,000 years—most of its time in existence—the Bible was preserved and reproduced by hand. Men copied it by hand! From 1500 B.C. to A.D. 1450, when printing was invented, it was copied by hand! In addition, many of those who preserved and copied it during the Dark Ages did not even understand what they were copying! Yet, it was preserved essentially error-free.

5. The Bible's accuracy is confirmed by archaeology—scientific historical study. The last 150 years have witnessed the birth, growth, and phenomenal development of the science of biblical archaeology. This new science has performed many wonders in furnishing background material and illustrating, illuminating, and in many cases authenticating the message and meaning of the Old and New Testament Scriptures. Think of just a few of these evidences.

The Rosetta Stone, now in the British Museum in London, was discovered in 1798 at Rosetta (Rashid), near the westernmost mouth of the Nile River, by an officer in Napoleon's expedition to Egypt. It was a slab of black basalt with an inscription written on it in three different languages—all saying the same thing. The discovery of this stone was the key that unlocked the door to knowledge of the language and literature of ancient Egypt. The three languages on the stone were Greek and two forms of Egyptian writing—the older, more complicated hieroglyphic script and the later simplified and more popular demotic writing, which was the common language of the people. Many artifacts from ancient Egypt had been found before which contained the hieroglyphic writing, but no one had ever been able to make any sense of it. Now since the Greek language on the stone could be read by many scholars it became the code-breaker for the Egyptian languages!

The <u>Moabite Stone</u> was another amazing discovery. This important inscription, found in 1868, dates from about 850 B.C. It was a stele or monument—an inscribed stone. It was erected by Mesha, king of Moab, and it is also called the Mesha Stone. It tells about the wars of Mesha of Moab with Omri, king of Israel, and Omri's successors. It also tells of Mesha's wars with the Edomites. The material recorded on this stone parallels biblical history recorded in 2 Kings 1 and 3. Many places mentioned in the Old Testament are noted on the Moabite Stone.

The discovery of the <u>Dead Sea scrolls</u> was the greatest archaeological discovery of modern times. In 1947 a young Bedouin shepherd stumbled upon a cave south of Jericho, containing many leather scrolls of Hebrew and Aramaic writing and about 600 fragmentary inscriptions. The scrolls had been sealed in clay vessels. After intensive study of the manuscripts from the Dead Sea area scholars were able to date them from a period of 300 B.C. to 30 B.C. The material contained partly biblical material and partly intertestamental documents. The biblical includes two scrolls of Isaiah, one complete, and most of the first two chapters of Habakkuk, and fragments of **all** the Old Testament books except Esther. The scroll of Isaiah, found in the initial finds from the Qumran area, has remained the best known of the discoveries. It was the first major biblical manuscript of great antiquity to be recovered. It is more than 1,000 years older than the most ancient Hebrew text, the Masoretic text, known to man before this discovery! The Dead Sea scrolls are the oldest existing manuscripts of the Bible in any language! The most amazing thing is that the text of Isaiah in these scrolls is essentially the same as we have today! To my mind this is a matter of divine providence.

6. The Bible's prophecies come true! We all are curious about the future. But who really knows what will happen in the future? Of course, only God does. The Bible makes many predictions both as to time and to events. If the Bible is true these predictions should come true. And they do! How can the Bible be a collection of myths, as some say? Let me share with you what the Bible says of itself. Then we can mention a few of its prophecies and their fulfillment. Peter said, "For we did not follow cunningly devised fables when we made known to you the power and coming of our Lord Jesus Christ, but were eyewitnesses of His majesty. For He received from God the Father honor and glory when such a voice came to Him from the Excellent Glory: 'This is My beloved Son, in whom I am well pleased.' And we heard this voice which came from heaven when we were with Him on the holy mountain. <u>We also have the prophetic word which is even more sure than this</u>, which you do well to heed as a light that shines in a dark place, until the day dawns and the morning star rises in your hearts. Knowing this first, that no prophecy of Scripture is of any private interpretation, for prophecy never came by the will of man, but holy men of God spoke as they were moved by the Holy Spirit" (2 Peter 2:16-21).

With this background I'll just list a few time prophecies and their fulfillments. For more detailed explanations see my book *Even at the Door*. Noah predicted that the Flood would come in 120 years. It did. God told Abraham that his descendants would be captives in Egypt for 400 years but that then they could come out with great substance. They were and they did—right on time. God predicted through His prophet Jeremiah that because of Israel's disobedience they would be taken captive by the Babylonians and would be captives for 70 years. It happened! God told Daniel, while he was a captive in Babylon, when the Messiah would be born. When the time came, He was born in Bethlehem—a city that another prophet predicted! The list could go on. The most interesting point about prophecy is that since we have seen the other prophecies fulfilled we can know that those yet to be fulfilled will come true as well!

7. The Bible's divine origin is proved by the testimony of transformed lives. I guess you could say that the proof is in the pudding. The Bible claims to have the ability by the power of God to reclaim man from sin and degradation and give him a positive and more abundant life. Is it true? I have seen it happen many times. It is the testimony of my own life! Where would I be today without the guidance of God's Word? What kind of people get involved in sharing their time and resources in helping others? Are they the atheists and agnostics? Or is it the worldly and self-abusers? No. It is those who follow the example of Jesus. If everyone practiced the principles taught in the Bible we would not have to lock anything. The streets in every city would be safe. There would be no need for a prison system. Those who follow God's Word are a living testimony of its divine origin.

The Great Standard of Truth

The seven points I have listed above could all be greatly expanded and verified. However, they are the simple basis for my belief in the authenticity of the Bible as the revealed will of God. To me, then, the Scriptures are the standard for my faith and practice as a Christian. There can be no other. The more we get to know about God through the study of His Word the deeper our understanding of His will and purpose for our lives. "The fear of the Lord is the beginning of wisdom, and the knowledge of the Holy One is understanding" (Proverbs 9:10).

"Bible religion is not one influence among many others, but its influence is supreme, pervading and controlling every other influence. Bible religion is to exercise control over life and conduct. It is not like a dash of color brushed here and there upon the canvas, but its influence is to evade the whole life, as though the canvas were dipped into the color until every thread of the fabric was dyed a deep, fast, unfading hue" *(The Youth's Instructor,* May 30, 1895).

The Bible says of itself, that it is true. "Sanctify them by Your truth, Your word is truth" (John 17:17). God's law is the truth (Psalm 119:142). Jesus said, "I am the way, the truth, and the life" (John 14:6). Since God and His Word are truth, that must be our ultimate and only standard. Even the Holy Spirit, called the Spirit of Truth, has the purpose of guiding us into all truth: to help us to better understand the truth of God's Word. Of course the Spirit does not supersede the Scripture. In fact, we are told to try or test the spirits in 1 John 4:1. And what is the standard for testing them? The Bible, of course! It is always and only the standard for the Christian. To submit all to the authority of Scripture is what Christianity does as part of its calling. It teachings are truth, not options. They are the standard and must be obeyed.

Problems Without a Standard

In the Roman Catholic system there is really not a standard. Let me explain. They teach that there is a triune or triple authority: the Bible, tradition, and the magisterium or teaching authority of the church. Here is the problem. For Catholics the Bible is not the standard alone. It must be interpreted by the other two sources of authority. Obviously, tradition and the teaching of the church changes over the years—so there is no real standard. For example, the new unabridged Catechism of the Catholic Church teaches Creation as the origin of man. However, since its printing the pope has declared that evolution is a more likely explanation for the origin of man than the biblical account. In addition, the pope announced in a sermon of February 16, 1997, that God will never again destroy the world no matter how sinful it gets. This is direct opposition to the promised destruction by fire predicted in 2 Peter and the book of Revelation.

For much of the Protestant world the picture is not much clearer because for many Protestants, however innocently they practice their religion, much of what they believe harks back to their Catholic heritage. The most clear example of this is Sundaykeeping, which is not found in Scripture by any stretch of the imagination. In addition, even for those who claim to take the Bible as their standard, in actual practice, many hold their own opinions and preconceptions above the plain meaning of Scripture.

Here are a couple of examples. In each edition of the Catholic weekly, *Our Sunday Visitor,* there is an "Ask Me a Question" section where questions that are sent in are answered by Father Frank Sheedy. In the December 29, 1996, edition the following question and answer appeared:

Question: In our Bible study, we couldn't find the term "ever-virgin" to describe the Blessed Virgin Mary. When did they start calling Mary "ever-virgin"?

—Name withheld, Long Beach, Calif.

Answer: Catholics have two sources of faith: the Bible and Tradition. One must be careful not to make the mistake of some Protestants—namely, if it isn't in the Bible, it is not so. Catholic teaching on "Mary ever-virgin" will be found in the Catechism of the Catholic Church.

Another common "worldly" perspective on the value of the Word of God was expressed this way: "I want my daughter to read the Bible, but I will explain to her that these are stories that people made up to teach people—it's not the rule." These words from pop-music icon and actress Madonna on how she will raise her daughter. Quoted in *World,* January 18, 1997.

What would happen if people actually immersed themselves in the Bible and studied its message for themselves? Let me give you the testimony of one man who did. At the age of 34 William Miller, a farmer and businessman, considered himself a deist. That is, he believed in natural law and morality but denied the existence of a Creator. He decided to study the Bible just to see what it had to say. Here is his report in one paragraph:

"I saw that the Bible did bring to view just such a Saviour as I needed; and I was perplexed to find how an uninspired book should develop principles so perfectly adapted to the wants of a fallen world. I was constrained to admit that the Scriptures must be a revelation from God. They became my delight; and in Jesus I found a friend. The Saviour became to me the chiefest among ten thousand; and the Scriptures, which before were dark and contradictory, now became the lamp to my feet and light to my path. My mind became settled and satisfied. I found the Lord God to be a Rock in the midst of the ocean of life. The Bible now became my chief study, and I can truly say, I searched it with great delight. I found the half was never told me. I wondered why I had not see its beauty and glory before, and marveled that I could have ever rejected it. I found everything revealed that my heart could desire, and a remedy for every disease of the soul. I lost all taste for other reading, and applied my heart to get wisdom from God" *(The Great Controversy,* p. 319). What a testimony! Maybe you, too, have found the Bible such a rich source of hope and confidence!

Jesus and the New Testament writers accepted the Hebrew Scriptures as having unquestioned authority. We are familiar with Paul's reminder to the young man, Timothy: "From childhood you have known the Holy Scriptures, which are able to make you wise for salvation through faith which is in Christ Jesus. All Scripture is given by inspiration of God, and is profitable for doctrine, for reproof, for correction, for instruction in righteousness, that the man of God may be complete, thoroughly equipped for every good work?" (2 Timothy 3:15-17). And Peter assures us that prophecy does not come from human sources, but "holy men of God spoke as they were moved by the Holy Spirit" (2 Peter 1:21).

As Christians we have a tremendous responsibility not only to be deep students of the Word ourselves, but also to foster a back-to-the-Bible movement that will help ourselves and our fellow believers prepare for the great tests that we will face in the last great crisis. We are warned, "None but those who have fortified the mind with the truths of the Bible will stand through the last great conflict. To every soul will come the searching test: Shall I obey God rather than men? The decisive hour is even now at hand. Are our feet planted on the rock of God's immutable word?" *(The Great Controversy,* pp. 593, 594).

A Divine Encounter

Because we believe the Bible is the Word of God, when we study it we actually have an encounter with God. He is speaking to us in His Word! A daily study of the Scriptures has an uplifting influence on the spirit and a broadening influence on the mind. "The Bible is God's voice speaking to us just as surely as though we could hear Him with our ears. The word of the living God is not merely written, but spoken. Do we receive the Bible as the oracle of God? If we realized the importance of this Word, with what awe would we open it, and with what earnestness would we search its precepts. The reading and contemplating of the Scriptures would be regarded as an audience with the Most High" *(In Heavenly Places,* p. 134).

So often throughout this book we have discovered the importance of being born again, of having the power of God's indwelling by the Holy Spirit transform us to be ready to meet our Lord in peace. The power for this transformation is in the Word of God. "The creative energy that called the worlds into existence is in the word of God. This word imparts power; it begets life. Every command is a promise; accepted by the will, received into the soul, it brings with it the life of the Infinite One. It transforms the nature and re-creates the soul in the image of God" *(Education,* p. 126). Again, "The whole Bible is a revelation of the glory of God in Christ. Received, believed, obeyed, it is the great instrumentality in the transformation of character. It is the grand stimulus, the constraining force, that quickens the physical, mental, and spiritual powers, and directs the life into right channels" *(The Ministry of Healing,* p. 458).

There are many voices calling people today. There is new age, astrology, science fiction, Eastern religions, materialism, Communism, and much more. But God has given ample evidence to the reasonable man that His word is true and can be trusted as the standard for faith and practice. "God will have a people upon the earth to maintain the Bible, and the Bible only, as the standard of all doctrines and the basis of all reforms. The opinions of learned men, the deductions of science, the creeds or decisions of ecclesiastical councils, as numerous and discordant as are the churches which they represent, the voice of the majority—not one nor all of these should be regarded as evidence for or against any point of religious faith. <u>Before accepting any doctrine or precept, we should demand a plain 'Thus saith the Lord' in its support</u>" *(The Great Controversy,* p. 595).

We must be a part of that people who stand on the foundation of truth—Thy Word is truth.

CHAPTER 9

The Dead Are Asleep

They were watching the skies—and the Internet—for a sign. And they found one. As Comet Hale-Bopp grew bright in the sky, the 39 members of Heaven's Gate descended into true darkness. They did it quietly, in a rich California suburb called Rancho Santa Fe. Orchestrated by a former choir director, their mass suicide was supposed to liberate them. The promise of their leader? He said that by dying, they would ascend on a cloud of light to a higher plane.

Astronomical charts may also have helped determine the timing of the Heaven's Gate suicides. They apparently began to kill themselves on the weekend of March 22, 23, 1997, around the time that Hale-Bopp got ready to make its closest approach to Earth. That weekend also witnessed a full moon and, in parts of the United States, a lunar eclipse. In addition the weekend included Palm Sunday, the beginning of the Christian Holy Week. Shrouds placed on the corpses were purple, the color of Passiontide, or, for New Agers, the color of those who have passed to a higher plane.

The 21 women and 18 men who took their lives engaged in a systematic, well-planned, and orchestrated suicide. From notes and videos they prepared ahead of time they all apparently willingly and cheerfully took part in what they termed "escaping their containers"—their bodies—so they could go on "to the next level."

The first news reports of the incident stated that the 39 people were all young men because they all had closely cropped hair, wore baggy black pants and shirts and identical black-and-white Nike running shoes. Not till the bodies were examined at the coroner's office was it discovered that 21 of the group were women. In addition, further examination of passports and personal identification showed that their ages ranged from 26 to 72.

The group had suitcases packed with clothes, spiral notebooks, and for some reason, lip balm. For some unknown reason, each of them had some quarters and a $5 bill in their pocket.

What really happened in this largest mass suicide in U.S. history? Yes, by their act they closed their probation. But did they go somewhere? Did they get to the spaceship they say was hidden behind the Hale-Bopp comet? Will they be back for a visit? How can we know? Should anyone follow them as they invited others to do? What really happens when one dies? Can we know these things? Yes, indeed!— and we must know the truth in order to be prepared against this and other last great deceptions of Satan.

The Powerful Deceptions of Spiritualism

We can answer these questions by looking at the origins of the Heaven's Gate cult and then comparing the beliefs of the cult with the great standard of truth. The tremendous deceptive power of spiritualism can be demonstrated in the activities of the people involved in the cult. The group's beliefs were a strange mixture of biblical expressions, astrological charts, new age, spiritualism, and science fiction television programs such as *Star Trek,* the *X-Files,* etc.

Cult leader Marshall Herff Applewhite was the son of a Presbyterian minister, who moved around Texas as a church builder. Applewhite was blessed with good looks and a powerful singing voice. At one point in his life he apparently had plans to study for the ministry himself, but gave up these plans to pursue a career in music. He seemed to enjoy life as a family man, with a wife and two children.

Then his struggle with homosexuality unraveled both his marriage and his academic post in a religious school. The Washington *Post* reported that in 1971 he checked into a psychiatric hospital to be cured of his homosexuality. He had been fired as a music professor at Houston's University of St. Thomas, a Roman Catholic school, after an affair with a student. He had been fired from another job for similar reasons in 1964.

"College records show that Applewhite left [the University of St. Thomas] in 1970 for 'health problems of an emotional nature.'

Suffering from depression and shame, hearing 'voices,' he checked into a hospital, asking to be 'cured' of his homosexual desires. He told his sister he had suffered a 'near death experience' after a heart attack, but he may actually have suffered from a drug overdose, according to Ray Hill, a radio-show host in Texas who knew Applewhite at the time. 'He was kind of a Timothy Leary type,' said Hill" *(Newsweek,* April 7, 1997).

According to *Time* magazine, "Applewhite spun his own myth: the personal turmoil was the result of his body's coming under the influence of a being from the 'Next level,' part of the discovery that he was one of 'the Two.'" The "Two" he referred to were the two witnesses of Revelation that were to prepare the way for the kingdom of heaven.

It was during his hospitalization that Applewhite met "the other half of the two." She was Bonnie Lu Nettles, then 44. She was a nurse and a wife and mother of four children. Her daughter Terrie who was interviewed by CNN after the suicide of the Heaven's Gate group, stated that her mother "dabbled in astrology and far-out religions and had been told by a couple of spiritualists that there was going to be this guy coming into her life. Then Herff showed up. They linked together on a spiritual plane." One can easily see the power and deception of spiritualism by the fact that he left his wife and two children and she left her husband and four children to become "the two witnesses of Revelation."

After "the Two linked up on the spiritual plane," "Nettles attended drama classes that Applewhite taught in Houston; she drew up his astrological charts and channeled her spiritual adviser 'Brother Francis' for guidance. In 1972 she helped him start the Christian Arts Center, a protocult that taught astrology and metaphysics. Applewhite had always been intense and charming. Now he became charismatic. Says Terrie Nettles: 'I felt like I was in the presence of an incredible human being. It was like I was being lifted.' She adds, 'I felt privileged to be with my mother and Herff. I was the only one who could talk with them together. Their followers had to talk to them in groups, not individually'" *(Time,* April 7, 1997).

In 1975 Nettles and Applewhite left Houston for California for speaking and recruiting trips in the West. Neither apparently ever saw their families again. Soon after arriving in California and beginning their cult the "Two" began calling themselves nicknames such as

"Guinea" and "Pig," "Bo" and "Peep"—a reference to their roles as shepherds. Later they were called "Him" and "Her" and finally the musical "Do" and "Ti."

The Powerful Pull of False Christs

The members of the Heaven's Gate cult believed that Applewhite—alias "Do" was "the One, a modern-day Christ." "The Two proclaimed that 'Bo' had been Jesus, Elijah, and Moses in his former lives." The real Jesus warned His followers, "Then if anyone says to you, 'Look, here is the Christ!' or 'There!' do not believe it. For false christs and false prophets will arise and show great signs and wonders, so as to deceive, if possible, even the elect. See, I have told you beforehand. Therefore if they say to you, 'Look, He is in the desert!' do not go out; or 'Look, He is in the inner rooms!' do not believe it" (Matthew 24:23-26). Now we can see why Jesus said, don't go, don't look, don't believe it. Let us learn a lesson from those who were deceived.

"John M. Craig of Durango, Colo., was 41 when he joined Applewhite's cult in 1975. Craig was a successful rancher and businessman, a strapping outdoors man who had bit parts as a cowboy in several movies. He also had six young children. One day in July an old college friend came to visit; two days later Craig drove off with him to hear Applewhite and his partner then, Bonnie Nettles, speak in Denver. The next morning, according to a family friend, Craig's wife woke up 'and there was a note that said he was gone to meet the spaceship because the end of the world was coming.' Craig never returned; his wife divorced him two years later and raised the children herself. Stories in the local papers last week mentioned rumors of financial troubles, but other sources, including his former wife, denied them. 'Nobody,' she said, 'will be able to explain why he did it.' He went to a meeting, and then he was gone" *(Newsweek,* April 7, 1997).

And then there was Yvonne McCurdy-Hill, 39, from Cincinnati, Ohio. "An employee at the U.S. post office, she loved to surf the Web, there entering Heaven's Gate. By August she had sold her BMW, cashed in her post office pension, sold her house and apportioned her five children, including infant twins, among her relatives. Then with her husband Steven, she joined Heaven's Gate in California. Steven didn't last as a cultist, but Yvonne did—to the finish. Her family and friends remain baffled. Said one, 'Yvonne is the last I would have thought would end like this'" *(Time,* April 7, 1997).

There were 37 others! Many with similar stories. They saw a flier, they went to a meeting—and they were gone. The Bible says "There is a way that seems right to a man, but its end is the way of death" (Proverbs 14:12). This verse is repeated word for word in Proverbs 16:25. It is apparently repeated for emphasis. Paul also gives a very strong warning of this very thing. "The coming of the lawless one is according to the working of Satan, with all power, signs, and lying wonders, and with all unrighteous deception among those who perish, **because they did not receive the love of the truth**, that they might be saved. And for this reason God will send them strong delusion, that they should believe the lie" (2 Thessalonians 2:9-11). The truth, as we have seen, is God's Word. One cannot have a hybrid religion and expect to avoid deception. How can we avoid being deceived by this powerful working of Satan? Only by a knowledge of God's Word and a determination to follow it.

What the Bible Says About Death

The Bible should be the full and ultimate authority for the Christian. That's why we want to know what the Bible has to say about death. Apparently, even in Old Testament times, men had a fascination with trying to communicate with the dead. The Bible counsel is, "When they say to you, 'Seek those who are mediums and wizards, who whisper and mutter,' should not a people seek their God? Should they seek the dead on behalf of the living? To the law and to the testimony! If they do not speak according to this word, it is because there is no light in them" (Isaiah 8:19, 20).

When I study the Bible topically, I attempt to look up every verse on a given topic. I can then get the big picture and follow up by looking at the details. This gives a true picture of what the Bible says on each topic that it mentions. Then my understanding of the topic becomes my doctrine on that subject.

Recently, on a flight from Chicago to Nashville, a young man next to me noted that I was looking at the *Newsweek* coverage of the Heaven's Gate cult. He asked if I had any idea why those people did that. I told him that I thought they had a wrong understanding of

Scripture and in addition they used extra-biblical sources for their understanding of life and death. That was a big mistake. Then I told him about my study method. I told him that one could more easily determine the truth about any topic by using this method. I told him, for example, that if one really wanted to know what the Bible taught about "baptism" he could simply look up in an exhaustive concordance, like Young's or Strong's, all the words that deal with baptism. There are 51 verses that use the word "baptized," 22 verses use the word "baptism," 7 verses use "baptize," and 4 use the word "baptizing." That is a total of 84 verses that one could study in their context to determine what the Bible teaches about baptism.

One quickly sees that, in the Bible context, one repents before he is baptized. This rules out infants, because they cannot understand the nature of sin and forgiveness. So the baptism the Bible teaches is a baptism of faith. In addition, when the Bible talks about a baptism taking place there are always two people involved. The one baptizing and the one being baptized. They go together down into the water and the one being baptized is dipped or immersed under the water. There are many other things that could be learned about baptism using this method. But you already know one thing for sure. If you were "sprinkled" as an "infant," you weren't "baptized" in the biblical sense.

This explanation seemed to make sense to the man I was talking with, so I told him the same thing could be done on the subject of death. I told him that the great preponderance of the evidence when one studies Christian anthropology indicates that when a person dies his breath returns to God (the breath of the good and the bad returns to God), and his body returns to dust. Man rests in his grave in a state of unconsciousness until the resurrection. The great mass of biblical evidence is that when one dies, "he sleeps with his fathers." The young man then said, "But didn't Jesus promise the thief who was hanging beside Him on the cross that he would be with Him in paradise that day?" I told him that many had drawn that conclusion from the reference, but when it is compared to others and studied in detail itself one can see that Jesus was giving the man assurance and not talking about what happens when you die.

But the young man persisted, "How do you know that Jesus wasn't promising the thief that he would be in heaven that day?" "By studying the story," I said. Let's look at the big picture. First we know that Jesus was crucified on Friday, the preparation day, He rested in the grave on Sabbath, and then on Sunday, He was resurrected.

When Mary came to the tomb on Sunday morning (the first day of the week), she was weeping because she thought Jesus was still in the tomb. But the tomb was empty and an angel told her, "He is not here, for He is risen!" (Matthew 28:6). Then a voice called her name—"Mary!" She immediately recognized the voice of Jesus and was so excited she wanted to embrace Him. But He stopped her by saying, "Do not cling to Me, for I have not yet ascended to My Father" (John 20:17).

In addition we are told that the Jews didn't want to keep those who had been crucified on the cross over the Sabbath. They broke the legs of the thieves so that they couldn't get away. But since Jesus was already dead, they did not break His legs (see John 19:31-33). So while Jesus died on Friday, the thief didn't. And even on Sunday Jesus had not ascended to heaven. The conclusion is simple and inescapable: neither Jesus nor the thief went to heaven on Friday.

Now here is the point: Either Jesus was lying to the thief about going to heaven that day or He was giving him assurance that day and not talking about what happens when one dies. The latter is the only possible conclusion! Any "problem" text that appears to conflict with the preponderance of the evidence can be explained by careful study. It made sense to my seatmate on the plane!

What Is Man?

The Creation account says, "And the Lord God formed man of the dust of the ground, and breathed into his nostrils the breath of life; and man became a living being" (Genesis 2:7). The King James Version says "a living <u>soul</u>." Here we have the basic constituent elements of man: the body (dust or earth) plus breath equals a living being or soul. Man does not have a soul. He is a soul. So what happens when one dies? The process is simply reversed. The breath returns to God and the body returns to dust. Man is no longer a living being. "Then the dust will return to the earth as it was, and the spirit [breath] will return to God who gave it" (Ecclesiastes 12:7).

This is the bottom line. Only God has immortality (1 Timothy 6:16). The devil's first recorded lie, spoken to Eve in the Garden of

Eden, was "You shall not surely die" (Genesis 3:4). So where do people get the idea that the soul escapes the body at death and lives on as a conscious entity? From Greek dualism, from Pythagoras (died in the 5th century B.C.); from Plato (died 350 B.C.); from Aristotle (died 320 B.C.); and from many others who were influenced by Greek philosophy—such as Thomas Aquinas (died 1274 A.D.). Aquinas, who was a pagan convert to Christianity, became a leading Roman Catholic theologian. But these ideas did not originate in the Scriptures, which are the standard of truth.

We all know what earth and dust are, but what is the breath of life? It is the spark of life. It is the vital force that enables man to function. It is the breath of God. The English Bible calls the breath "Spirit."

In the Old Testament two words are used to denote spirit or breath. They are *N'shamah* and *Ruach*. *N'shamah* is used 21 times in the Old Testament. It can mean either the physical act of breathing or the breath itself. Most frequently it refers to respiration.

A typical example of the use of this word is found in Genesis 7, when the Bible describes the results of the Flood. "And all flesh died that moved on the earth: birds and cattle and beasts and every creeping thing that creeps on the earth, and every man. All in whose nostrils was the breath of the spirit of life, all that was on the dry land died" (Genesis 7:21, 22). According to this verse and many others, all living creatures, man and animals, have the same breath or life principle. If when the breath returns to God some conscious entity "goes to heaven," then both animals and man "go to heaven at death"—and there is no distinction between the righteous and the wicked! This conclusion is obviously absurd. Not one passage of the 21 in the Old Testament that uses *N'shamah* says anything about man being immortal!

Ruach occurs 377 times in the Old Testament. The King James Version translates the word as "spirit" 232 times; as "wind" 91 times; as "breath" 28 times; and the balance is of various other uses. Obviously, the three uses above are the most common as in Genesis 8:1 where God caused a wind to pass over the earth. "It is also used to denote vitality (Judges 15:19), courage (Joshua 2:11), temper or anger (Judges 8:3), disposition (Isaiah 54:6), moral character (Ezekiel 11:19), and the seat of the emotions (1 Samuel 1:15).

"In the sense of breath, the *ruach* of men is identical with the *ruach* of animals (Eccl. 3:19). The *ruach* of man leaves the body at death (Ps. 146:4) and returns to God (Eccl. 12:7; cf. Job 34:14). *Ruach* is used frequently of the Spirit of God, as in Isaiah 63:10. <u>Never in the Old Testament, with respect to man, does *ruach* denote an intelligent entity capable of sentient existence apart from a physical body</u>.

"The New Testament equivalent of *ruach* is *pneuma,* 'spirit,' from *pneo,* 'to blow,' or 'to breathe.' As with *ruach*, there is nothing inherent in the word *pneuma* denoting an entity in man capable of conscious existence apart from the body, nor does the New Testament usage with respect to man in any way imply such a concept" *(Seventh-day Adventists Believe,* p. 83).

The Biblical Meaning of Soul

The word translated "soul" in the English Bible is *nephesh* in the Old Testament and *psuche* in the New Testament. *Nephesh* is used about 750 times in the Old Testament. It can mean breath, life, person, or appetite. The Hebrew *Nephesh chayyah* has been translated "living being" or "living soul." But the Bible also uses the same term to refer to marine animals, insects, reptiles, and beasts (Genesis 1:20, 24; 2:19). So the "breath of life" is not limited to people. Every living creature possesses it. *Psuche* is used in the New Testament 155 times. It also refers to a person, a personal pronoun (as in "my soul" or simply "me"), life, emotional life, or animals. In total there are over 900 passages where *nephesh* or *psuche* are used, and not one passage mentions immortal in connection with these words. The Old and New Testaments are in complete agreement on this topic. These words are not used as being part of a person but rather it <u>is</u> the person (see Genesis 14:21; Numbers 5:6; and Deuteronomy 10:22).

"The biblical evidence indicates that sometimes *nephesh* and *psuche* refer to the whole person and at other times to a particular aspect of man, such as the affections, emotions, appetites, and feelings. This usage, however, in no way shows that man is a being made up of two separate and distinct parts. The body and the soul exist together; together they form an indivisible union. <u>The soul has no conscious existence apart from the body</u>. There is no text that indicates that the soul survives the body as a conscious entity" *(ibid.,* pp. 82, 83).

What Difference Does It Make?

So what difference does it make, anyway, what a person believes about man's condition in death? We will all find out eventually, won't we? Yes, but "the doctrine of man's consciousness in death, especially the belief that spirits of the dead return to minister to the living, has prepared the way for modern spiritualism. If the dead are admitted to the presence of God and holy angels, and privileged with knowledge far exceeding what they before possessed, why should they not return to the earth to enlighten and instruct the living? If, as taught by popular theologians, spirits of the dead are hovering about their friends on earth, why should they not be permitted to communicate with them, to warn them against evil, or to comfort them in sorrow? How can those who believe in man's consciousness in death reject what comes to them as divine light communicated by glorified spirits. <u>Here is a channel regarded as sacred, through which Satan works for the accomplishment of his purposes</u>" *(The Great Controversy,* pp. 551, 552).

There is ample evidence that millions of people believe in the unbiblical teaching of the immortality of the soul. Let me share just two illustrations of this. On the back cover of the Catholic weekly, *Our Sunday Visitor,* April 6, 1997, a book is advertised under the heading "Help Those Who Have Died." The book is titled *Charity for the Suffering Souls.* The advertising is as follows:

"Father John A. Nageleisen provides proof from Scripture on the existence and torments of Purgatory. Tells what the fire is like. Gives the conditions of the suffering souls as to pain and consolations. Analyzes the credibility of departed souls that have returned to warn those on earth. Covers the means of relieving the poor souls—holy water, mass, alms, fasting, etc. Includes motives for helping the poor souls, and how they assist their benefactors. Contains novenas and prayers. Beautiful illustrations, 408 pp. PB. Imprimatur of several bishops."

This idea of departed souls returning to warn those on earth is pure spiritualism, yet it is openly advertised in *Our Sunday Visitor.* Thankfully, many Catholic believers are beginning to realize that such teachings of their church do not harmonize with the Scriptures. In the "Ask Me a Question" section of the March 9, 1997, edition of *Our Sunday Visitor* a person writes this question:

"**Question:** The Church teaches that when we die, we are judged and go to heaven or hell. Are we not awaiting the Second Coming, when all will be resurrected and judged?"

Then "Father" Frank Sheedy gives this answer:

"**Answer:** The Church teaches that there are two judgments, particular and general. The Catechism tells us that each person receives eternal retribution in his or her **immortal soul** at the very moment of death—either heaven (immediately or through purification) or everlasting damnation. This is the particular judgment.

"After the Second Coming of Christ there will be a general, or Last Judgment, when our souls will be reunited to our bodies and a different judgment will be for all to understand (see Mt. 25)."

Preparing for the Great Deception

In a chapter titled "Spiritualism," in *Early Writings,* Ellen White warns, "I saw that the saints must have a thorough understanding of present truth, which they will be obliged to maintain from the Scriptures. They must understand the state of the dead; for the spirits of devils will yet appear to them, professing to be beloved relatives or friends, who will declare to them unscriptural doctrines" *(Early Writings,* p. 262). What are these "unscriptural doctrines" that the spirits of devils will teach? She gives a more specific answer when talking about the same topic earlier. "They [the saints] must understand the state of the dead; for the spirits of devils will yet appear to them, professing to be beloved friends and relatives, who declare to them that the Sabbath has been changed, also other unscriptural doctrines" *(ibid.,* p. 87).

She goes on to say, "They [the spirits of devils] will do all in their power to excite sympathy and will work miracles before them to confirm what they declare. The people of God must be prepared to withstand these spirits with the Bible truth that the dead know not anything, and that they who thus appear are the spirits of devils.

"We must examine well the foundation of our hope: for we shall have to give a reason for it from the Scriptures. This delusion will spread, and we shall have to contend with it face to face; and unless we are prepared for it, we shall be ensnared and overcome. But if we do what we can on our part to be ready for the conflict that is just before us, God will do His part, and His all-powerful arm will protect us. He would sooner send every angel out of glory to make a hedge about faithful souls, than have them deceived and led away by the lying wonders of Satan" *(ibid.,* p. 262).

We must thoroughly study this topic so that our minds will be fortified against the deceptions of Satan. One can easily see how spiritualism is invading television programing, including movies, serials, and even cartoons! No doubt the most insidious deception regarding spiritualism is that it is being taught right in the churches—places where poor souls should be able to seek a refuge from Satan.

"Satan has long been preparing for his final effort to deceive the world. The foundation of his work was laid by the assurance given to Eve in Eden: 'Ye shall not surely die.' 'In the day ye eat thereof, then your eyes shall be opened, and ye shall be as gods, knowing good and evil.' Genesis 3:4, 5. Little by little he has prepared the way for his masterpiece of deception in the development of spiritualism. . . . Except those who are kept by the power of God, through faith in His word, the whole world will be swept into the ranks of delusion. The people are fast being lulled to a fatal security, to be awakened only by the outpouring of the wrath of God" *(The Great Controversy,* p. 561).

We must remember the Bible declares: "For the living know that they will die; but the dead know nothing, and they have no more reward, for the memory of them is forgotten. Also their love, their hatred, and their envy have now perished; nevermore will they have a share in anything done under the sun" (Ecclesiastes 9:5, 6).

CHAPTER 10

Miracles Versus Miracles

By definition a miracle is an extraordinary event manifesting divine intervention in human affairs. Mankind has always had a fascination with signs, wonders, and miracles. Apparently, God has used this interest to get man's attention and give evidence of His power. However, the devil also has supernatural power, and he uses it to perform signs, wonders, and miracles as well. Used in this context these "wonders" are supernatural events and could not be performed by man alone—without some power outside of himself. It stands to reason, therefore, that a miracle itself is not necessarily a sign of divine intervention.

Numerous Old Testament Miracles

God intervened in human affairs many times during the Old Testament era. There was Enoch's translation; the preservation of Noah and his family during the Flood; the birth of Isaac to aged parents; the burning bush; the miracles in Egypt; the Exodus; the crossing of the Red Sea; the provision of the manna; fresh water from rocks; the conquest of Jericho; deliverance from the fiery furnace; the handwriting on the wall; Daniel's protection from the lions. The list is long and God's power amply proven in each case.

Miracles have an unusual impact on those who witness them. They seem to have a "wow" effect at first and then people seem to forget them. For example, Pharaoh saw a whole river turn to blood and many other amazing miracles, yet he hardened his heart against God and His people. The children of Israel saw many amazing miracles, and yet so often when faced with adversity they would cry out, "Would to God that we had died by the hand of the Lord in the land of Egypt." And at the time of the first advent, Jesus performed many awesome miracles, including the raising of three people from the dead—one of whom had been dead four days and was already in his grave, yet the people killed Jesus. So why does the Lord use miracles anyway? Apparently He does because He wants to help His people and see His cause go forward. Sometimes God uses miracles to encourage believers. "The signs and miracles performed in the presence of Pharaoh were not given for his benefit alone, but for the advantage of God's people, to give them more clear and exalted views of God, and that all Israel should fear Him, and be willing and anxious to leave Egypt, and choose the service of the true and merciful God. Had it not been for these wonderful manifestations, many would have been satisfied to remain in Egypt rather than to journey through the wilderness" *(Spiritual Gifts,* vol. 3, p. 205).

God was faithful in His miraculous provisions to Israel. And in spite of this the people didn't even seem aware of what He was doing for them. He provided manna, for example, for 40 years (see Exodus 16:35) and associated with this provision was a triple miracle—every week for 40 years. First, was God's daily provision of the manna itself. Second, was the double portion on Friday. Third, was the preservation of the second portion over the Sabbath when no new manna came. All this was done to show them that the Sabbath was a sacred day.

We occasionally experience something that we call "a once in a lifetime experience." Some in the Old Testament saw many of these types of experiences. For example, some saw a parting of the waters twice! "Many who passed through the Red Sea when they were children, now, by a similar miracle, crossed over Jordan, men of war, equipped for battle." Listen to the thrilling conclusion to the crossing of Jordan: "After the host of Israel had all passed over, Joshua commanded the priests to come up out of the river. When they, bearing the ark of the covenant, stood safe upon the farther shore, God removed His mighty hand, and the accumulated waters rushed down, a mighty cataract, in the natural channel of the stream. Jordan rolled on, a resistless flood, overflowing all its banks" *(Testimonies for the Church,* vol. 4, p. 158).

Miracles in the New Testament

Beginning with the changing of the water to wine at the wedding feast at Cana Jesus began a ministry that lasted three and a half years—a ministry filled with miracles of compassion. His miracles had an impact on those who saw and heard. "Many believed when they saw the miracles which He did" (John 2:23, KJV). And when Nicodemus came to see Jesus at night, he stated, "We know that you are a teacher come from God: for no man can do these miracles that thou doest, except God be with him" (John 3:2, KJV).

Jesus did not perform miracles or exercise His divine power for His own benefit or to relieve Himself from suffering. He had volunteered to take this upon Himself. He came to save others. He sought to bring blessing, hope, and life to the afflicted and oppressed. In fact, "during His ministry Jesus devoted more time to healing the sick than to preaching. His miracles testified to the truth of His words, that He came not to destroy but to save. . . . Wherever He went, the tidings of His mercy preceded Him. Where He had passed, the objects of His compassion were rejoicing in health, and making trial of their new-found powers. Crowds were collecting around them to hear from their lips the works that the Lord had wrought. His voice was the first sound that many had ever heard, His name the first word they had ever spoken, His face the first they had ever looked upon. Why should they not love Jesus, and sound His praise? As He passed through the towns and cities He was like a vital current, diffusing life and joy wherever He went" *(The Desire of Ages,* p. 350).

These miracles were "wonders to behold." And yet, perhaps the greatest evidence of Jesus' divinity was expressed to the dejected disciples when Jesus walked and talked with them undetected as the risen Lord. He took the Scriptures and pointed out the prophecies that His life and ministry had fulfilled. "It is the voice of Christ that speaks through patriarchs and prophets, from the days of Adam even to the closing scenes of time. The Saviour is revealed in the Old Testament as clearly as in the New. It is the light from the prophetic past that brings out the life of Christ and the teachings of the New Testament with clearness and beauty. The miracles of Christ are a proof of His divinity; but a stronger proof that He is the world's Redeemer is found in comparing the prophecies of the Old Testament with the history of the New" *(ibid.,* p. 799).

The Jewish leaders objected to the fact that Jesus performed so many miracles. They objected because He was destroying their influence with the people. In addition, they looked upon the helpless with heartless indifference, while Jesus was moved with compassion toward them. In many cases their selfishness and oppression had actually caused the affliction that Jesus relieved.

But Jesus' crowning miracle—the raising of Lazarus—was the miracle that sealed the decision of the Jews to have Him crucified. Then a very strange thing happened. They captured Jesus and took Him first to the high priest, then Pilate and then Herod, each one realizing that Jesus was really innocent of the charges against Him—but they all went along with the wishes of those who desired to have Him killed.

Herod, in the course of his interrogation of Jesus promised to release Him if He would work a miracle. At this His accusers were seized with fear. They had seen Jesus perform many miracles. They had even seen Him raise Lazarus. They feared that Jesus would perform a miracle and be released, so they all shouted together, "He works His miracles through the power given Him by Beelzebub, the prince of devils." They accused the One who lived to bless others with being used by Satan!

Miracles were wrought by the disciples and apostles as well, but they of necessity used a different method of healing. Whereas Jesus would say, "Rise and be healed," they would have to say, "In the name of Jesus, rise and be healed." Jesus used His divinity and they too used His divinity!

A Change in New Testament Times

Miracles were one of the major gifts given to the church according to 1 Corinthians 12. But Jesus also warned, "For false Christs and false prophets will arise and show great signs and wonders [miracles], so as to deceive, if possible, even the elect" (Matthew 24:24).

In Revelation we read about Satan working through the second beast of Revelation 13:

"He performs great signs, so that he even makes fire come down from heaven on the earth in the sight of men. And he deceives those who dwell on the earth by those signs which he was granted to do in the sight of the beast, telling those who dwell on the earth to make an image to the beast who was wounded by the sword and lived. He was granted power to give breath to the image of the beast, that the image of the beast should both speak and cause as many as would not worship the image of the beast to be killed. And he causes all, both small and great, rich and poor, free and slave, to receive a mark on their right hand or on their foreheads, and that no one may buy or sell except one who has the mark or the name of the beast, or the number of his name" (Revelation 13:13-17).

Two chapters later John warns of the same type of miraculous workings that prepare the world for the last great battle.

"And I saw three unclean spirits like frogs coming out of the mouth of the dragon, out of the mouth of the beast, and out of the mouth of the false prophet. For they are the spirits of demons, performing signs, which go out to the kings of the earth and of the whole world, to gather them to the battle of the great day of God Almighty. 'Behold, I am coming as a thief. Blessed is he who watches, and keeps his garments, lest he walk naked and they see his shame'" (Revelation 16:13-15).

When the final warning is given to the inhabitants of the earth, the great controversy will come to its ultimate climax. Everyone living will have to make a decision for one side or the other. The picture will look like this: "Servants of God, with their faces lighted up and shining with holy consecration, will hasten from place to place to proclaim the message from heaven. By thousands of voices, all over the earth, the warning will be given. Miracles will be wrought, the sick will be healed, and signs and wonders will follow the believers. Satan also works, with lying wonders, even bringing down fire from heaven in the sight of men. Revelation 13:13. **Thus the inhabitants of the earth will be brought to take their stand**" (*The Great Controversy*, p. 612).

If people are brought to make a decision, they will have to have some criterion upon which to decide. But it will not be easy. "So closely will the counterfeit resemble the true that it will be impossible to distinguish between them except by the Holy Scriptures. By their testimony every statement and every miracle must be tested" (*ibid.*, p. 593).

Testing the Miracles

Obviously we must test the statements made by those performing the miracles, as well as testing the miracles themselves. The first and primary test is by the Word of God. Here are three tests that I have found to "try the spirits."

1. Does the miracle or its message agree with Scripture?
2. Does the miracle worker uphold God's law, including the Sabbath?
3. Does the life of the miracle worker show evidence of the fruits of the Spirit?

Miracles don't just happen. They have a point to prove—a deception to get across. From what source do they come? That's why we have the test. Let's look at them in order.

1. Does the miracle or its message agree with Scripture? The big question here is regarding the miracle worker and the miracle and their relation to Scripture—the great standard of truth. This test is the same as the first test of a prophet. "To the law and to the testimony! If they do not speak according to this word, it is because there is no light in them" (Isaiah 8:20). "The people of God are directed to the Scriptures as their safeguard against the influence of false teachers and delusive power of spirits of darkness. Satan employs every possible device to prevent men from obtaining a knowledge of the Bible; for its plain utterances reveal his deceptions" (ibid.). "The only safety for the people of God is to be thoroughly conversant with their Bibles, and be intelligent upon the reasons of our faith in regard to the sleep of the dead" (Evangelism, p. 604).

The most interesting and at the same time most frightening thing about miracles is that many take these supernatural events and do not test them but take them as "gospel" above what has already been revealed in the Scriptures. Many of those currently involved in the "Vineyard" churches claim to have miraculous spiritual experiences that in essence transcend Scripture. They say, "God is above His Word," or "God is not limited by His Word." If this were true, there is no standard—no way to test the spirits!

Ellen White faced this very type of experience early in her work. "Forty-five years ago, when I began my labors, we met with some of the most erroneous doctrines. One would say, 'I have the truth because my feelings tell me so.' Another would say, 'The Spirit tells me that I have the truth.' <u>But how were they to know that they had the right spirit</u>? **There are two spirits in the world, the Spirit of Christ, and the spirit of Antichrist.** They declared that they had gone beyond the Bible, and left that for those not so far advanced as themselves; for the Lord talked directly with them. As I stood with my Bible before them, pleading with them, they pushed me away, saying, 'No, no, I don't want to hear anything about it. God has told me the way.' <u>We must know what saith the Scriptures. Let God be true and every man a liar</u>. Not one of us must lose the eternal treasure that is laid up for the overcomer. A great sacrifice was made for us because God loved us" *(Review and Herald,* June 10, 1890).

The false miracles at the end of time will be so deceptive that they will be impossible to distinguish except by the Bible. Think of the significance in this. If you judge only by your natural senses, you will believe these false miracles to be from God! We must be willing to elevate the Word of God above our senses! "We must all now seek to arm ourselves for the contest in which we must soon engage. <u>Faith in God's word, prayerfully studied and practically applied, will be our shield from Satan's power</u> and will bring us off conquerors through the blood of Christ" *(Testimonies for the Church,* vol. 1, p. 461).

2. Does the miracle worker uphold God's law, including the Sabbath? When the apostles were imprisoned for preaching about Christ, the Lord miraculously freed them from prison. They went right back to preaching, and when they were brought before the authorities, they stated, "We ought to obey God rather than men." And speaking of Jesus they said, "And we are His witnesses to these things, and so also is the Holy Spirit <u>whom God has given to those who obey Him</u>" (Acts 5:29, 32).

This second point of the test might seem rather narrow, but there is good evidence for it. If the law of God and the Sabbath in particular will be the great test at the end, does it make sense that God will be working miracles on both sides? Hardly. Here is the evidence that the true miracles will be performed by Sabbathkeepers.

"It is impossible to give any idea of the experience of the people of God who shall be alive upon the earth when celestial glory and a repetition of the persecutions of the past are blended. They will walk in the light proceeding from the throne of God. <u>By means of the angels there will be constant communication between heaven and earth</u>. And Satan, surrounded by evil angels, and claiming to be God, will work miracles of all kinds, to deceive, if possible, the very elect. <u>God's people will not find their safety in working miracles, for Satan will counterfeit the miracles that will be wrought</u>. **God's tried and tested people will find their power in the sign spoken of in Exodus 31:12-18.** They are to take their stand on the living word: 'It is written.' <u>This is the only foundation upon which they can stand securely</u>" *(Maranatha,* p. 205).

What is the sign from Exodus 31 that God has written in His Word? It is none other than the true seventh-day Sabbath.

"And the Lord spoke to Moses, saying, 'Speak also to the children of Israel, saying: "Surely my Sabbaths you shall keep, for it is a **sign** between Me and you throughout your generations, <u>that you may know that I am the Lord who sanctifies you</u>. . . . Therefore the children of Israel shall keep the Sabbath, to observe the Sabbath throughout their generations as a <u>perpetual covenant</u>. It is a **sign** between Me and the children of Israel <u>forever</u>; for in six days the Lord made the heavens and the earth, and on the seventh day He rested and was refreshed."' And when He had made an end of speaking with him on Mount Sinai, He gave Moses two tablets of the Testimony, **tablets of stone, written with the finger of God**" (Exodus 31:12, 13, 16-18).

The Lord says that the Sabbath is a sign between Him and His people forever. He wrote this sign in stone for a perpetual covenant. Will He then come as a Sundaykeeper to perform miracles? The answer is quite logical and consistent with His dealings. There is more "sign" evidence.

"Moreover I also gave them My Sabbaths, to be a **sign** between them and Me, that they might <u>know</u> that I am the Lord who sanctifies them. . . . Hallow My Sabbaths, and they will be a **sign** between Me and you, <u>that you may know that I am the Lord your God</u>" (Ezekiel 20:12, 20). What's the sign? It is the Sabbath! There is more evidence:

"The time is not far distant when Satan will come down having great power, and will work wonderful signs and great miracles; and with his delusions he will sweep away every one who does not stand upon the rock of eternal truth. God is even now proving us. <u>We see some who claim to be followers of Christ working miracles; **but do**</u>

they keep the commandments of God? [The Sabbath is one of the commandments!] We will go to the inspired word, and try every one of them. 'To the law and to the testimony; if they speak not according to this word, it is because there is no light in them.' When the youth go out from our schools, they will have to meet these people; and we want them to be firmly established in the truth. We want them to have a training that will prepare them to withstand error, and will guide their feet in the narrow, upward way" *(Signs of the Times,* December 10, 1885). There is safety in the Sabbath sign!

3. Does the life of the miracle worker show evidence of the fruits of the Spirit? Jesus told us how to tell true from false. He said, "Beware of false prophets, who come to you in sheep's clothing, but inwardly they are ravenous wolves. You will know them by their fruits" (Matthew 7:15, 16). In other words, what kind of life do they live? What are the fruits of their "ministry"?

"Those who look for miracles as a sign of divine guidance are in grave danger of deception. It is stated in the Word that the enemy will work through his agents **who have departed from the faith,** and they will seemingly work miracles, even to the bringing down of fire out of heaven in the sight of men. By means of 'lying wonders' Satan would deceive, if possible, the very elect" *(Selected Messages,* vol. 3, p. 408). Those who perform the false miracles will either be those who have left the faith or have never been a part of it.

Don't Depend on Miracles

"We are not to establish our faith on the hope of seeing miracles. Satan will work miracles to accomplish his purposes. We must rely on a 'Thus saith the Lord.' It is the word of God, and perfect, sanctified unity that are to make Christ's waiting ones complete in Him" *(The Southern Watchman,* March 1, 1904).

As miracles increase near the end, people will demand miracles of God's people to "prove" they have the truth. But miracles are never given on demand. "Spiritualists are increasing in numbers. They will come to men who have the truth as Satan came to Christ, tempting them to manifest their power, and work miracles, and give evidence of their being favored of God, and of their being the people who have the truth. Satan said to Christ, 'If thou be the Son of God, command these stones that they be made bread.' Herod and Pilate asked Christ to work miracles when He was on trial for His life. Their curiosity was aroused, but Christ did not work a miracle to gratify them" *(The Signs of the Times,* April 12, 1893).

Unfortunately, for those who are looking for miracles, Satan will supply them. "The man who makes the working of miracles a test of his faith will find that Satan can, through a species of deceptions, perform wonders that will appear to be genuine miracles" *(Maranatha,* p. 156).

It is interesting to note that John the Baptist, the "Elijah" forerunner of Christ's first advent, did not perform any miracles. Yet Jesus spoke of him as the greatest prophet born of women. "John performed no sign, but all the things that John spoke about this Man were true. And many believed on Him there" (John 10:41, 42). "It was not given to John to call fire down from heaven, or to raise the dead, as Elijah did, nor to wield Moses' rod of power in the name of God. He was sent to herald the Saviour's advent, and to call upon the people to prepare for His coming. So faithfully did he fulfill his mission, that as the people recalled what he had taught them of Jesus, they could say, 'All things that John spake of this Man were true.' Such witness to Christ every disciple of the Master is called upon to bear" *(The Desire of Ages,* p. 219).

Did Ellen White work miracles in her ministry? When the pioneers of our church were working to establish sanitariums for the sick, many asked her, "Do you have power to work miracles and to heal the sick? I answer, I have never worked a miracle in my life; but I have presented many suffering ones in faith to Christ, and the mighty Healer has rebuked disease and raised the suffering ones to health. Christ alone can heal the sick and raise the dead" (Letter 278, 1908, *Manuscript Releases,* vol. 7, p. 381).

The very best evidence of God's miraculous power is found in the transformed life of one who trusts in Him. It is a true miracle of grace when the heart is changed; and we love Jesus, and desire to do those things that please Him.

Don't Expect a Miracle

God does not work miracles when one is not necessary or the cause does not merit one. Let me give some examples. "Do you pray for the advancement of the truth? Then work for it, and show that your prayers rise from sincere and earnest hearts. God does not work miracles where He has provided the means by which the work may be accomplished. Use your time and talents in His service, and He will not fail to work with your efforts. <u>If the farmer fails to plow and sow, God does not work a miracle to undo the results of his neglect</u>. Harvest-time finds his fields barren—there are no sheaves to be reaped, no grain to be garnered. God provided the seed and the soil, the sun and the rain; and if the agriculturist had employed the means that were at his hand, he would have received according to his sowing and labor" *(Christian Education,* p. 116).

Now, having shown this basic illustration, let me get more specific in two areas—our children and our health. How can we expect God to work miracles to save our children when we have knowingly placed them in harm's way? If we have lived in the city and allowed our children to watch hours and hours of television with all of its crime, violence, drug abuse, immorality, silliness, and commercials designed for children's minds, how can we expect anything other than a harvest of tares? "By beholding we are changed." "Parents who denounce the Canaanites for offering their children to Moloch, what are you doing? You are making a most costly offering to your mammon god; and then, when your children grow up unloved and unlovely in character, when they show decided impiety and tendency to infidelity, you blame the faith you profess because it was unable to save them. <u>You are reaping that which you have sown,—the result of your selfish love of the world and neglect of the means of grace</u>. **You moved your families into places of temptation, and the ark of God, your glory and defense, you did not consider essential; and the Lord has not worked a miracle to deliver your children from temptation**" *(Signs of the Times,* January 31, 1884).

Later that same year in another *Signs* article Ellen White stated, "God will not work a miracle to change natural causes which you can control. <u>If you place yourself and family in the current of the world, you and your children will be borne downward by it</u>. Be wise and discriminating in regard to spiritual advantages, and gather about yourself and your children correct influences. . . . The habits and customs with which we have become familiar may cling to us, and we may find that we have assimilated to them more than we were aware. This is a risk that we cannot afford to run. We might better lose every worldly advantage than to lose Jesus, or dishonor Him by our careless inattention to His requirements. It is best to obey God at any sacrifice" *(ibid.,* May 8, 1884).

With regard to our health, we all know much more than we practice. But it seems that some completely disregard the counsel that God has been pleased to give us in regard to healthful living.

"God will not work a miracle to keep those from sickness who have no care for themselves, but are continually violating the laws of health and make no efforts to prevent disease. When we do all we can on our part to have health, then may we expect that the blessed results will follow, and we can ask God in faith to bless our efforts, for the preservation of health. He will then answer our prayer, if His name can be glorified thereby. But let all understand that they have a work to do. **God will not work in a miraculous manner to preserve the health of persons who by their careless inattention to the laws of health are taking a sure course to make themselves sick**" *(Counsels on Health,* p. 59).

How can we possibly think that God will bless us with good health when we knowingly violate the laws of health? "No man or woman has any right to form habits which lessen the healthful action of one organ of mind or body. He who perverts his powers is defiling the temple of the Holy Spirit. The Lord will not work a miracle to restore to soundness those who **continue** to use drugs which so degrade the soul, mind, and body that sacred things are not appreciated. **Those who give themselves up to the use of tobacco and liquor do not appreciate their intellect.** They do not realize the value of the faculties God has given them. They allow their powers to wither and decay" *(Review and Herald,* November 6, 1900).

The bottom line on the health question is very simple. "If, after so much light has been given, God's people still cherish wrong habits, indulging self and refusing to reform, they will suffer the sure consequence of transgression. If they are determined to gratify perverted appetite at any cost, God will not work miracle after miracle to save them. They shall lie down in sorrow" *(Pacific Union Recorder,* October 9, 1902).

The same principle that applies to family and health applies to other areas of life. For example, it will take a lot of money to finish the work; but God does not plan to sustain His work by miracles. God never personally signs or send the check. The money comes from people like you and me who feel impressed to support a particular project.

The fact that God works in mighty ways when we do our work is presented in a classic statement found in *Prophets and Kings.* On his deathbed, Elisha told King Joash how to defeat the Syrians. He first asked the king to shoot arrows out the window in the direction of Syria. "And now the prophet tested the faith of the king. Bidding Joash take up the arrows, he said, 'Smite upon the ground.' Thrice the king smote the ground, and then he stayed his hand. 'Thou shouldest have smitten five or six times,' Elisha exclaimed in dismay; 'then hadst thou smitten Syria till thou hadst consumed it: whereas now thou shalt smite Syria but thrice.' 2 Kings 13:15-19.

"The lesson is for all in positions of trust. <u>When God opens the way for the accomplishment of a certain work and gives assurance of success, the chosen instrumentality must do all in his power to bring about the promised result.</u> **In proportion to the enthusiasm and perseverance with which the work is carried forward will be the success given.** God can work miracles for His people only as they act their part with untiring energy. He calls for men of devotion to His work, men of moral courage, with ardent love for souls, and with a zeal that never flags" *(Prophets and Kings,* pp. 262, 263).

"Lying Wonders"

Already we see the beginning of "lying wonders"—and more are coming! We have been warned, "As spiritualism more closely imitates the nominal Christianity of the day, it has greater power to deceive and ensnare. . . . Through the agency of spiritualism, miracles will be wrought, the sick will be healed, and many undeniable wonders will be performed. And as the spirits profess faith in the Bible, and manifest respect for the institutions of the church, their work will be accepted as a manifestation of divine power" *(The Great Controversy,* p. 588).

In the foreword of the book *The Thunder of Justice,* Malachi Martin wrote: "Literally, every decade of this one century alone has piled one on another, what Christ called 'the signs of the times' (Matt. 16:1-4). In a general way of speaking, it is quasi-impossible to have totally escaped any awareness of these events, and the clamor of the claimant participants. Visions. Appearances. Messages. Predictions. Warnings. Interpretations. Weeping statues and bleeding icons. Miraculous spring waters. Spontaneous cures. Spinning dances of the sun, and eclipses of the moon. Little children telling the future. Uneducated men and women instructing popes and presidents. Nationwide publicity tours by bearers of special revelations. Throughout all of this, an obvious emphasis on the singular role of the Blessed Virgin Mary of Nazareth as Queen of Heaven, Mother of All the Living, and—not surprisingly—as the Mediatrix of All Graces is pervasive."

We can now add to this list that the pope wants to bring "Mary" to the United States! In the May 1997 issue of *Inside the Vatican,* editor Robert Moynihan dedicates his entire editorial to Mary with the headline: **THE CONSECRATION, Let Us Make the Third Millennium the Millennium of Mary.** I will now quote a portion of the editorial:

"The Holy Father longs to visit the United States one more time. That is the report from those closest to Him. . . . Monsignor Stanislaw Dziwisz, the Pope's private secretary and long-time friend and collaborator, says behind John Paul II's longing to see America again is his wish to honor the Blessed Virgin, <u>to urge Americans to turn to her, and</u> **<u>to dramatically and symbolically link the great Western democracy more closely to her.</u>**

" 'I have no doubt he would go,' said Dziwisz in a conversation with *Inside the Vatican,* 'if his pilgrimage could be related to some Marian occasion.'

"The Monsignor could not say exactly what kind of an event that would be. He pointed out that if the United States had a national Marian shrine such as those in many other countries—Guadalupe in Mexico, Lourdes in France, Fatima in Portugal, Czestochowa in Poland—the visit could be tied in with a pilgrimage to that shrine.

"It is apparent the Vatican, <u>aware of the role America plays in the world,</u> aware also of the grave moral and spiritual crisis America is facing, is groping for a way to reach America, through Mary, for the gospel.

"The dedication of a great national Marian shrine and the consecration of America to 'Our Lady of Fairest Love' would be an appropriate occasion for John Paul to visit the U.S. one last time."

So the pope wants to dedicate a national shrine to Mary and consecrate America to Mary. There is also more to this issue. It seems likely that in May of 1998 the pope will "exercise the charism of papal infallibility and declare the third Marian Dogma." That being that she is now our "Co-Redemptrix."

On a related subject, the same issue of *Inside the Vatican* (May 1997) reported that on February 16, 1997, the pope pronounced that "God will never destroy the world again as He did with the Great Flood at the time of Noah." The magazine goes on to report, "Pope John Paul II said [this] in a sermon today at a Rome parish before retiring to the Vatican for a week-long Lenten retreat. The Holy Father said that after the Great Flood, God forged a covenant with Noah. 'From the words of the covenant between God and Noah, it is understood that now <u>no sin could bring God to destroy the world He created</u>,' the pope said." So according to the pope, the earth will not be destroyed by a great earthquake and fire and the second coming of Jesus Christ. Things are just going to get better as we prepare for the great Jubilee beginning in the year 2000. The festivities planned to welcome the third millennium—the great Jubilee in the year 2000— are causing more than a little turmoil in Rome. "It might have been expected in Rome. With 1,000 days left before the Great Jubilee of the year 2000, preparations for the event are in turmoil. <u>Crowds of 20 million, 30 million, maybe 40 million tourists and pilgrims</u> are expected to descend on Rome in 2000 to celebrate the third Christian millennium" *(Inside the Vatican,* May 1997, p. 26).

I believe that the time is at hand when Satan will go into overdrive to deceive people with his lying wonders. The multiplication of Marian apparitions and other "miracles" illustrate this activity. Now the misdirected plans for the great Jubilee millennium in this statement should give us some cause for serious reflection. "I saw our people in great distress, weeping, and praying, pleading the sure promises of God, while the wicked were all around us, mocking us, and threatening to destroy us. They ridiculed our feebleness, they mocked at the smallness of our numbers, and taunted us with words calculated to cut deep. They charged us with taking an independent position from all the rest of the world. They had cut off our resources so that we could not buy nor sell, and referred to our abject poverty and stricken condition. They could not see how we could live without the world; we were dependent upon the world, and we must concede to the customs, practices, and laws of the world, or go out of it. If we were the only people in the world whom the Lord favored the appearances were awfully against us. They declared that they had the truth, **that miracles were among them,** that angels from heaven talked with them, and walked with them, that great power, **and signs and wonders were performed among them,** and this was the **Temporal Millennium,** which they had been expecting so long. The whole world was converted and **in harmony with the Sunday law,** and this little feeble people stood out in defiance of the laws of the land, and the laws of God, and claimed to be the only ones right on the earth" *(Maranatha,* p. 209).

But there is good news. "Satan will work his miracles to deceive; he will set up his power as supreme. The church may appear as about to fall, but it does not fall. It remains, while the sinners in Zion will be sifted out—the chaff separated from the precious wheat. This is a terrible ordeal, but nevertheless it must take place. None but those who have been overcoming by the blood of the Lamb and the word of their testimony will be found with the loyal and true, without spot or stain of sin, without guile in their mouths" *(ibid.,* p. 32).

Let us not allow these precious days of probation to pass without seeking God with all our hearts and seeking a knowledge of His Word. We want to be among those who are not deceived but stand firm on the platform of truth—holding up the sign of the Sabbath.

CHAPTER 11

Beware of False Prophets

From the beginning—at Creation—God has used various channels in communicating His will to His creatures. With such an abundant revelation mankind is left without any excuse regarding a knowledge of God's will and the way we are to live. In the beginning God spoke with Adam and Eve face-to-face. Man was then in a state of innocence—it was before sin. Sin changed all that: fallen man could no longer have direct, face-to-face contact with God. "Your iniquities have separated you from your God; and your sins have hidden His face from you" (Isaiah 59:2). But God is determined to communicate with mankind and to share a knowledge of His will. He chose alternative ways to give direction, counsel, and an overall knowledge of His will.

God's Methods of Communication

1. Angel messengers. On many occasions God sent messages to earth by heavenly angels. These glorious beings spoke directly with the persons to whom they were sent. They were recognized as angels by those they spoke with. In this manner an angel spoke to Hagar (Genesis 16:7-12), to Lot (Genesis 19:1, 12, 13, 15), to Jacob (Genesis 32:1), to Moses (Exodus 3:2), to Balaam (Numbers 22:32), to all the children of Israel (Judges 1:1-4), to Gideon (Judges 6:11-22), to the mother of Samson (Judges 13:3-5), to Elijah (1 Kings 19:5-7), to Daniel (Daniel 9:21, 22), to Zechariah (Zechariah 1:9, 11-14), to Joseph, husband of Mary (Matthew 1:20, 21; 2:13, 19), to Zacharias, father of John the Baptist (Luke 1:11-20), to Mary (Luke 1:26-38), to the shepherds (Luke 2:8-14), to the women at the tomb (Luke 24:23), to the apostles in jail (Acts 5:19, 20), to Cornelius (Acts 10:3-6), and to Paul (Acts 27:23, 24). We could list others, but these give a good cross section. An unfortunate consequence of sin is that Satan also tries to communicate with men in ways that counterfeit God's methods. For example, Satan will disguise himself as an angel of light—as he did at the temptation of Christ.

2. The Urim and Thummim. This method of communicating God's will is described in the Bible in this way: "And you shall put in the breastplate of judgment the Urim and the Thummim, and they shall be over Aaron's heart when he goes in before the Lord" (Exodus 28:30). In some manner not clearly explained in the Bible, God revealed His will to the high priest by means of these precious stones. The little evidence suggests that a light rested on the right stone when God indicated a positive answer, and a cloud or shadow covered the left stone to indicate a negative answer to whatever question had been asked by the high priest.

3. The Shekinah. Again, we don't know much about this method of communication, but apparently, God made His will known by the light between the cherubim on the mercy seat of the ark. Sometimes a voice from the light answered the high priest. When the light was there it seemed to show approval and a shadow indicated disapproval.

4. Dreams. God frequently spoke directly to individuals in a dream. We have record of this when He spoke to Abimelech "in a dream" (Genesis 20:3); to Jacob (Genesis 28:12); to Laban (Genesis 31:24); to Joseph (Genesis 37:5); to Pharaoh (Genesis 47:7); to Solomon (1 Kings 3:5); and to Nebuchadnezzar (Daniel 2:1), as well as to many others.

These are all ways that God has communicated to men. When Saul was king of Israel, he inquired of the Lord, and "the Lord answered him not, neither by dreams, nor by Urim, nor by prophets." As a result Saul was convinced, as he stated it himself, that "God is departed from me" (1 Samuel 28:6, 15).

5. Prophets. Beyond these various methods of communication with man there is one other that God has used more than any other over the centuries. Down through the ages God has made known His commandments and guidance in the way of truth through the prophets. In fact, He has told us: "Surely the Lord God does nothing, unless He reveals His secret to His servants the prophets" (Amos 3:7).

Beware of False Prophets

There have also been false prophets, inspired by Satan, down through the ages, and many have been deceived and led astray by them. In the days of Elijah, for example, there were 450 prophets of Baal and 400 prophets of Asherah "who ate at Jezebel's table." You could say that there were 850 false prophets serving the "royal family" of Israel!

In His sermon on the mount Jesus stated that on the judgment day many false prophets would seek admission to heaven and be turned away. "Many will say to Me in that day, 'Lord, Lord, have we not prophesied in Your name, cast out demons in Your name, and done many wonders in Your name?' And then I will declare to them, 'I never knew you; depart from Me, you who practice lawlessness!'" (Matthew 7:22, 23). Apparently, many false prophets are actually deceived themselves and expect to be admitted to heaven. -

Just what is a false prophet? <u>A false prophet is any person who claims to speak for God but doesn't meet the biblical tests of a prophet</u>. The person must meet all four tests. It's just that simple. We will look at those tests later in this chapter.

Rather than spending a lot of time talking about false prophets we should rather answer two basic questions. The first is: Will there be prophets in the post-New Testament church? If the answer to this question is no, then we don't need to ask the second question, because anyone who claimed to be a prophet after John the revelator would simply be a false prophet. If the answer to the first question is yes—there will be prophets in the post-New Testament times—then we must ask and answer the second question: What are the tests of a prophet?

Will There Be Prophets in the Christian Era?

I have discovered seven points of evidence that build a case for the gift of prophecy in the Christian Era—the time from when Jesus was on earth to the Second Coming. I doubt that any readers have questions about whether or not Moses, Isaiah, Daniel, or John the revelator were prophets. But did God intend that the gift of prophecy be manifest in the Christian church and especially at the time of the end? That is the question I will address in this section. The following seven points indicate that the answer is yes. What do you think?

1. Just plain logic and reason. Though this is a philosophical approach, we are invited by God to use our reason. He says, "Come now, and let us reason together" (Isaiah 1:18). Philosophers tell us that if there is a God, He will reveal Himself. He will let His subjects know about Himself in some way. In other words, He will establish some way of communicating with them. This point establishes a foundation upon which to add the remaining evidence.

2. We are all modern Israel. We are God's people. Though we live in an age of computers, cellular phones, microwave ovens, and credit cards, we still need to communicate with our God. But you say, "Why do we need a prophet? We have the Bible. We have it on cassette, diskette, compact disk, in modern English, in living sound." We need prophets because we are modern Israel. We should never forget that. We should study it thoroughly and know it for ourselves. Dr. Hans LaRondelle has written a very insightful book on this subject. It is titled *The Israel of God in Prophecy* (Andrews University Press, 1983). If the Bible were being written today, we would be the Bible characters. Our response to God and our work for Him would be the story line. We are the people that God will communicate with just like He did in Old Testament times and in the days of the apostles. We are the Israel of God today! And by the way, we have every indication that God is writing such a story in heaven.

3. God has a modus operandi. God has an M.O.—a way He operates. When you study and learn about God in His prior revelations to man, you quickly observe that He likes to communicate with man. You see His love. He wants to be with us. He wants to talk with us and listen to us. He wants to let us know "what's going on" and what will happen in the latter days. "Surely the Lord God does <u>nothing</u>, unless He reveals His secret to His servants the prophets" (Amos 3:7). It simply would not be like God to bring a flood on the whole earth and not give a warning by Noah. It wouldn't be like Him to deliver His people from bondage in Egypt without the prophet Moses.

Remember that Moses worked some time in Egypt just to convince the Israelites that God was going to deliver them and that they should prepare to leave. God didn't just come to them the night they were supposed to leave and say, "It's time to go, everybody!" It wasn't a voice from heaven or a mental impression. It was the work of the great prophet Moses to prepare Israel for the Exodus. "By a prophet the Lord brought Israel out of Egypt, and by a prophet he was preserved" (Hosea 12:13). It's not like God to come to earth the first time without the ministry of John the Baptist. And it is not like God to come the second time, the great climax of the great controversy, without revealing this event to a prophet who would work to prepare the people for it.

4. The testimony of Jesus Himself. Jesus frequently spoke of the prophets and had very high regard for them. He wept in lamenting Israel's treatment of the prophets. "O Jerusalem, Jerusalem, the one who kills the prophets and stones those who are sent to her! How often I wanted to gather your children together, as a hen gathers her chicks under her wings, but you were not willing" (Matthew 23:37)! It is obvious that Jesus recognized that there would be a continuing ministry of prophets, because He warned the disciples to beware of false prophets. "For false christs and false prophets will rise, and show signs and wonders to deceive, if possible, even the elect" (Mark 13:22). It is understood from Jesus' language that there would be true prophets, because He warns us to beware of false prophets—three times in Matthew 24 alone! So not every person who claims to be a prophet is a true prophet—one who is gifted from God. But there obviously will be true prophets or He would have said, "Anyone who claims to be a prophet is a false prophet." He was warning us that Satan will take this prophetic gift that God is planning to use and send in his false prophets—wolves in sheep's clothing—in an attempt to deceive mankind. So how do we tell the difference and avoid being deceived? We apply the four tests of a prophet!

5. The testimony of the apostle Paul. Discussing God's great gifts to the church, Paul includes a total of five lists. It is significant to note that the words "prophets" or "prophecy" appear in all five of the gift lists. It may be even more noteworthy that it is the only gift to appear in all five lists. Let's take a quick look at just one of the gift lists and note the timing and purpose of the gifts. Jesus, having completed His earthly work for the salvation of men, returned to heaven. At His ascension He gave His church the gift of prophecy. He had laid the foundation for His church in the saving work of His death, burial, resurrection, and ascension. After that, the building of His church was to be turned over to men, who were directed by the Holy Spirit. These men were not qualified by any natural endowments or talents. It was not by natural ability or wisdom that they could hope to successfully accomplish and to bring to completion the work that Christ had begun and left to them in the Great Commission. Jesus knew this, and accordingly, He gave them spiritual endowments. The first and greatest gift was the powerful gift of the Holy Spirit, granted to all who believe and accept it as the indwelling Christ to guide us into all truth. And then He gave special gifts, to fit and prepare men to do His work, to qualify them for success in spiritual endeavors, to enable them to achieve His purposes on the earth.

Paul details when these gifts were made, names some of the most important of them, reveals their purpose, and makes known how long they would remain in the church.

"When He [Christ] ascended on high, He led captivity captive, and gave gifts to men. . . . And He Himself gave some to be apostles, some prophets, some evangelists, and some pastors and teachers, for the equipping of the saints for the work of ministry, for the edifying of the body of Christ, till we all come to the unity of the faith and the knowledge of the Son of God, to a perfect man, to the measure of the stature of the fullness of Christ; that we should no longer be children, tossed to and fro and carried about with every wind of doctrine, by the trickery of men, in the cunning craftiness by which they lie in wait to deceive, but speaking the truth in love, may grow up in all things into Him who is the head—Christ—from whom the whole body, joined and knit together by what every joint supplies, according to the effective working by which every part does its share, causes growth of the body for the edifying of itself in love" (Ephesians 4:8, 11-16).

Wow! What a long sentence! Verses eleven through sixteen are all part of one long sentence. At least we are sure of the context. We can see that the gift of prophecy was given by Jesus Himself to benefit the church to bring about unity of the faith and so that we could have sound doctrine and not be tossed about in our beliefs. This will enable us to preach the truth in love.

Paul also counsels, "Do not despise prophecies. Test all things; hold fast what is good" (1 Thessalonians 5:20, 21). And how can we test prophecies? By the four tests. It is very important that we understand this process of testing.

6. The witness of the Old Testament. The Old Testament predicts that there would be prophets working in New Testament times—during the Christian Era. One passage in particular is quite noteworthy.

"And it shall come to pass afterward that I will pour out My Spirit on all flesh; your sons and your daughters shall prophesy, your old men shall dream dreams, your young men shall see visions; and also on My menservants and on My maidservants I will pour out My Spirit in those days. And I will show wonders in the heavens and in the earth: Blood and fire and pillars of smoke. The sun shall be turned into darkness, and the moon into blood, before the great and terrible day of the Lord" (Joel 2:28-31).

Some who are critics of last-day prophets say that this passage applies to the preaching on the day of Pentecost, since Peter makes reference to it. Pentecost was a partial fulfillment, to be sure; just as the early rain was a forerunner of the latter rain. But it is easy to see that Pentecost was not the complete fulfillment of Joel's prediction, because that is in connection with the great and terrible day of the Lord. That event will be accompanied by signs and wonders in the heavens—something which clearly did not occur on the day of Pentecost.

Another Old Testament passage predicting the gift of prophecy in the last days is Malachi 4: "Behold, I will send you Elijah the prophet before the coming of the great and dreadful day of the Lord" (Malachi 4:5). The Elijah message is a prophetic message of preparation for the way of the Lord. Like the work of the prophet Elijah it will urge repentance and revival—just before the great and dreadful day of the Lord.

7. The testimony of the book of Revelation. Revelation 10 reveals a people with prophetic roots—a prophetic movement. Revelation 12 and 19 reveal a people with a prophetic messenger. And Revelation 14 reveals a people with a prophetic message. There was indeed a movement, which came to activity at the right time (see the historical context of Revelation 12), one which fulfilled all of these characteristics—and it still continues to do so.

The evidence given in these seven points has convinced me that God intends to continue to communicate with man in the Christian Era—the time in which we live—using the methods He has used in the past—including the use of the prophetic gift.

How the Prophetic Gift Functioned in the Early Church

The New Testament gives prophecy a prominent place among the gifts of the Holy Spirit, once ranking it first and twice second among the gifts or ministries most useful to the church (see Romans 12:6; 1 Corinthians 12:28; Ephesians 4:11). It encourages believers to especially desire this gift (1 Corinthians 14:1, 39). The reference book *Seventh-day Adventists Believe* suggests that prophets performed the following functions in the early church:

"**1. They assisted in founding of the church.** The church was 'built on the foundation of the apostles and prophets, Jesus Christ Himself being the chief cornerstone' (Eph. 2:20, 21).

"**2. They initiated the church's mission outreach.** It was through prophets that the Holy Spirit selected Paul and Barnabas for their first missionary journey (Acts 13:1, 2) and gave direction as to where missionaries should labor (Acts 16:6-10).

"**3. They edified the church.** 'He who prophesies,' Paul said, 'edifies the church.' Prophecies are spoken 'to men for their upbuilding, and encouragement and consolation' (1 Cor. 14:4, 3, RSV). Along with other gifts, God gave prophecy to the church to prepare believers 'for the work of ministry, for the edifying of the body of Christ' (Eph. 4:12).

"**4. They united and protected the church.** Prophets helped to bring about 'the unity of the faith,' protect the church against false doctrines so believers would 'no longer be infants tossed back and forth by the waves, and blown here and there by every wind of teaching and by the cunning craftiness of men in their deceitful scheming' (Eph. 4:14, NIV).

"**5. They warned of future difficulties.** One New Testament prophet warned of an approaching famine. In response the church initiated a relief program to assist those who suffered because of that famine (Acts 11:27-30). Other prophets warned of Paul's arrest and imprisonment in Jerusalem (Acts 20:23; 21:4, 10-14).

"**6. They confirmed the faith in times of controversy.** At the first church council the Holy Spirit guided the church to a decision on a controversial issue dealing with the salvation of Gentile Christians. Then, through prophets, the Spirit reaffirmed the believers in the true doctrine. After conveying the council's decision to the membership, 'Judas and Silas, who themselves were prophets, said much to encourage and strengthen ["confirm," KJV] the brothers' (Acts 15:32, NIV)" *(Seventh-day Adventists Believe,* pp. 218, 219).

It seems that the answer is a ringing yes to the question of whether or not God planned to continue the use of prophets in the New Testament church. The seven points of evidence above and the six functions of prophets in the New Testament church are sufficient proof that God is continuing His communication with man to the very end of time. Paul says that the spiritual gifts have been given to bring the church "to the unity of the faith and of the knowledge of the Son of God, to a perfect man, to the measure of the stature of the fullness of Christ" (Ephesians 4:13). Because the church has not yet reached this experience, it still needs all the gifts of the Spirit. These gifts, including the gift of prophecy, will continue to operate for the benefit of God's people until Christ returns.

With this background, we can now discuss the second major question. What are the tests of a true prophet? How can one tell the difference between a true and a false prophet?

The Tests of a Prophet

Since the Bible is our only and ultimate standard of truth, we must find the tests of a prophet in its teachings. "Beloved, do not believe every spirit, but test the spirits, whether they are of God; because many false prophets have gone out into the world" (1 John 4:1). The Bible indicates that there are four basic tests to determine whether or not one claiming the gift is a true prophet. Accordingly, any person claiming to have the prophetic gift should be subjected to these biblical tests. If he or she measures up to these criteria we can have confidence that indeed the Holy Spirit has given that individual the gift of prophecy.

Here are the four tests:

1. Do the teachings of the prophet agree with the Scriptures— the biblical canon? Do their teachings harmonize with the Bible? "To the law and to the testimony! If they do not speak according to this word, it is because there is no light in them" (Isaiah 8:20). This is the basic overall test of a prophet and the real bottom line. A true prophet's message must be in harmony with God's unchanging law and the testimony given throughout the Bible. A later prophet must not conflict with the earlier prophets. The Holy Spirit, Who inspires all true prophets, will not contradict His previously given testimony, because God "does not change like shifting shadows" (James 1:17, NIV).

2. Do the prophet's predictions come true? As we have seen above, the role and function of a prophet is much broader than merely making predictions. However, when predictions are made they must come true. Many biblical prophecies are conditional—such as Jonah's prediction of the destruction of Nineveh. Accordingly, unless a prophecy is conditional, it must come true. "When a prophet speaks in the name of the Lord, if the thing does not happen or come to pass, that is the thing which the Lord has not spoken" (Deuteronomy 18:22). "When the word of the prophet comes to pass, the prophet will be known as one whom the Lord has truly sent" (Jeremiah 28:9).

3. Does the prophet acknowledge the incarnation of Christ? This test applies most specifically to the New Testament and Christian Era prophets. "By this you will know the Spirit of God: Every spirit that confesses that Jesus Christ has come in the flesh is of God, and every spirit that does not confess that Jesus Christ has come in the flesh is not of God" (1 John 4:2, 3). This test requires more than a simple acknowledgment that Jesus Christ lived on earth. The true prophet will confess to the biblical teachings about Christ. He must believe in Christ's deity, that He is the Creator, His virgin birth, true humanity, sinless life, atoning sacrifice, resurrection, ascension, intercessory ministry, and second advent.

4. Do the life and teaching of the prophet bear good or bad fruit? The Bible says, "You will know them by their fruits. . . . A good tree cannot bear bad fruit, nor can a bad tree bear good fruit. . . . Therefore by their fruits you will know them" (Matthew 7:16, 18, 20). In fact, the Scriptures declare that the Holy Spirit inspired "holy men of God" (2 Peter 1:21). This, of course, does not mean that the prophet himself must of necessity be absolutely sinless and perfect. Not at all. In fact, we are told that "Elijah was a man of like passions as we are" (James 5:17, KJV). But the prophet's life must be characterized by the fruit of the Spirit, and not by the works of the flesh which we discussed earlier. In addition, it is important to observe the influence of the prophet. Does the prophet's influence and/or message help to fulfill the functions of a true prophet? For example, does the prophet's ministry help to equip the saints for the work of ministry and help to bring unity of faith and fellowship in the church?

The Prophetic Gift and Ellen G. White

Has the prophetic gift been manifested in the last-day church in the ministry of Ellen G. White? While you are beginning to contemplate this question let me pose another, hypothetical, question. Suppose that I were to announce to you that I had been given the gift of prophecy and the call to be a prophet? How would you determine the validity of such a claim? Obviously, you would utilize the four tests of a prophet. But we don't always do that. We often scrutinize our prophets and forget the message. In other words, we often want to know personal details, such as when they stopped using salt on the table.

It is interesting to note that many of the Old Testament prophets were actually <u>killed</u>. Who killed them? They were often killed by God's professed people. <u>They</u> actually killed God's prophets! Not just the wicked unbelievers. (See 1 Kings 19:10, 14.) This attitude was also evidenced toward the life and ministry of Jesus. He said, "A prophet is not without honor except in his own country, among his own relatives, and in his own house" (Mark 6:4). Jesus was never recognized as a prophet or the Messiah in His hometown of Nazareth. He was born and raised there, but on both occasions that He visited Nazareth, they tried to kill Him and ran Him out of town. "You couldn't be the Messiah," they said. "We know you. You are the carpenter's son."

You get the picture. Somehow familiar things get criticized. Ellen White has had more scrutiny than Dan Quayle and Clarence Thomas combined! Sometimes you just have to feel sorry for her. Sometimes it might be good to reread the testimonies that she bore—sometimes unwillingly, but always in love and in response to the charge laid on her by the Lord.

Just two months after the Great Disappointment, in December of 1844, she had her first vision. She was only 17 years old. The Lord told her that she needed to share the message with others. Do you think she was eager to do this? Not at all. She knew what the people had just gone through. They had just experienced the Great Disappointment as a result of studying the prophecies. So people gave her the third degree. And so do we—every word she wrote, we scrutinize it. Every bite of food she ate, we ask when she stopped eating this food or that. This has little to do with the four tests, of course, but we give her the third, fourth, and fifth degree. So let's just apply the four tests and see how she relates to them.

1. Did what she said agree with Scripture?
2. Did her predictions come true?
3. Did she uphold Christ?
4. Was her life and her work a positive influence?

1. Do Ellen White's writings agree with Scripture? The answer to this question becomes more significant when the scope of her work is analyzed. She exercised her gift of prophecy for 70 years. From 1844, when she was 17, until 1915—the year of her death—she had more than 2,000 visions. Her writings fill more than 80 books, 200 tracts and pamphlets, and 4,600 periodical articles. Sermons, diaries, special testimonies, and letters comprise another 60,000 pages of manuscript material. Today, virtually all of this material is available on a single CD-ROM, allowing anyone instant access to this tremendous volume of writing. Her abundant literary production includes tens of thousands of Bible texts, often coupled with detailed expositions. Careful study by many has shown that her writings are consistent, accurate, and in full agreement with the Scriptures.

2. Did her predictions come true? As with the ministry of most other prophets only a very small percentage of Ellen White's writings contain predictions. But those she did make have been fulfilled with an amazing accuracy. Two examples are in the area of the growth of spiritualism and the development of a close working relationship between the United States and the Roman Catholic Church.

In her early ministry spiritualism was in its infancy. She predicted that it would eventually have a worldwide influence and in the process would be "Christianized." Since that time spiritualism has indeed spread worldwide and gained millions of adherents. Mary, the mother of Jesus, is actually dead and resting in her grave. But today the rise of Mariology has her not only worshiped as divine but portrayed as attempting to communicate with men on earth. The current pope has dedicated himself and his entire pontificate to Mary. (For more information on this, see *Sunday's Coming,* the chapter "Spiritualism Joins the Church.")

During Ellen White's entire lifetime a great gulf existed between Protestants and Roman Catholics that seemed to preclude any cooperation between the two. Yet she predicted that they would eventually work together. She even predicted how it would happen. She stated that changes within Protestantism would bring about a departure from the faith of the Reformation. Today many Protestant leaders are saying that the Protestant Reformation was a great misunderstanding. In addition, organizations like the Christian Coalition and Promise Keepers are working actively to bridge the gap between Protestants and Catholics.

During his presidency Ronald Reagan established full diplomatic relations with the Holy See—the central government of the Roman Catholic Church. On January 1, 1995, the pope was featured as "Man of the Year" on the cover of *Time* magazine. A great many details and events Ellen White predicted years ago are the then unforeseen present reality.

3. Did Ellen White uphold the incarnation of Christ? Two of her most popular books, *The Desire of Ages* and *Steps to Christ,* have led millions of people to a deep relationship with Christ. Her speaking and writing clearly portray Christ as fully God and fully man. She emphasized the value of developing a personal and intimate relationship with Jesus Christ. She acknowledged Christ as her Creator, Saviour, Lord, and Coming King.

4. The influence of her life and ministry. Many of the major positive endeavors of the Seventh-day Adventist Church were initiated and encouraged by Ellen White. To name a few of the more well-known, we might mention the publishing work, the medical/health work, the health food industry, and the educational program of the church. In 1982 Roger L. Dudley and Des Cummings, Jr., printed the results of a study they had conducted while working at the Institute of Church Ministries at Andrews University regarding the influence of the writings of Ellen White. They surveyed a sample of 8,200 Seventh-day Adventist church members from 193 churches. Even today many major network political opinion surveys talk to only 500 people, so a survey of over 8,000 people is quite significant. The survey compared the Christian attitude and behavior of Adventists who regularly read Ellen White's writings with those who don't. The study reached conclusions which I think are quite remarkable.

"Readers have a closer relationship with Christ, more certainty of their standing with God, and are more likely to have identified their spiritual gifts. They are more in favor of spending for public evangelism and contribute more heavily to local missionary projects. They feel more prepared for witnessing and actually engage in more witnessing and outreach programs. They are more likely to study the Bible daily, to pray for specific people, to meet in fellowship groups, and to have daily family worship. They see their local church more positively. They are responsible for winning more converts" *(Seventh-day Adventists Believe,* p. 227).

Has the ministry of Ellen White, the fruits of her labors, been positive? Who could draw a negative conclusion?

Inspiration and Copying

A number of years ago, a man who had been a much better than average student of the writings of Ellen White was shocked to discover that significant portions of the book *The Desire of Ages* used wording that was similar to or actually copied from the works of other Christian authors. This experience and his subsequent actions caused many Adventists to question the inspiration of Ellen White and not a few felt compelled to separate from our fellowship.

It is my belief that this was all the result of faulty reasoning regarding the nature of inspiration and of holding Ellen White to a higher and more rigid standard than we have maintained for the Bible writers. Many have accepted the concept of person and thought inspiration for the Bible writers, but these same individuals have wanted to hold Ellen White to the standard of verbal or actual word inspiration—something she never claimed for herself. Perhaps it was our misuse of and arguing over various portions of her writings that caused us to make her bigger than life.

Let me illustrate what I mean. The book of Revelation borrows heavily from other parts of the Bible. So much so that it is impossible to understand Revelation without a good working knowledge of the rest of God's Word. This point is clearly made when one notices how frequently allusions or references to previously written portions of Scripture occur in Revelation. <u>More than 1,000 times in its 404 verses Revelation lifts phrases or sentences out of the writings of the prophets and uses them to build the New Testament Apocalypse</u>. And yet Revelation makes so many claims for special revelation. For example:

1:1—The Revelation of Jesus Christ . . . unto His servant John.

1:10—I was in the Spirit on the Lord's day.

1:19—Write the things which thou hast seen.

6:1—And I saw.

6:3—And I heard.

This type of "special revelation" language occurs again and again in Revelation. And yet even much of the three angels' messages contain quotations from the Old Testament Scriptures.

The gospel of Luke is another example of inspired copying. Luke was not an eyewitness of the events in his gospel, but he relied on the testimony of eyewitnesses and written sources (see Luke 1:1-4). He carefully investigated and arranged material and presented it to Theophilus. Many Bible scholars believe that Theophilus probably assumed responsibility for publishing Luke and Acts so that they would be available to Gentile readers.

Does it bother you that these inspired writers copied from other sources? It certainly won't if you subscribe to the most biblical and traditional Adventist view of inspiration. The very first chapter in the book *Seventh-day Adventists Believe* is written to convey our understanding of the inspired Word of God. I will excerpt a few thoughts from this chapter.

"'All Scripture,' Paul says, 'is given by inspiration of God' (2 Timothy 3:16). The Greek word *theopneustos*, translated as 'inspiration,' literally means 'God-breathed.' God breathed truth into men's minds. They, in turn, expressed it in the words found in the Scriptures. Inspiration, therefore, is the process through which God communicates His eternal truth.

"Divine revelation was given by inspiration of God to 'holy men of God' who were 'moved by the Holy Spirit' (2 Peter 1:21). These revelations were embodied in human language with all its limitations and imperfections, yet they remained God's testimony. God inspired men—not words.

"Inspiration acts not on the prophet's words or his expressions but on the man or woman, who, under the influence of the Holy Ghost, is imbued with thoughts. The words receive the impress of the individual mind. . . .

"As to contents, to some the Spirit revealed events yet to occur (Daniel 2; 7; 8; 12). Other writers recorded historical events, either on the basis of personal experience or through selecting materials from existing historical records (Judges, 1 Samuel, 2 Chronicles, the Gospels, Acts).

"The biblical assertion that 'All Scripture is inspired of God' or 'God-breathed,' profitable and authoritative for moral and spiritual living (2 Timothy 3:15, 16, RSV; NIV) leaves no question about divine guidance in the selection process. Whether the information came from personal observation, oral or written sources, or direct revelation, it all came to the writer through the Holy Spirit's guidance. This guarantees the Bible's trustworthiness. . . .

"The Bible's writers viewed all the historical narratives it contains as true historical records, not as myths or symbols. Many contemporary skeptics reject the stories of Adam and Eve, Jonah, and the Flood. Yet Jesus accepted them as historically accurate and spiritually relevant (Matthew 12:39-41; 19:4-6; 24:37-39).

"The Bible does not teach partial inspiration or degrees of inspiration. These theories are speculation that robs the Bible of its divine authority."

Ellen White's View of Inspiration

In the author's introduction to *The Great Controversy,* Ellen White outlines her understanding of inspiration and how she was inspired. She states:

"The Bible points to God as its author; yet it was written by human hands; and in the varied style of its different books it presents the characteristics of the several writers. The truths revealed are all 'given by inspiration of God' (2 Timothy 3:16); yet they are expressed in the words of men. The Infinite One by His Holy Spirit has shed light into the minds and hearts of His servants. He has given dreams and visions, symbols and figures; and those to whom the truth was thus revealed have themselves embodied the thoughts in human language. . . .

"The Spirit was not given—nor can it ever be bestowed—to supersede the Bible; for the Scriptures explicitly state that the Word of God is the standard by which all teaching and experience must be tested. Says the apostle John, 'Believe not every spirit, but try the spirits whether they are of God: because many false prophets are gone out into the world.' 1 John 4:1. And

Isaiah declares: 'To the law and to the testimony: if they speak not according to this word, it is because there is no light in them.' Isaiah 8:20. . . .

"As the Spirit of God has opened to my mind the great truths of His Word, and the scenes of the past and future, I have been bidden to make known to others that which has thus been revealed— to trace the history of the controversy in past ages, and especially so to present it as to shed a light on the fast-approaching struggle of the future. In pursuance of this purpose, I have endeavored to select and group together events in the history of the church in such a manner as to trace the unfolding of the great testing truths that at different periods have been given to the world."

Seventh-day Adventists do not claim to be better than other religious groups or to believe that God's prophets were given only to them. We do, however, simply claim to be unique in three ways. We are a people with prophetic roots (Revelation 10), a people with a prophetic messenger (Revelation 12; 19), and a people with a prophetic message (Revelation 14).

And so I encourage you in the words of Paul: "Do not despise prophecies. Test all things; hold fast what is good" (1 Thessalonians 5:20, 21).

CHAPTER 12

He Restores My Soul

One of the most familiar and often-quoted portions of the Old Testament is the twenty-third psalm. "He restores my soul. He leads me in the paths of righteousness for His name's sake" (Psalm 23:3). What is this restoration that God does for me? Many of us have been involved in restoration projects of one kind or another. Some restore antiques, others old cars, still others old homes. Somehow an old object that may be hard to recognize for what it once was catches our imagination and a process of restoration begins.

When Adam and Eve came from the Creator's hand, they bore, in their physical, mental, and spiritual natures, a likeness to their Maker. "God created man in His own image" (Genesis 1:27). It was God's purpose that the longer man lived the more fully he should reveal this image—the more fully he would reflect the glory of the Creator. Originally man had the high privilege of face-to-face and heart-to-heart communion with His Maker. If he had remained loyal to God, all this would have been his forever. But by disobedience this awesome relationship was broken.

"Through sin the divine likeness was marred, and well-nigh obliterated. Man's physical powers were weakened, his mental capacity was lessened, his spiritual vision dimmed. He had become subject to death. Yet the race was not left without hope" *(Education,* p. 15). Now comes the great plan of salvation that demonstrates to the universe God's great love for mankind. It was not an afterthought. Jesus is "the Lamb slain from the foundation of the world" (Revelation 13:8). But really, what is the purpose for this great plan? Why was God willing to go through with the plan? The what and why questions are answered in this important statement.

"By infinite love and mercy the plan of salvation had been devised, and a life of probation was granted.

"**To restore in man the image of his Maker,**

"To bring him back to the perfection in which he was created,

"To promote the development of body, mind, and soul, that the divine purpose in his creation might be realized—this was to be the work of redemption.

"**This is** the object of education, **the great object of life**" *(ibid.,* pp. 15, 16).

Is this good news or what? The whole plan of salvation, the sacrificial system, the sanctuary services, the birth, life, and death of Christ—all were initiated by God to bring us back, to restore us to the perfection in which man was created!

Tiny Parable—Big Lesson

Tucked away in two of the Gospels is a tiny one-verse parable that explains the process of conversion, being born again, restoration, and regeneration. It is the parable of the leaven. This is a most unique parable in that it is only one verse long; and unlike the parable of the wheat and the tares, for example, no explanation is given by Jesus. Apparently, He felt that it was self-evident to His hearers.

The parable says, "The kingdom of heaven is like leaven, which a woman took and hid in three measures of meal till it was all leavened" (Matthew 13:33).

The Gospel of Luke also records this parable. Although almost identical to Matthew, it begins with a question: "To what shall I liken the kingdom of God? It is like leaven, which a woman took and hid in three measures of meal till it was all leavened" (Luke 13:20, 21).

Perhaps the most unusual thing about this parable is that in most Bible passages leaven is something to be avoided. In Old Testament times leaven was symbolic of evil. Prior to the Passover service every trace of leaven had to be removed from the homes of the people as being symbolic of sin (see Leviticus 23:6). Jesus told His followers to beware of the leaven of the Pharisees and of the Sadducees (Matthew 16:6). From the context of that verse it is evident that He was speaking of their hypocrisy. They were white on the outside but dirty on the inside. "Good" leaven works on the inside and produces positive results that can be seen as a result.

In both Matthew and Luke the leaven parable is preceded by the parable of the mustard seed. "As the parable of the Mustard Seed represents the extensive growth of the kingdom in numbers, so the parable of the Leaven represents the intensive, qualitative growth of the individual members of the kingdom" *(Seventh-day Adventist Bible Commentary,* vol. 5, p. 409). As leaven permeates every part of the dough in which it is placed, so the teachings of Christ through the study of His Word would penetrate the lives of those who received them and were willing to be transformed thereby.

In this parable the leaven cannot symbolize sin because eventually "the whole [lump of dough] was leavened," and Christ would certainly not mean that His kingdom was to become completely permeated with evil. The "bread" would be ruined.

The book *Christ's Object Lessons* devotes an entire chapter explaining the significance of this simple one-verse parable. The insights are awesome and very relevant to this chapter and the entire focus of the book—preparation for the Second Coming and living in heaven. Let's look at a few of these very significant points.

"In the Saviour's parable, leaven is used to represent the kingdom of heaven. It illustrates the quickening, assimilating power of the grace of God.

"None are so vile, none have fallen so low, as to be beyond the working of this power. In all who will submit themselves to the Holy Spirit a new principle of life is to be implanted; the lost image of God is to be restored in humanity.

"But man cannot transform himself by the exercise of his will. He possesses no power by which this change can be effected. The leaven— something wholly from without—must be put into the meal before the desired change can be wrought in it. **So the grace of God must be received by the sinner before he can be fitted for the kingdom of glory.** . . . The renewing energy must come from God. The change can be made only by the Holy Spirit. **All who would be saved, high or low, rich or poor, must submit to the working of this power.**

"As the leaven, when mingled with the meal, works from within outward, so it is by the renewing of the heart that the grace of God works to transform the life. <u>No mere external change is sufficient to bring us into harmony with God</u>. There are many who try to reform by correcting this or that bad habit, and they hope in this way to become Christians, <u>but they are beginning in the wrong place. Our first work is with the heart</u>. . . .

"The mere knowledge of truth is not enough. We may possess this, but the tenor of our thoughts may not be changed. <u>The heart must be converted and sanctified</u>."

So how does obedience fit into all of this? It is vital, but it must come from the heart and not be just an outward compliance. "The man who attempts to keep the commandments of God from a sense of obligation merely—because he is required to do so—will never enter into the joy of obedience. <u>He does not obey</u>. <u>When the requirements of God are accounted a burden because they cut across human inclination, we may know that the life is not a Christian life</u>. True obedience is the outworking of a principle within. It springs from the love of righteousness, the love of the law of God. <u>The essence of all righteousness is loyalty to our Redeemer</u>. **This will lead us to do right because it is right—because right doing is pleasing to God**" *(Christ's Object Lessons,* pp. 96-98).

This heartfelt obedience coming from a transformed life relates to what Jesus told Nicodemus: "Except a man be born from above, he can not see the kingdom of God." In the encounter with Nicodemus Jesus used the wind as His illustration. One cannot "see" the wind but he can see its effects. In the same way we really can't "see" the yeast or baking powder once it is placed in the flour, but the results are very visible. In fact we expect results.

Let me illustrate. My mother-in-law is a pro at making biscuits. She has prepared them so many times it seems that it just comes natural. Right after my wife and I were married, some 30 years ago now, she decided to make biscuits. She had seen her mother make them so many times she just did what she had always seen her mother do. However, when she took the biscuits out of the oven they were flat—almost like communion bread. She later discovered that her mom always used self-rising flour; while the flour she had used was just regular flour. It didn't have any leavening in it! Now my wife also makes famous biscuits!

The right kind of leavening is very vital. As many families, we now have a bread-making machine. It sits on the kitchen counter and can take the ingredients for bread and essentially perform the entire bread-making process from that point on to completed loaves—including the baking! Because of our busy schedules we use this machine on a regular basis—we still prefer my wife's handmade bread, but . . .

Recently a loaf of bread from the machine didn't come out right. The loaf was very small and when we cut it open it was still "gooy" inside. We checked the date on the yeast packet and discovered that it was way beyond its useful life. Apparently, that was the problem.

A very interesting factor about yeast or leavening is that, as the Bible says, it leavens the whole lump. When you make a pan of biscuits or some loaves of bread, you don't see just one here and one there that rise. They either all rise or they all don't! That's why if we have the Spirit of God in our lives we have all of the "fruits" present—love, joy, peace, etc.

"The leaven hidden in the flour works invisibly to bring the whole mass [of dough] under its leavening process; so the leaven of truth works secretly, silently, steadily, to transform the soul. The natural inclinations are softened and subdued. New thoughts, new feelings, new motives, are implanted. A new standard of character is set up—the life of Christ. The mind is changed; the faculties are roused to action in new lines. Man is not endowed with new faculties, but the faculties he has are sanctified. The conscience is awakened. We are endowed with traits of character that enable us to do service for God" *(ibid.,* pp. 98, 99).

Paul, when writing to the Ephesians, explained this process. Since the power of the Creator is contained in His Word, I will simply quote the words of Scripture and let the Holy Spirit do the work of transfer to our lives.

"And you He made alive, who were dead in trespasses and sins, in which you once walked according to the course of this world, according to the prince of the power of the air, the spirit who works in the sons of disobedience, among whom also we all once conducted ourselves in the lusts of our flesh, fulfilling the desires of the flesh and of the mind, and were by nature children of wrath, just as others.

"But God, who is rich in mercy, because of His great love with which He loved us, even when we were dead in trespasses, made us alive together with Christ (by grace you have been saved), and raised us up together, and made us sit together in the heavenly places in Christ Jesus, that in the ages to come He might show the exceeding riches of His grace in His kindness toward us in Christ Jesus.

"For by grace you have been saved through faith, and that not of yourselves, it is the gift of God, not of works, lest anyone should boast.

[Now here comes the leaven part.] "For we are His workmanship, created in Christ Jesus for good works, which God prepared before-hand that we should walk in them" (Ephesians 2:1-10).

As Christ's workmanship, created for good works, we experience restoration, conversion—the leavening process—the good kind! It seems that there is very little interest in godly living, yet that is what Christ wants to do through us. *Christ's Object Lessons* asks some very pointed questions and then gives a very startling and frank answer.

"Often the question arises,

"Why, then, are there so many, claiming to believe God's word, in whom there is not seen a reformation in words, in spirit, and in character?

"Why are there so many who cannot bear opposition to their purposes and plans, who manifest an unholy temper, and whose works are harsh, overbearing, and passionate?

"There is seen in their lives the same love of self, the same selfish indulgence, the same temper and hasty speech, that is seen in the life of the worldling. There is the same sensitive pride, the same yielding to natural inclination, the same perversity of character, as if the truth were wholly unknown to them. [Why?] **The reason is that they are not converted.** They have not hidden the leaven of truth in the heart. It has not had opportunity to do its work. Their natural and cultivated tendencies to evil have not been submitted to its transforming power. Their lives reveal the absence of the grace of Christ, an unbelief in His power to transform the character" *(ibid.,* pp. 99, 100).

Last-day Christians often have a form of godliness, but deny that Christ has the power to transform them. Without the leaven of God's Spirit we will end up as crackers instead of loaves. Oh, how we need the heavenly yeast in our hearts.

Adding Leaven to the Life

The Bible says, "Faith cometh by hearing, and hearing by the word of God" (Romans 10:17). "<u>The Scriptures are the great agency for the</u> <u>transformation of character</u>. Christ prayed, 'Sanctify them through Thy truth; Thy word is truth.' John 17:17. <u>If studied and obeyed, the word</u> <u>of God works in the heart, subduing every unholy attribute</u>. The Holy Spirit comes to convict of sin, and the faith that springs up in the heart works by love to Christ, conforming us in body, soul, and spirit to His own image. Then God can use us to do His will. <u>The power given us</u> <u>works from within outwardly, leading us to communicate to others the</u> <u>truth that has been communicated to us</u>" *(ibid.)*.

But how does it actually work? When we study conversion closely we recognize that it is a gift. It is a miracle. It is just what the doctor [the Great Physician] ordered. The study of the Bible plays a major role in the conversion process. It is because the power of the Creator is in His word. When we study the Word of God we have an encounter with the Almighty. While we are in the process of Bible study the Holy Spirit that inspired the Bible writers in the first place will inspire us and write God's Word in our hearts and minds as well.

"<u>The truths of the word of God meet man's great practical neces-</u> <u>sity—the conversion of the soul through faith</u>" *(ibid.)*. The leaven of truth is a great regulator. It is the active agent used by the Holy Spirit to bring about regeneration—considered by many, because of its miracu- lous nature, to be a mystery. But just as we can observe the properties of yeast when introduced into the dough, we can observe the life-chang- ing power in God's Word at work. "Received into the heart, the leaven of truth will regulate the desires, purify the thoughts, and sweeten the disposition. It quickens the faculties of the mind and the energies of the soul. It enlarges the capacity for feeling, for loving. . . .

"The word of God is to have a sanctifying effect on our association with every member of the human family. . . .

"The leaven of truth works a change in the whole man, making the coarse refined, the rough gentle, the selfish generous. By it the impure are cleansed, washed in the blood of the Lamb. <u>Through its life-giving</u> <u>power it brings all there is of mind and soul and strength into harmony</u> <u>with the divine life</u>. Man with his human nature becomes a partaker of divinity. Christ is honored in excellence and perfection of character" *(ibid., pp. 101, 102)*.

So this tiny parable illustrates clearly what it takes to get ready, be prepared, be fitted for the future life with the heavenly family. It takes transformation. It takes a change in desire. It is our great practical necessity. But it is something that we cannot accomplish ourselves. It takes the leaven of truth to permeate the whole body to effect this change. It takes the power of God as expressed in His Word and applied to our hearts by His Spirit to restore us to the image of God.

The First Promise of Redemption

The great controversy—the struggle between good and evil—was explained to Adam and Eve, when God, in their presence, told Satan that he would at last be destroyed. He explained that there would be a dynamic tension between right and wrong—between the law of God and the kingdom of Satan. This tension would also exist between the followers of God and the followers of Satan. Jesus told Satan, "I will put enmity between thee and the woman, and between thy seed and her seed; it shall bruise thy head, and thou shalt bruise his heel" (Genesis 3:15). "The divine sentence pronounced against Satan after the fall of man was also a prophecy, embracing all the ages to the close of time and foreshadowing the great conflict to engage all the races of men who should live upon the earth.

"God declares: 'I will put enmity.' This enmity is not naturally entertained. When man transgressed the divine law, his nature became evil, and he was in harmony, and not at variance, with Satan. There exists naturally no enmity between sinful man and the originator of sin. Both became evil through apostasy. The apostate is never at rest, except as he obtains sympathy and support by inducing others to follow his example. For this reason fallen angels and wicked men unite in desperate companionship. Had not God specially interposed, Satan and man would have entered into an alliance against Heaven; and instead of cherishing enmity against Satan, the whole human family would have been united in opposition to God" (The Great Controversy, p. 505).

What is this "enmity" that Jesus promised to place between Satan and His people? It is a hatred, a distaste for sin. But because of our fallen nature it doesn't occur naturally. We must request it from God. To the ordinary person sin is enjoyable. The big problem with sin is that its pleasure doesn't last and it leads to destruction. Sin is a terrible addiction and we can't help ourselves. We need the change of heart that God promised to give us in this first great promise of the Bible. Ellen White gives the definition of enmity this way: "In the statement, 'I will put enmity between thee and the woman, and between thy seed and her seed,' God has pledged Himself to introduce into the hearts of human beings a new principle,—a hatred of sin, of deception, of pretense, of everything that bears the marks of Satan's guile" (Testimonies for the Church Containing Letters to Physicians and Ministers, p. 6).

Without Christ's help we are stuck in sin—stuck on death row—all our good intentions notwithstanding. We can quickly and easily identify with the struggles of Paul as outlined in Romans. The things that we want to do we seem powerless to accomplish, and the things that we know we shouldn't do we find ourselves doing.

The whole world is in a big mess because the world is at enmity with the law of God. Sinners are at enmity with their Maker; and as a result they are at enmity with one another. The world is clearly coming to an end, and men are desperate to find a solution to the inherent problem of the sinful nature. There is a divine solution. "It is the grace that Christ implants in the soul which creates in man enmity against Satan. Without this converting grace and renewing power, man would continue the captive of Satan, a servant ever ready to do his bidding. But the new principle in the soul creates conflict where hitherto had been peace. **The power which Christ imparts enables man to resist the tyrant and usurper. Whoever is seen to abhor sin instead of loving it, whoever resists and conquers those passions that have held sway within, displays the operation of a principle wholly from above**" (The Great Controversy, p. 506).

This is an awesome statement and an even more awesome condition to be in. King David expressed his conversion experience so frequently in the Psalms in words such as "Oh how I love your law, it is my meditation all day" and "I long for Your salvation, O Lord, and Your law is my delight." "All who are not decided followers of Christ are servants of Satan. In the unregenerate heart there is a love of sin and a disposition to cherish and excuse it. In the renewed heart there is a hatred of sin and a determined resistance against it" (ibid., p. 508).

The Way Out

"God's forgiveness is not merely a judicial act by which He sets us free from condemnation. <u>It is not only forgiveness *for* sin **but reclaiming *from* sin.**</u> It is the outflow of redeeming love that transforms the heart. David had the true conception of forgiveness when he prayed, 'Create in me a clean heart, O God; and renew a right spirit within me.' Ps. 51:10" *(The Faith I Live By,* p. 129).

We must not be satisfied just to be forgiven: we must also ask for and receive transformation. That is what fits us for heaven. But just as it is impossible to pay for our own sins and still have eternal life, it is also impossible on our own to change our natures. Here also, we need Christ.

"It is impossible for us, of ourselves, to escape from the pit of sin in which we are sunken. Our hearts are evil and we cannot change them. 'Who can bring a clean thing out of an unclean? Not one.' 'The carnal mind is enmity against God: for it is not subject to the law of God, neither indeed can be.' Job 14:4; Romans 8:7. <u>Education, culture, the exercise of the will, human effort, all have their proper sphere, but here they are powerless</u>. They may produce an outward correctness of behavior, but they cannot change the heart; they cannot purify the springs of life. <u>There must be a power working from within</u> [the Spirit of God illustrated by the leaven], <u>a new life from above, before men can be changed from sin to holiness</u>. **That power is Christ.** His grace alone can quicken the lifeless faculties of the soul, and attract it to God, to holiness" *(Steps to Christ,* p. 18).

As I have stated earlier, God wants us to be ready when He comes again. If we are not ready we will be lost! The problem is we can't get ready on our own. We need what only Jesus can provide: the wedding garment, the robe of righteousness, the leaven to change our hearts, and the enmity—the hatred for sin—that God has promised. When we accept these gifts from God we are ready for heaven!

It Takes a Miracle

All of us are naturally selfish, materialistic, and greedy, but "with the gentle touch of grace the Saviour banishes from the soul unrest and unholy ambition, changing enmity to love and unbelief to confidence. When He speaks to the soul, saying, 'Follow Me,' the spell of the world's enchantment is broken. At the sound of His voice the spirit of greed and ambition flees from the heart and men arise, emancipated, to follow Him" *(Prophets and Kings,* p. 60).

There are many people today, as in Christ's day, that demand to see a miracle in order to believe. And indeed the devil is supplying such miracles as weeping statues, bleeding icons, etc. The Jews demanded of Christ, "Show us a sign, work us a miracle." But He would not. Neither did He perform a miracle when Satan asked Him to during the temptations in the wilderness. "He does not impart to us power to vindicate ourselves or to satisfy the demands of unbelief and pride. But the gospel is not without a sign of its divine origin. Is it not a miracle that we can break from the bondage of Satan? Enmity against Satan is not natural to the human heart; it is implanted by the grace of God. When one who has been controlled by a stubborn, wayward will is set free, and yields himself wholeheartedly to the drawing of God's heavenly agencies, **a miracle is wrought;** so also when a man who has been under delusion comes to understand moral truth. Every time a soul is converted, and learns to love God and keep His commandments, the promise is fulfilled, 'A new heart also will I give you, and a new spirit will I put within you.' Ezek. 36:26. The change in human hearts, the transformation of human characters, is a miracle that reveals an ever-living Saviour, working to rescue souls. **A consistent life in Christ is a great miracle"** *(The Desire of Ages,* p. 407).

The miraculous change in the life of a Christian is also the greatest sermon that can be preached in the sharing of the gospel as well. It is more powerful than all the sermons that could be preached. It is a miracle when a heart is changed! It is a miracle when we have love for Jesus and His law when the natural inclination of the carnal mind is enmity against God and His law. It is a miracle when we actually enjoy being obedient to God and we find pleasure in doing those things that please Him.

God has declared, "I will put enmity." It is a supernatural act. It is a gift from God that must be requested by the sinner. We can desire to be changed, but God must provide the power.

Apparently, we all have enmity—either for God or for Satan. There is no such thing as neutral enmity. Jesus said, "No one can serve two masters; for either he will hate the one and love the other, or else he will be loyal to the one and despise the other. You cannot serve God and mammon" (Matthew 6:24). There is another interesting and very significant feature about this enmity business. One cannot serve God halfway. It is either all or not at all. Since it is natural to have enmity against God and His law, unless we completely change we are still on Satan's side. This causes tremendous frustration for those who claim to be Christians but still hold on to the world and love the things of the world. Again Jesus said, "You shall love the Lord your God with <u>all</u> your heart, with <u>all</u> your soul, and with <u>all</u> your mind" (Matthew 22:37). This was not a new concept to God's people, and it certainly is not to us. Jesus was here quoting from Deuteronomy 6:5.

No More Friendship With the World

John warns us, "Do not love the world or the things in the world. <u>If anyone loves the world, the love of the Father is not in him</u>. For all that is in the world—the lust of the flesh, the lust of the eyes, and the pride of life—is not of the Father but is of the world" (1 John 2:15, 16). James makes a similar point. "<u>Do you not know that friendship with the world is enmity with God</u>? Whoever therefore wants to be a friend of the world makes himself an enemy of God" (James 4:4).

How do we then relate to the world? "We often hear the remark, 'You are too exclusive.' As a people we would make any sacrifice to save souls, or lead them to the truth. But to unite with them, to love the things that they love, and have friendship with the world, we dare not, for we should then be at enmity with God" *(Testimonies for the Church,* vol. 1, p. 73). We are in the world but not of the world. We are not to be conformed to this world but to stay "unspotted" from the world.

Since serving two masters is not possible, the attempt to do so causes real stress. Happiness can be found only when we are fully submitted to God and we are being molded by the Holy Spirit into His image.

Enmity Heats Up at the End

Because one either loves and serves God or Satan the intensity of the battle really heats up as the great controversy draws to its conclusion. Satan works with great diligence, because he knows that time is short. But correspondingly God pours out His Spirit in unprecedented proportions. The battle lines are drawn and the "time of trouble" begins. "The dragon was wroth with the woman, and went to make war with the remnant of her seed, which keep the commandments of God, and have the testimony of Jesus Christ" (Revelation 12:17). When adversity comes to the one who has been changed by the miracle of God's grace, he clings to Jesus and longs for heaven. The unconverted person, on the other hand, curses and questions God, and turns away from Him.

"Great scenes are soon to open before us. The Lord is coming with power and great glory. And Satan knows that his usurped authority will soon be forever at an end. His last opportunity to gain control of the world is now before him, and he will make most decided efforts to accomplish the destruction of the inhabitants of the earth. . . . The enmity of Satan against good will be manifested more and more as he brings his forces into activity in his last work of rebellion; and every soul that is not fully surrendered to God, and kept by divine power, will form an alliance with Satan against heaven, and join in battle against the Ruler of the universe" *(Testimonies to Ministers,* pp. 464, 465).

In fact, "The whole world is to be stirred with enmity against Seventh-day Adventists, because they will not yield homage to the papacy, by honoring Sunday, the institution of this antichristian power. It is the purpose of Satan to cause them to be blotted from the earth, in order that his supremacy of the world may not be disputed" *(Maranatha,* p. 217).

But we do not need to be afraid. "Those who are true to God need not fear the power of men nor the enmity of Satan. <u>In Christ their eternal life is secure.</u> Their only fear should be lest they surrender the truth, and thus betray the trust with which God has honored them" *(The Desire of Ages,* p. 356).

The Stewardship Connection

When the leaven is in our hearts, with the Holy Spirit as the active agent, we are changed from selfishness to love. Our stewardship relationships and attitudes change as well. "When divine love transforms the heart, working out of it everything that is selfish and covetous, <u>we shall bring **all** our tithes and offerings into the storehouse of the Lord</u>, and He will pour us out a 'blessing that there shall not be room enough to receive.' And by and by, when we have kept the truth even to the end, the gates of the heavenly city will be opened to us, and we shall hear the voice of our Saviour saying, 'Come, ye blessed of my Father, inherit the kingdom prepared for you from the foundation of the world'" *(Signs of the Times,* December 10, 1885).

Since we know that under the influence of the Spirit of God the selfish become generous, it is quite a serious fact to consider the large number of professed Christians who have become so preoccupied with life and selfish with their possessions that they give hardly any support to the cause of God. In our church alone this number is nearly two thirds of the book membership!

But in her comments on the parable of the talents in Matthew 25, Ellen White gives a warning as to the results of this type of lifestyle. "Let none suppose that they can live a life of selfishness, and then, having served their own interests, enter into the joy of their Lord. In the joy of unselfish love they could not participate. They would not be fitted for the heavenly courts. They could not appreciate the pure atmosphere of love that pervades heaven" *(Christ's Object Lessons,* p. 364).

Finishing the Work

The words "finishing the work" have almost become Adventist jargon. But from God's perspective, He is very excited with this prospect and pledges to provide great power and guidance in its accomplishment. The work of regeneration will play a big part in this final effort.

"Very precious to God is His work in the earth. Christ and heavenly angels are watching it every moment. As we draw near to the coming of Christ, more and still more of missionary work will engage our efforts. The message of the renewing power of God's grace will belt the world. Those that will be sealed will be from every nation and kindred and tongue and people. From every country will be gathered men and women who will stand before the throne of God and before the Lamb in worship, crying, 'Salvation to our God which sitteth upon the throne and unto the Lamb.' But before this work can be accomplished, we must experience right here in our own country the work of the Holy Spirit upon our hearts" *(Review and Herald,* February 6, 1908).

Knowing where we are in this world's history gives us special impetus to seek pardon for our transgressions and power for transformation. A very amazing feature about the last message to the world is that the message involves the regeneration made possible by God's Spirit and it is given by those who have experienced this regeneration!

"During the loud cry, the church, aided by the providential interpositions of her exalted Lord, will diffuse the knowledge of salvation so abundantly that light will be communicated to every city and town. The earth will be filled with the knowledge of salvation. <u>So abundantly will the renewing Spirit of God have crowned with success the intensely active agencies, that the light of present truth will be seen flashing everywhere</u>" *(Maranatha,* p. 27).

At this time in the history of the world we should have but one object in view—to gain eternal life. Every other desire should be subordinate to this. As we discussed in the last chapter, our redemption includes justification and sanctification in the here and now. Our glorification is the work of God alone and takes place at the Second Coming.

Forgiven and Cleansed

This book is written to underscore the need of spiritual preparation for eternity. "This is the will of God, even your sanctification" (1 Thessalonians 4:3). Justification (forgiveness) and sanctification (cleansing and regeneration) are linked in both the Bible and the Spirit of Prophecy. "If we confess our sins, He is faithful and just to forgive us our sins **and** to cleanse us from all unrighteousness" (1 John 1:9). Conversion has been almost wholly lost sight of in some circles. But "to be pardoned in the way that Christ pardons, is <u>not only to be forgiven</u> **but** <u>to be renewed in the spirit of our mind</u>. The Lord says, 'A new heart will I give unto thee.' The image of Christ is to be stamped upon the very mind, heart, and soul. The apostle says, 'But we have the mind of Christ' (1 Cor. 2:16). <u>Without the transforming process which can come alone through divine power, the original propensities to sin are left in the heart in all their strength, to forge new chains, to impose a slavery that can never be broken by human power</u>. But men can never enter heaven with their old tastes, inclinations, idols, ideas, and theories" *(Selected Messages,* vol. 3, p. 190). It is all a wonderful and complete gift, but we must accept it.

Jesus did not leave anything out that was necessary for our salvation. "How wonderful is the plan of redemption in its simplicity and fullness. <u>It not only provides for the full pardon of the sinner</u> **but also** <u>for the restoration of the transgressor</u>, in making a way whereby he may be accepted as a son of God" *(Review and Herald,* March 3, 1891).

When the heavenly angel told Joseph that his fiancée, Mary, was pregnant by the Holy Spirit, the angel also told him the sex of the child,

His name, and the purpose of His life. "And she will bring forth a <u>Son</u>, and <u>you shall call His name Jesus</u>, for <u>He will save His people **from their sins**</u>" (Matthew 1:21). So "God's forgiveness is not merely a judicial act by which He sets us free from condemnation. <u>It is not only forgiveness *for* sin, but reclaiming *from* sin</u>. It is the outflow of redeeming love that transforms the heart" *(Thoughts From the Mount of Blessing,* p. 114).

The Work of the Holy Spirit

In God's plan He has assigned the work of changing hearts—regeneration—to the Holy Spirit. It is the power of the indwelling Spirit that withdraws our affections from worldly interests, instructs us in the things of God, guides us into all truth, develops in us the attributes of God, fills the soul with the desire for holiness—in short brings about the new birth—conversion. There are things that we can do to bring this about, as we shall see elsewhere. There are literally dozens of texts that give us insights into the work of God's Spirit. Just a few are:

"It is the Spirit who gives life" (John 6:63).

"But if the Spirit of Him who raised Jesus from the dead dwells in you, He who raised Christ from the dead will also give life to your mortal bodies through His Spirit who dwells in you" (Romans 8:11).

"Restore to me the joy of Your salvation and <u>uphold me with your generous Spirit</u>" (Psalm 51:12).

"When the enemy comes in like a flood, the Spirit of the Lord will lift up a standard against him" (Isaiah 59:19). This one is an awesome promise.

"I will give you a new heart and put a new spirit within you; I will take the heart of stone out of your flesh and give you a heart of flesh. <u>I will put My Spirit within you and cause you to walk in My statutes, and you will keep My judgments and do them</u>" (Ezekiel 36:26, 27).

Paul prayed that the Ephesians would "be strengthened with might through His Spirit in the inner man" (Ephesians 3:16).

"Not by works of righteousness which we have done, but according to His mercy He saved us, <u>through the washing of regeneration and renewing of the Holy Spirit</u>" (Titus 3:5).

God's final stamp of approval is placed on His redeemed as the seal of God. This is also the work of the Spirit. "And do not grieve the Holy Spirit of God, by whom you were sealed for the day of redemption" (Ephesians 4:30).

When we begin to see the role of the Holy Spirit in the process of sanctification the logical question is: "How can we receive the Spirit into our lives?" The Bible gives the answer.

"And I say to you, ask, and it will be given to you; seek, and you will find; knock, and it will be opened to you. For everyone who asks receives, and he who seeks finds, and to him who knocks it will be opened. If a son asks for bread from any father among you, will he give him a stone? Or if he asks for a fish, will he give him a serpent instead of a fish? Or if he asks for an egg, will he offer him a scorpion? If you then, being evil, know how to give good gifts to your children, how much more will your heavenly Father give the Holy Spirit **to those who ask Him!**" (Luke 11:9-13).

Ellen White makes several interesting statements regarding the work of the Holy Spirit in the work of sanctification.

"The Lord Jesus acts through the Holy Spirit; for it is His representative. Through it He infuses spiritual life into the soul, quickening its energies for good, cleansing it from moral defilement, and giving it a fitness for His kingdom. Jesus has large blessings to bestow, rich gifts to distribute among men. He is the wonderful Counselor, infinite in wisdom and strength; and if we will acknowledge the power of His Spirit, and submit to be molded by it, we shall stand complete in Him" *(Review and Herald,* February 10, 1903).

"Genuine faith is followed by love, and love by obedience. All the powers and passions of the converted man are brought under the control of Christ. His Spirit is a renewing power, transforming to the divine image all who will receive it. It makes me sad to say that this experience is understood by but few who profess the truth" *(Testimonies for the Church,* vol. 5, p. 219).

While on her tour of duty in Australia, just a year after writing *Steps to Christ,* Ellen White wrote a very concise statement outlining the important work of the Holy Spirit in fitting us for heaven. "Through faith the Holy Spirit finds access to the heart, and creates holiness therein. Man cannot become an agent to work the works of

Christ unless he is in communion with God through the Holy Spirit. We are fitted for heaven only through a transformation of character; we must have Christ's righteousness as our credentials, if we would find access to the Father. We must be partakers of the divine nature, having escaped the corruption that is in the world through lust. We must daily be transformed by the influence of the Holy Spirit; for it is the work of the Holy Spirit to elevate the taste, to sanctify the heart, to ennoble the whole man, by presenting to the soul the matchless charms of Jesus" *(Bible Echo and Signs of the Times,* February 15, 1893).

I have previously written about the great time prophecies and world conditions that indicate strongly that we are right at the end of time. "Life is too short, the hours of probation too precious, for us to make a mistake in our religious life. Earnest men and women, filled with courage and devotion, are needed in the Master's service. The call comes to us, 'Be not conformed to this world; but be ye transformed by the renewing of your mind.' As we obey this command, the power of the Holy Spirit will come upon mind and body, bringing us into conformity to the will of Christ, and renewing us in His likeness. **The hereditary and cultivated tendencies to wrong will die,** and Christ will be formed within, the hope of glory. It will be seen that we are indeed followers of Christ" *(Signs of the Times,* June 21, 1905).

It was because of this life-changing power that impetuous Peter was able to inspire the believers down through time with his wonderful Epistles. These letters bear testimony that he had been transformed by grace, and that his hope of eternal life was sure and steadfast. It is the agency of the Holy Spirit to do the work of the leaven in our lives and to fill us with love for God and His laws, and place enmity in our hearts against Satan and the ways of the world. This is God's great plan for man. "Thus it is that God desires to fulfill for us His purpose of grace. By the power of His love, through obedience, fallen man, a worm in the dust, is to be transformed, fitted to be a member of the heavenly family, a companion, through eternal ages, of God and Christ and the holy angels. **Heaven will triumph; for the vacancies made by the fall of Satan and his host will be filled by the redeemed of the Lord"** (Australasian Union Conference Record, June 1, 1900).

CHAPTER 13

More Than a Relationship

The love between a Christian and his God is more than a friendship or an acquaintance. Some say that "I love God and He loves me and that's all there is to it." But is that really all there is to it? Jesus says, "If you love Me, keep My commandments," and "He who does not love Me does not keep My words" (John 14:15, 24). In his first Epistle John is even more explicit: "Now by this we know that we know Him, if we keep His commandments. He who says, 'I know Him,' and does not keep His commandments, is a liar, and the truth is not in him. But whoever keeps His word, truly the love of God is perfected in him. By this we know that we are in Him. He who says he abides in Him ought himself also to walk just as He walked" (1 John 2:3-6).

In His sermon on the mount Jesus talked about the true way into the kingdom. "Not everyone who says to Me, 'Lord, Lord,' shall enter the kingdom of heaven, but he who does the will of My Father in heaven. Many will say to Me in that day, 'Lord, Lord, have we not prophesied in Your name, cast out demons in Your name, and done many wonders in Your name?' And then I will declare to them, 'I never knew you; depart from Me, you who practice lawlessness!'" (Matthew 7:21-23). Of course lawlessness is disobedience. The wise man is the one who hears the sayings of God and does them.

Just what part does obedience play in the life of a Christian? Does our obedience gain us any merit in terms of salvation? We must by now understand that our efforts could never legally qualify us for salvation. Victory is certainly given to those who accept the power of God for forgiveness and cleansing. However, obedience is the outward evidence of our saving relationship with God. Whenever the Israelites were in a right relationship with God, they obeyed Him and they were blessed. When they disobeyed, they broke their covenant relation with Him and they were cursed. In Moses' last counsel to the children of Israel, recorded in the book of Deuteronomy, he reviewed God's plan for prosperity. "Now it shall come to pass, if you diligently obey the voice of the Lord your God, to observe carefully all His command-ments which I command you today, that the Lord your God will set you high above all nations of the earth. And all these blessings shall come upon you and overtake you, because you obey the voice of the Lord your God" (Deuteronomy 28:1, 2). Then follows a long list of promised blessings.

The Two Errors

The devil tries to divert the Christian into one ditch or the other in-stead of letting him walk down the correct path on the way of truth. "There are two errors against which the children of God—particularly those who have just come to trust in His grace—especially need to guard. The first, . . . is that of looking to their own works, trusting to anything they can do, to bring themselves into harmony with God. He who is trying to become holy by his own works in keeping the law, is attempting an impossibility. All that man can do without Christ is pol-luted with selfishness and sin. It is the grace of Christ alone, through faith, that can make us holy.

"The opposite and no less dangerous error is that belief in Christ releases men from keeping the law of God; that since by faith alone we become partakers of the grace of Christ, our works have nothing to do with our redemption.

"But notice here that obedience is not a mere outward compliance, but the service of love. The law of God is an expression of His very na-ture; it is an embodiment of the great principle of love, and hence is the foundation of His government in heaven and earth. If our hearts are re-newed in the likeness of God, if the divine love is implanted in the soul, will not the law of God be carried out in the life? When the prin-ciple of love is implanted in the heart, when man is renewed after the image of Him that created him, the new-covenant promise is fulfilled. 'I will put My laws into their hearts, and in their minds will I write them.' Hebrews 10:16. And if the law is written in the heart, will it not shape the life? **Obedience—the service and allegiance of love—is the true sign of discipleship.** Thus the Scripture says, 'This is the love of God, that we keep His commandments.' 'He that saith, I know Him, and keepeth not His commandments, is a liar, and the truth is not in him.' 1 John 5:3; 2:4. Instead of releasing man from obedience, **it is faith,** and faith only, that makes us partakers of the grace of Christ, **which enables us to render obedience.**

"We do not earn salvation by our obedience; for salvation is a free gift of God, to be received by faith. **But obedience is the fruit of faith.** 'Ye know that He was manifested to take away our sins; and in Him is no sin. Whosoever abideth in Him sinneth not: whosoever sinneth hath not seen Him, neither known Him.' 1 John 3:5, 6. **Here is the true test.** If we abide in Christ, if the love of God dwells in us, our feelings, our thoughts, our purposes, our actions, will be in harmony with the will of God as expressed in the precepts of His holy law" *(Steps to Christ,* pp. 59-61).

It could not be made much plainer than that. If we love Jesus and invite Him to dwell in us, it will be a natural response to love His law and obey Him. The following quotation develops this thought in a careful and logical progression.

"God's commands are designed to guide you to life's very best. You will not obey Him, however, if you do not believe Him and trust Him. You cannot believe Him, if you do not love Him. You cannot love Him, unless you know Him. If, however, you really come to know Him as He reveals Himself to you, you will love Him. If you love Him, You will believe and trust Him. If you believe and trust Him, you will obey Him. God has given His commands so you may prosper and live life to its fullest measure. If you love Him, you will obey Him! If you do not obey Him, you do not really love Him (see John 14:24). God is love. Because of His love, His will for you is always best. God is also all-knowing, so His directions are always right" (Henry T. Blackaby, *Experiencing God* [Nashville: Broadman & Holman, 1994], p. 14).

It's More Than Profession

"Religion is something more than a profession, something deeper than an impulsive feeling. It is doing the will of God" *(That I May*

Know Him, p. 113). Since the fall of Adam and Eve there has always been one central difference between the faithful and the unfaithful—the saved and the lost. It is the matter of obedience. Those who obey receive life—more abundantly—and in the end eternal life. Those who disobey receive death—eternal death. To obey or not to obey focuses attention on the law of God. God's law is the basis of His government. It is the demonstration of His character. It is the standard in the judgment. The law's eternal nature is the reason Christ died for man's transgression. God couldn't just change the law or look the other way.

"Obedience or disobedience decides every man's destiny. Those who obey God are counted worthy to share His throne, while those who disobey will be forever lost. But sin has weakened our powers of obedience, and in our own strength we can never obey God. Knowing this, God sent Jesus to our world to live His law. Only the mind that is trained to obedience to God can do justice to His divine claims, and God gave Christ up to humiliation and suffering, to be afflicted with all the temptations wherewith humanity is afflicted, that in His strength we might be enabled to keep His law. It was for the recovery of man that Christ came into the world, and it is to the will of man that He appeals. The knowledge of God through Jesus Christ brings every thought into obedience to His will" *(Review and Herald,* December 15, 1896).

This is quite an insightful and positive statement. Obedience or disobedience determines who is saved and who is lost. This is not because our works or obedience are meritorious in any way. They are not! But the fact remains that those who accept the great gift of Christ in justification (forgiveness) and sanctification (transformation) will be cheerfully obedient in a service and allegiance of love. "There is not a point that needs to be dwelt upon more earnestly, repeated more frequently, or established more firmly in the minds of all than the impossibility of fallen man meriting anything by his own best good works. Salvation is through faith in Jesus Christ alone" *(Faith and Works,* p. 19). David explained his relationship to obedience this way: "I delight to do Your will, O my God, and Your law is within my heart" (Psalm 40:8). He was enjoying a new covenant experience. "This is the covenant that I will make with them after those days, says the Lord: I will put My laws into their hearts, and in their minds I will write them" (Hebrews 10:16).

How does God actually do this—write His law in our hearts? He does it by dwelling in us at our invitation and by His Holy Spirit. God's law and His character are virtually synonymous in the Scriptures:

God is good (Luke 18:19)	His law is good (1 Timothy 1:5)
God is holy (Isaiah 5:16)	His law is holy (Romans 7:12)
God is perfect (Matthew 5:48)	His law is perfect (Psalm 19:7)
God is pure (1 John 3:3)	His law is pure (Psalm 19:8)
God is just (Deuteronomy 32:4)	His law is just (Romans 7:12)
God is true (John 3:33)	His law is true (Psalm 19:9)
God is spiritual (1 Corinthians 10:4)	His law is spiritual (Romans 7:14)
God is righteous (Jeremiah 23:6)	His law is righteous (Psalm 119:172)
God is faithful (1 Corinthians 1:9)	His law is faithful (Psalm 119:86)
God is love (1 John 4:8)	His law is love (Romans 13:10)
God is unchangeable (James 1:17)	His law is unchangeable (Matthew 5:18)
God is eternal (Genesis 21:33)	His law is eternal (Psalm 111:7, 8)

This comparison has tremendous implications. The ten-commandment law is God's character in written form! It is no more possible to change God's law than it would be to pull God out of heaven and change Him. When He is in our hearts by faith, His law will be lived out in our lives.

"The commandments of God are not dry theories and maxims growing on the trunk of Phariseeism. Every jot and tittle of the law of God is a pledge of perfect rest and assurance in obedience. If you will obey these commandments, you will find, in every specification, a most precious promise. **Take Jesus as your partner. Ask Him to help you keep God's law**. He will be to you a safeguard and counselor, a guide that will never mislead" *(Review and Herald,* January 26, 1897).

Another very simple statement shows the tremendous significance of God's great law. "The ten commandments, Thou shalt, and Thou shalt not, are ten promises, assured to us if we render obedience to the law governing the universe. 'If ye love Me, keep my commandments' (John 14:15). Here is the sum and substance of the law of God. The

terms of salvation for every son and daughter of Adam are here outlined" *(God's Amazing Grace,* p. 134).

God's Law the Standard

"The condition of eternal life is now just what it always has
been,—just what it was in Paradise before the fall of our first parents,—perfect obedience to the law of God, perfect righteousness. If
eternal life were granted on any condition short of this, then the happiness of the whole universe would be imperiled. The way would be
open for sin, with all its train of woe and misery, to be immortalized"
(Steps to Christ, p. 62).

Hatred of God's law comes from Satan. He is the great apostate.
"The great conflict that Satan created in the heavenly courts is soon,
very soon, to be forever decided. Soon all the inhabitants of the earth
will have taken sides, either for or against the government of heaven.
Now, as never before, Satan is exercising his deceiving power to mislead
and to destroy every unguarded soul. We are called upon to arouse the
people to prepare for the great issues before them. We must give warning to those who are standing on the brink of ruin. God's people are to
put forth every power in combating Satan's falsehoods and pulling down
his strongholds. To every human being in the wide world who will give
heed, we are to make plain the principles at stake in the great controversy—principles upon which hangs the eternal destiny of the soul. To
the people far and near we are to bring home the question: **'Are you following the great apostate in disobedience to God's law, or are you
following the Son of God, who declared, "I have kept My Father's
commandments"'"** *(Testimonies for the Church,* vol. 7, p. 141).

The Covenant Relation

Many Bible writers equate man's obedience to his covenant relationship to God. Indeed the law is the basis of the covenant. Note the
parallel language of this psalm:

"They did not keep the covenant of God;

They refused to walk in His law" (Psalm 78:10).

From earliest Bible times God has entered into covenants or agree-
ments with men. In fact, all mankind is able to enter into this type of
agreement with God. We learn from Scripture and our own personal

experience that God never goes back on His Word, but, unfortunately, man seems to have a very hard time keeping his end of the bargain. And like clockwork, when men have honored their covenant with God by being obedient to His laws they have prospered; when they didn't they had serious problems.

Time after time the Bible records how men forgot or transgressed their covenant with God. One such example was the defeat of Israel at Ai. Upon the occasion of the conquest of Jericho God had instructed the Israelites to bring the silver and gold they found in the city to the Temple to start the Temple economy. "All the silver and gold, and vessels of bronze and iron, are consecrated to the Lord; they shall come into the treasury of the Lord" (Joshua 6:19).

Only one man in all of Israel disobeyed, but the results were felt by the entire nation. In the next battle—the struggle for the little city of Ai—36 Israelites were killed. Joshua fell on his face before the Lord, and God said to him, "Israel has sinned and they have also transgressed My covenant which I commanded them. For they have even taken some of the accursed things, and have both stolen and deceived. . . . There is an accursed thing in your midst, O Israel; **you cannot stand before your enemies until you take away the accursed thing from among you**" (Joshua 7:11, 13). They could not stand before their enemies because one man broke the covenant! "Achan's sin brought disaster upon the whole nation. For one man's sin the displeasure of God will rest upon His church till the transgression is searched out and put away. **The influence most to be feared by the church is not that of open opponents, infidels, and blasphemers, but of inconsistent professors of Christ.** These are the ones that keep back the blessing of the God of Israel and bring weakness upon His people" *(Patriarchs and Prophets,* p. 497).

"If the presence of one Achan was sufficient to weaken the whole camp of Israel, can we be surprised at the little success which attends our efforts when every church and almost every family has its Achan?" *(Testimonies for the Church,* vol. 5, p. 157).

Josiah's Revival

The Bible records the story of a tremendous revival in the days of King Josiah. Again it centered around the restoration of the covenant relation with God. Apparently, the Temple had fallen into disrepair and in the eighteenth year of Josiah's reign he ordered that the temple be cleaned out and repaired. In the process the high priest found the Book of the Law. When the scribe read it to the king, he tore his clothes in fear and consternation. Immediately the king asked the priest to inquire of the Lord to see whether or not their lives could be spared. The reading of the law had revealed to him that God's people were far from the standard. They were in great apostasy. They had fallen so far from God's will that the king was fearful of God's wrath.

The priest returned with the message from God that the calamity the king feared would not come until after his death. Josiah then called for a great reformation and revival. The Bible describes it this way: "Then the king [Josiah] sent them to gather all the elders of Judah and Jerusalem to him. And the king went up to the house of the Lord with **all the men of Judah,** and with him all the inhabitants of Jerusalem— **the priests and the prophets and all the people,** both small and great; and he read in their hearing all the words of the Book of the Covenant which had been found in the house of the Lord.

"Then <u>the king</u> stood by a pillar <u>and made a covenant before the Lord</u>, **to follow the Lord and to keep His commandments and His testimonies, and His statutes**, with all his heart and all his soul, and to perform the words of this covenant that were written in this book. **And all the people took their stand for the covenant**" (2 Kings 23:1-3).

What a picture! Led by their king, all the people took their stand for the covenant. Then Josiah called for a great spiritual convocation. It apparently was a once-in-a-lifetime experience.

"There had been no Passover kept in Israel like that since the days of Samuel the prophet; and none of the kings of Israel had kept such a Passover as Josiah kept, with the priests and the Levites, all Judah and Israel who were present, and the inhabitants of Jerusalem" (2 Chronicles 35:18).

Why couldn't we have such a revival today? We surely need one! Let it begin with me. Let it continue with you! What would such a commitment to faithfulness do to our families, our churches, our conferences? And it must happen! It is predicted and it will happen! Even now, it is happening in many places!

The Appeal in Malachi

The setting of the book of Malachi is another time of great apostasy. A careful reading of the book indicates not only the great need for revival in Malachi's day but it also points forward to the time of preparation for the Second Coming—our day. Chapter 3 records God's appeal to man:

"'I am the Lord, I do not change'" (v. 6).

"'You have gone away from My ordinances and have not kept them.

"'Return to Me, and I will return to you,' says the Lord of hosts.

"'But you said, "In what way shall we return?"'" (v. 7).

And God says, "Stop robbing Me of tithes and offerings!" (vs. 8-10).

In the days of Achan only one man in the camp was unfaithful, now the whole nation was in apostasy. Today we note that less than half of God's professed remnant are faithful in the area of tithes and offerings. When I made my baptismal vow—my covenant with God — I decided to be faithful in my tithes and offerings. It is at the heart of my covenant relation with God. Let us all renew and continue to maintain that covenant today!

The Consequences of Sin

The New Testament story of Ananias and Sapphira recorded in Acts 5:1-11 underscores the fact that there are consequences to sin. This couple made a commitment to God and then decided to "keep back **part** of the money." The results of that decision are well known to us. Do we really think that we can rob God with impunity in this life and then be welcomed to heaven when Jesus returns? It would be a fatal mistake to believe it. Note Ellen White's comments on the story in Acts 5: "There are those who are **guilty of the same sin as Ananias and Sapphira, thinking that if they withhold a portion of what God claims in the <u>tithing system</u>** the brethren will never know it. Thus thought the guilty couple whose life is given as a warning. . . . <u>Although no visible marks of God's displeasure follow the repetition of the sin of Ananias and Sapphira **now,** yet the sin is just as heinous in the sight of God and will as surely be visited upon the transgressor in the day of judgment</u>, and many will feel the curse of God even in this life" *(Testimonies for the Church,* vol. 4, pp. 469, 470).

My work assignment and personal interest leads me to learn more of the biblical principles of personal money management. It seems that unfaithfulness in stewardship is always a part of apostasy and faithfulness in stewardship always accompanies times of revival and reformation.

Early in Adventist history a stewardship revival occurred in the Battle Creek, Michigan, church. In was the fall of 1888. In those days Battle Creek was the world headquarters of the Seventh-day Adventist Church. Special meetings were held at the headquarters church. Ellen White recorded regarding the meetings: "A decided advancement in spirituality, piety, charity, and activity, has been made as the result of the special meetings in the Battle Creek church. **Discourses were preached on the sin of robbing God in tithes and offerings. . . . Many confessed that they had not paid tithes for years; and we know that God cannot bless those who are robbing Him, and that the church must suffer in consequence of the sins of its individual members.** There are a large number of names on the church books; and if all would be prompt in paying an honest tithe to the Lord, which is His portion, the treasury would not lack for means. . . . **As the sin of robbing God was presented, the people received clearer views of their duty and privilege in this matter**" *(Counsels on Stewardship,* pp. 95, 96).

I believe that if we would all be faithful in this area that a great revival would take place in the church. Why? Because, where your treasure is, there will your heart be also. And with our hearts in the work our bodies would follow in service—I think you get the picture. The revival will start one commitment at a time. Will you join me in making that recommitment now?

Politically Incorrect

Society has reached such a degenerate level that right seems wrong and wrong seems right. The Bible says that in the last days "men will be . . . without natural affection" (2 Timothy 3:1, 3, KJV). In their inmost heart anyone with a general knowledge of Scripture understands that homosexuality is a sinful perversion. Yet how many say anything about it?

"The men of Sodom were exceedingly wicked and sinful against the Lord" (Genesis 13:13). God was so displeased with the fact that Sodom had "given themselves over to sexual immorality and gone after strange flesh" (Jude 1:7), that He destroyed them with eternal fire. They received their final reward—the second death! God says that the destruction of Sodom and Gomorrah was an example of what would happen "to those who afterward would live ungodly" (2 Peter 2:6). In the days that Isaiah was writing apparently there was open sin then, too, but he says that Jerusalem had stumbled, Judah had fallen. "The look on their countenance witnesses against them, <u>and they declare their sin as Sodom; **they do not hide it.**</u> Woe to their soul! For they have brought evil upon themselves" (Isaiah 3:9).

The climate in America today is to accept homosexuality as a perfectly acceptable "alternative lifestyle," rather than to condemn it as a sinful perversion. *Time* magazine April 14, 1997, featured a smiling "out of the closet" lesbian, Ellen DeGeneres, as its cover feature! The same person and her "friend" were invited to the White House by President Clinton and featured in photos with the president in the national papers. "She" is the star of an ABC prime-time TV series, according to the media. Real Christians should properly boycott ABC. Why should we support the glorification of perversion? It is common knowledge that the vast majority of those who work in the television industry are not planning to go to heaven. In fact, many of them ridicule those who do. Why support such a selfish, worldly group? Remember the principle—by beholding we become changed. We need to set our affections on heavenly things!

In the days of John the Baptist, King Herod had taken his brother's wife and was living in adultery with her. John said to Herod, "It is not lawful for you to have your brother's wife" (Mark 6:18). John literally lost his head over that statement. But Jesus said of him, "Among those born of women there is not a greater prophet than John the Baptist" (Luke 7:28). John the Baptist was a type of Elijah, of which we as God's remnant are also a type (see Malachi 4:5). Where are the men and women who will stand up and fight for truth today?

"The <u>greatest want</u> of the world is the want of men—men who will not be bought or sold, men who in their inmost souls are true and honest, men who do not fear to call sin by its right name, men whose conscience is as true to duty as the needle to the pole, men who will stand for the right though the heavens fall" *(Education,* p. 57). Where are the men (and women) prepared to stand today as did Joseph and Daniel in past times of crisis?

Adultery seems almost as common in the church as in the world today. In a joint statement signed by James and Ellen White, regarding the topic of unfaithfulness in marriage, they asked, "<u>Why! oh, why! will men and women who might be respectable and good and reach heaven at last sell themselves to the devil so cheap, wound their bosom friends, disgrace their families, bring a reproach upon the cause, and go to hell at last</u>? God have mercy! Why will not those who are taken in crime manifest repentance proportionate to the enormity of their crime and fly to Christ for mercy and heal, as far as possible, the wounds they have made?" *(The Adventist Home,* p. 346).

Why do I mention these specific things? The answer is simple. Those who claim to be children of God; those who claim to be preparing for a home in heaven will not condone and practice the lifestyle of the world. Those presently living in immoral relationships and are thinking that they will be saved at last are wrong! We cannot pretend that things are OK when they are not! Now, in the final hours of probation God is pleading with us to be overcomers by His power.

A Perfect Heart

On the occasion of the great thanksgiving celebration when the building materials for the Temple had all been provided, King David had a public prayer of dedication and thanks. In this prayer he prayed for his son who would succeed him on the throne of Israel. "And give my son Solomon a loyal heart to keep Your commandments and Your testimonies and Your statutes, to do all these things, and to build the temple for which I have made provision" (1 Chronicles 29:19).

Should we not pray for such a loyal (perfect KJV) heart to keep the commandments of the Lord? And pray for the same thing for our children? "The idea prevails that Christ has done all for us, and that we can go on transgressing the commandments and will not be held accountable for it. <u>This is the greatest deception that the enemy ever devised</u>. We must take our position that we will not violate the commandments at any cost, and be in that spiritual condition that we can educate others in spiritual things" *(Selected Messages,* vol. 3, p. 153).

The Lord told Israel through Isaiah, "If you are willing and obedient, you shall eat the good of the land; but if you refuse and rebel, you shall be devoured by the sword, for the mouth of the Lord has spoken" (Isaiah 1:19, 20).

Jesus holds up a high standard but offers help to achieve it. Several short statements make this point. "Christ came to this earth and lived a life of perfect obedience, that men and women, through His grace, might also live lives of perfect obedience. This is necessary to their salvation. Without holiness no man shall see the Lord" *(Review and Herald,* March 15, 1906).

"Great possibilities, high and holy attainments, are within our reach. Sanctification means perfect love, perfect obedience, entire conformity to God's will. It means unreserved surrender to Him. It means to be pure and unselfish, without spot or blemish" *(Signs of the Times,* May 28, 1902).

"He who has the love of God in his heart has no enmity against the law of God, but renders willing obedience to all His commandments, **and this constitutes Christianity**. He who has supreme love to God will reveal love to his fellow men, who belong to God both by creation and redemption. Love is the fulfilling of the law; and it is the duty of every child of God to render obedience to His commandments" *(Sons and Daughters of God,* p. 51). The bottom line of Christianity is willing obedience to God and His law. We say the Sabbath will be the issue at the end. It is true it is the main focus, but the real issue is the validity and perpetuity of God's law of which the Sabbath is a part.

There is great cause for rejoicing and thanksgiving when we realize what Jesus has done for us. He has forgiven us our sins and made it possible for us, with His power, to overcome evil and live lives that will prepare us to live in the company of heavenly beings. "We have reason for ceaseless gratitude to God that Christ, by His perfect obedience, has won back the heaven that Adam lost through disobedience. Adam sinned, and the children of Adam share his guilt and its consequences; but Jesus bore the guilt of Adam, and all the children of Adam that will flee to Christ, the second Adam, may escape the penalty of transgression. Jesus regained heaven for man by bearing the test that Adam failed to endure; for He obeyed the law perfectly, and all who have a right conception of the plan of redemption will see that they cannot be saved while in transgression of God's holy precepts. They must cease to transgress the law and lay hold on the promises of God that are available for us through the merits of Christ" *(Faith and Works,* p. 88).

By the Power of God

The standard is high and the reason is justified. God aims to eradicate the world of sin. He wants to fit us to live in the company of holy beings. He intends that sin will not rise up the second time. He not only want us to be obedient, He wants us to have a hatred for sin—to have enmity against evil. And so He has made His power available to assure our success—if we are willing. "Divine power is brought to man in order that his human effort may be wholly successful" *(Selected Messages,* vol. 3, p. 190). "It is not only at the beginning of the Christian life that this renunciation of self is to be made. At every advance step heavenward it is to be renewed. All our good works are dependent on a power outside of ourselves; therefore there needs to be a continual reaching out of the heart after God, a constant, earnest confession of sin and humbling of the soul before Him. Perils surround us; and we are safe only as we feel our weakness and cling with the grasp of faith to our mighty Deliverer" *(The Ministry of Healing,* p. 455).

Whenever we accomplish anything worthwhile it is because God is with us. We are totally dependent on Him for goodness—righteousness. But we must cooperate with God. "The work of transformation from unholiness to holiness is a continuous one. Day by day God labors for man's sanctification, and man is to co-operate with Him, putting forth persevering efforts in the cultivation of right habits. He is to add grace to grace; and as he thus works on the plan of addition, God works for him on the plan of multiplication. Our Saviour is always ready to hear and answer the prayer of the contrite heart, and grace and peace are multiplied to His faithful ones. Gladly He grants them the blessings they need in their struggle against the evils that beset them" *(The Acts of the Apostles,* p. 532).

On the same page another awesome "how to" statement offers hope. "Before the believer is held out the wonderful possibility of being like Christ, obedient to all the principles of the law. But of himself man is utterly unable to reach this condition. The holiness that God's word declares he must have before he can be saved is the result of the working of divine grace as he bows in submission to the discipline and restraining influences of the Spirit of truth. Man's obedience can be made perfect only by the incense of Christ's righteousness, which fills with divine fragrance every act of obedience. The part of the Christian is to persevere in overcoming every fault. Constantly he is to pray to the Saviour to heal the disorders of his sin-sick soul. He has not the wisdom or the strength to overcome; these belong to the Lord, and He bestows them on those who in humiliation and contrition seek Him for help" *(ibid.)*.

Man's Part

On his way back home, Jacob prepared for his meeting with Esau in every way possible. He sent gifts, apologies, divided his group into sections—all in preparation for the encounter. Then he left the whole matter in God's hands.

The same was true with Joshua during the conquest of Canaan. "Joshua had received the promise that God would surely overthrow these enemies of Israel, yet he put forth as earnest effort as though success depended upon the armies of Israel alone. He did all that human energy could do, and then he cried in faith for divine aid. The secret of success is the union of divine power with human effort. Those who achieve the greatest results are those who rely most implicitly upon the Almighty Arm" *(Patriarchs and Prophets, p. 509)*.

God doesn't need our money or anything else we have. He wants our hearts. And "when it is in the heart to obey God, when efforts are put forth to this end, Jesus accepts this disposition and effort as man's best service, and He makes up for the deficiency with His own divine merit. But He will not accept those who claim to have faith in Him, and yet are disloyal to His Father's commandment. We hear a great deal about faith, but we need to hear a great deal more about works. Many are deceiving their own souls by living an easygoing, accommodating, crossless religion. But Jesus says, 'If any man will come after Me, let him deny himself, and take up his cross, and follow Me'" *(Signs of the Times, June 16, 1890)*.

"Blessed is the man who walks not in the counsel of the ungodly, nor stands in the path of sinners, nor sits in the seat of the scornful; but his delight is in the law of the Lord, and in His law he meditates day and night. He shall be like a tree planted by the rivers of water, that brings forth its fruit in its season, whose leaf also shall not wither; and whatever he does shall prosper" (Psalm 1:1-3).

CHAPTER 14

He Is Able

The little book of Jude is tucked away in an almost invisible part of the Bible. For many of us its place in the Bible is mostly as a help in finding the book of Revelation. You remember your mental exercise; First and Second Peter, First, Second, and Third John, **Jude**, and REVELATION. But this little book itself is a gold mine of inspired counsel.

The book of Jude was written by "Jude, the servant of Jesus Christ, and brother of James." It is generally agreed that James, the Lord's brother, is the James who presided at the Council of Jerusalem. (See Acts 12:17; 15:13.) This James may also have later written the Epistle of James. The writer of Jude, therefore, may well have been the brother of this James, and thus a brother of the Lord Jesus.

Since the book of Jude was not written to a specific church or group it is considered to be a "general Epistle" written for the benefit of all the believers—including us. In just 25 verses, Jude covers a variety of critically important topics. He begins by telling the believers to "earnestly contend for the faith which was once delivered unto the saints" (v. 3). Ellen White notes, "Romanists have persisted in bringing against Protestants the charge of heresy and willful separation from the true church. But these accusations apply rather to themselves. They are the ones who laid down the banner of Christ and departed from 'the faith which was once delivered unto the saints.' Jude 3" *(The Great Controversy,* p. 51).

Jude notes the contrast between those who will be saved and those who will be destroyed. The enormous magnitude of sin is emphasized when he points out that even the angels who have fallen from their first estate with Satan are now reserved unto judgment—which will be eternal death by fire, as shown by the example of the destruction of Sodom and Gomorrah. As noted earlier, we have a heaven to win and a hell to shun. Right now the forces of the great controversy are pulling everyone into one camp or the other! "We are nearing the close of this earth's history, when two parties alone can exist, and every man, woman, and child will be in one of these armies. Jesus will be the General of one army; of the opposing army, Satan will be the leader. All who are breaking, and teaching others to break, the law of God, the foundation of His government in heaven and in earth, are marshaled under one superior chief, who directs them in opposition to the government of God. And 'the angels which kept not their first estate, but left their own habitation' (Jude 6) are rebels against the law of God, and enemies to all who love and obey His commandments. These subjects, with Satan their leader, will gather others into their ranks through every possible means, to strengthen his forces and urge his claims" *(Selected Messages,* vol. 3, p. 422).

Of particular interest to those who recognize who real players in the great controversy are, is the way in which Christ dealt with the devil. When contending over the body of Moses, Christ did not argue with Satan, but simply said, "The Lord rebuke thee." And later in His own incarnate state, during His temptation in the wilderness, Jesus did not argue with Satan but simply responded with Scripture. His defense was, "It is written!" Again and again in the Bible and the Spirit of Prophecy we are counseled not to argue with Satan or his followers. We are counseled to say to Satan, "In the name of the Lord Jesus Christ, get thee behind me Satan." And when confronted by those who are filled with his spirit we simply respond with our scriptural defense, "It is written." Never argue with Satan.

It is Jude and not any recorded words of Enoch himself that points out that Enoch, as the seventh from Adam, was given a vision of the great controversy and the Second Coming when the Lord will come with ten thousand of His saints. And then as does the apostle Peter, Jude warns of the mockers (scoffers) of the last days. Some will apparently call themselves Christians but still walk after their ungodly lusts because they have not the Spirit. These are the ones who do not have the leaven of the Holy Spirit in their hearts necessary to change their natural enmity against God and His law to repugnance of Satan and his ways. The wedding garment, the robe of righteousness, the leaven of God's Spirit, and the enmity that God has promised to put between us and Satan is the difference between being saved and being lost—between going to heaven with Christ when He comes or experiencing God's wrath and the resulting eternal death!

Reminding us of God's awesome power to save, Jude encourages us to keep ourselves in the love of God and to have compassion on those who are lost. He points out that though some appear so far gone that they are already literally on fire, we can in effect "pull them out of the fire," and save their lives.

Visit any large city and you will see the thousands who have almost entirely destroyed their minds and bodies through intemperance. When I was a boy these consisted largely of older men who had become alcoholics, or winos, as they were called. But today, in addition to this group, there is a much larger group who have become enslaved in the use of mind-altering drugs and Satanic music. They seem to be binding themselves in bundles to be burned. And yet the Scriptures declare about the power of Jesus: "He is able to save to the uttermost those who come to God through Him, since He ever lives to make intercession for them" (Hebrews 7:25). This is the primary purpose of our health and medical outreach programs—to save sinners and point them to the great healer.

"I have been instructed that the medical missionary work will discover, in the very depths of degradation, men who, though they have given themselves up to intemperate, dissolute habits, will respond to the right kind of labor. But they need to be recognized and encouraged. Firm, patient, earnest effort will be required in order to lift them up. They cannot restore themselves. They may hear Christ's call, but their ears are too dull to take in its meaning; their eyes are too blind to see anything good in store for them. They are dead in trespasses and sins. Yet even these are not to be excluded from the gospel feast. They are to receive the invitation: 'Come.' Though they may feel unworthy, the Lord says, 'Compel them to come in.' Listen to no excuse. By love and kindness lay right hold of them. 'Ye, beloved, building up yourselves on your most holy faith, praying in the Holy Ghost, keep yourselves in the love of God, looking for the mercy of our Lord Jesus Christ unto eternal life. <u>And of some have compassion, making a difference: and others save with fear, pulling them out of the fire.</u>' Jude 20-23. Press home upon the conscience the terrible results of the transgression of God's law. Show that it is not God who causes pain and suffering, but that man through his own ignorance and sin has brought this condition upon himself" *(Testimonies for the Church,* vol. 6, pp. 279, 280).

And now follows the conclusion of Jude's Epistle. It is a statement of hope and assurance. "Now unto him that is able to keep you from falling, and to present you faultless before the presence of his glory with exceeding joy, to the only wise God our Saviour, be glory and majesty, dominion and power, both now and ever. Amen" (Jude 24, 25, KJV).

He Is Able

God is able. We could just stop right there. He is able. That's all we need to know! Whatever it takes, He is able to do it. The more we study about Christ and His work and ministry on our behalf, the more we begin to recognize that we are dependent 100 percent on His mercy and power for our salvation. But our decision and cooperation is vital to the unleashing of His awesome power. "What God promises He is able at any time to perform, and the work which He gives His people to do He is able to accomplish by them. If they will live according to every word He has spoken, every good word and promise will be fulfilled unto them" *(Counsels on Health,* p. 378).

Many who are stuck in the ruts of sin, when presented with the way of God, almost despair because it seems so far above them. "I could never live like that," they exclaim. And it is true that in their own strength they can't—but God is able! "You can fight against the enemy, not in your own strength, but in the strength God is ever ready to give you. Trusting in His word, you will never say, 'I can't'" *(The Adventist Home,* p. 357).

God Is on Our Side

For those who have decided to follow Jesus to His kingdom, there is good news—lots of good news. Not only does He offer forgiveness of our sins and power for transformation, but He has also demonstrated that He is able to do what He has promised! We can understand from reading His Word that God is immortal, all-powerful, all-knowing,

above all, and ever-present. He is infinite and beyond human comprehension, and yet He makes Himself known through His self-revelation.
He has revealed Himself in His inspired Word, the Bible, in the works
of nature, His creation, and in His providential leading in our lives.

The Bible does not attempt to prove God's existence. It assumes it.
Its opening sentence declares, "In the beginning God created the heavens and the earth" (Genesis 1:1). The Bible describes God as the
Creator, Sustainer, and Ruler of all creation. God's revelation through
creation is so powerful that there is no excuse for atheism, which arises
from a suppression of divine truth in a mind that refuses to acknowledge the evidence that God exists. "The fool has said in his heart,
'There is no God.'" (Psalm 14:1).

There is enough evidences for God's existence to convince anyone
who seriously tries to discover the truth about Him. Faith is a prerequisite, for "without faith it is impossible to please Him, for he who
comes to God must believe that He is, and that He is a rewarder of
those who diligently seek Him" (Hebrews 11:6).

Faith in God, however, is not blind. It is based on sufficient evidence
found in God's revelations through the Scriptures and through nature.
Having said this, there are other very significant evidences of God's existence. There is the evidence of a changed life. We can't see the power,
like the wind or the leaven, but we can see the results. There is also the
evidence of God's protection and provision for His faithful followers.

We can better respond to God's instructions when we believe God
is who He says He is; when we believe that God can do what He says
He will do. A good example of this is the experience of Abram when
God promised him a son in his old age. God introduced Himself to
Abram by saying, "I am Almighty God, walk before me and be blameless" (Genesis 17:1). He wanted Abram to believe that He could do
what He told him He would do. There are steps that we can take from
faith to knowledge.

- "• You will have to *believe* God is who He says He is.
- You will have to *believe* God can do what He says He
  will do.
- You will have to *adjust* your thinking in light of this belief.
- Trusting that God will demonstrate Himself to be who He
  says He is, you then *obey* Him.

- When you *obey*, God does His work through you and demonstrates that He is who He says He is.
- Then you will *know* God by experience.
- You will *know* He is who He says He is" (Henry T. Blackaby, *Experiencing God,* p. 98).

So when did Abram know that God was Almighty? He had faith to believe it in his mind as soon as God said it. But he came to know it by experience when God did something in his life that only God could do. When he was 100 years old and his wife Sarah was 90, they had a son—then he knew by experience that God was the Almighty God. He knew that God was able to do what He said He would do.

We are encouraged to put our faith in the promises of God, today, on our own behalf. We must believe through experimental, experiential knowledge that God will do what He says He will do for us—forgive us and cleanse us from sin. In other words, fit us for heaven. Doubting this promise can have serious consequences.

The Ten Spies

God had promised it to them, and now He was about to give the land of Canaan to Israel. Moses sent 12 men into the Promised Land to explore it and bring back a report. The land, they reported, was beautiful and very fruitful, but the people living there seemed as giants (Numbers 13; 14). Two of the spies, Joshua and Caleb, were ready to trust God. They said, "Let us go up at once and take possession, for we are well able to overcome it." But the ten other spies were fearful and unbelieving. They said, "We are not able to go up against the people, for they are stronger than we" (Numbers 13:30, 31). When Joshua and Caleb saw that the report of the ten faithless spies was convincing the people that what God had promised was impossible, they tried once more to convince the people that God could do what He said He would do. Their final appeal was strong and direct. "The land we passed through to spy out is an exceedingly good land. If the Lord delights in us, then He will bring us into this land and give it to us, a land that flows with milk and honey. Only do not rebel against the Lord, nor fear the people of the land, for they are our bread; their protection has departed from them, and the Lord is with us. Do not fear them"

(Numbers 14:7-9). But the people took up stones to stone them; and the Lord was not able to take them in because of their unbelief.

Rather than looking to the strength of God they looked at themselves and gave up. They didn't see how in their own strength they could defeat the enemy. Little did they know that God had already prepared the way for the conquest of Canaan by putting fear into the hearts of the inhabitants. Forty years later Rahab, who lived in Jericho, described what God had done. She explained that when the people heard about the way God delivered Israel from the Egyptians, "our hearts were melted; neither did there remain any more courage in anyone because of you, for the Lord your God, He is God in heaven above and on earth beneath" (Joshua 2:11). Not believing that God could do what He said He would do cost Israel 40 years of waiting in the wilderness! Do you believe that God was able to take them in the first time they came to the borders of Canaan? Of course, you do! And so do I. But what about my life of sin? Do I believe that God is able to do what He says He will do with it? Remember, He is able.

God the Giant Killer

When Israel was being harassed by the Philistines, God asked Samuel the prophet to select a deliverer/king from among the sons of Jesse. When Samuel met with him, Jesse made seven of his sons to pass before Samuel. But Samuel said, "The Lord has not chosen these. Are all your sons here?" And Jesse responded, "There is one more. He is the youngest and he is keeping the sheep." They sent for young David and when Samuel saw him the Lord spoke to him and said, "Arise, anoint him; for this is the one!" Saul, although still the king of Israel, had been rejected by the Lord because of his incomplete obedience.

When Israel's army next mobilized to fight the Philistines, the talk in the camp was of a giant named Goliath. He was taunting the Israelites and cursing their God. For 40 days Goliath had taunted the Israelites.

David's three oldest brothers had gone to fight with Saul in this battle against the Philistines. Near the end of this period Jesse sent David with some care packages from home for his brothers. When David entered the camp of Israel he heard the giant's boasting and asked, "Who is this uncircumcised Philistine, that he should defy the armies of the living God?"

You well remember this awesome story. David volunteered to fight the giant. The king offered David the use of his personal armor, but David didn't feel comfortable with it. He ended up taking only his shepherd's staff and his sling and five smooth stones. Goliath was furious that Israel would send a mere youth to fight him. As David approached he roared that he would feed him to the birds and beasts. David responded with words worth noting, "You come to me with a sword, with a spear, and with a javelin. But I come to you in the name of the Lord of hosts, the God of the armies of Israel, whom you have defied. This day the Lord will deliver you into my hand, and I will strike you and take your head from you. And this day I will give the carcasses of the camp of the Philistines to the birds of the air and the wild beasts of the earth, that all the earth may know that there is a God in Israel. For all this assembly shall know that the Lord does not save with sword and spear; for the battle is the Lord's and He will give you into our hands" (1 Samuel 17:45-47). David killed the giant with the first stone, which came with such force that it embedded itself in his forehead. Then David took Goliath's sword and cut off his head with it.

This story contains the fascinating detail that after Israel routed the Philistines, King Saul asked his general, Abner, "Whose son is this youth?" Abner responded, "I don't know." There was such a lack of faith in Israel that they had allowed an unknown youth to do what they were afraid to do. But David knew that God was able. We face challenges today—Goliaths of equally blasphemous size. Are we operating our lives with the understanding that God is able? He is able.

David Acknowledges God's Power

Throughout his 40-year reign, acknowledged as the high point in Israel's history, King David always acknowledged God as his strength. He knew it was God's ability that was his strength. So many statements made by David convey his faith in God. I want to list just a few to build our own confidence. These were made by a man who knew by experience that God could and would do what He said He would do.

"The Lord is my rock and my fortress and my deliverer; my God, my strength, in whom I will trust; my shield and the horn of my salvation, my stronghold" (Psalm 18:2).

"Let the words of my mouth and the meditation of my heart be

acceptable in Your sight, O Lord, my strength and my Redeemer"
(Psalm 19:14).

"The Lord is my light and my salvation; whom shall I fear?
The Lord is the strength of my life; of whom shall I be afraid?"
(Psalm 27:1).

"But the salvation of the righteous is from the Lord; <u>He is their
strength in the time of trouble</u>" (Psalm 37:39).

"God is our refuge and strength, a very present help in trouble"
(Psalm 46:1).

"The Lord of hosts is with us; the God of Jacob is our refuge"
(Psalm 46:7).

"He only is my rock and my salvation; He is my defense; I
shall not be shaken" (Psalm 62:2).

"He who dwells in the secret place of the Most High shall abide
under the shadow of the Almighty. I will say of the Lord, 'He is my
refuge and my fortress; my God, in Him I will trust" (Psalm 91:1, 2).

If you were there to ask David, "Is God able to do what He says
He will do?" David would respond, "He is able!"

Isaiah's Affirmation

Isaiah, referred to as the gospel prophet, includes in his book a
view of God's power and its availability to mankind.

"Have you not known? Have you not heard? The everlasting God,
the Lord, the Creator of the ends of the earth, neither faints nor is
weary. There is no searching of His understanding. He gives power to
the weak, and to those who have no might He increases strength. Even
the youths shall faint and be weary, and young men shall utterly fall,
but those who wait on the Lord shall renew their strength; they shall
mount up with wings like eagles, they shall run and not be weary, they
shall walk and not faint" (Isaiah 40:28-31).

Those who trust in God are rewarded with fulfilled promises and a
confidence that carries them through the trials of life and fits them for
a place in the heavenly kingdom. I want to be in that group, don't you?
God Himself lets us in on the secret: it is 100 percent trust in Him and
not in self. "Thus says the Lord: 'Let not the wise man glory in his wisdom, let not the mighty man glory in his might, nor let the rich man
glory in his riches; but let him who glories glory in this, that he under-

stands and knows Me, that I am the Lord, exercising lovingkindness, judgment, and righteousness in the earth. For in these I delight,' says the Lord" (Jeremiah 9:23, 24).

Trial by Fire

The third chapter of Daniel records the wonderful deliverance of three young men from certain death by fire. Sometime after his vision of the great metal image that portrayed the rise and fall of nations, King Nebuchadnezzar decided to ignore the revelation given him by God and to build a large image similar to the one he had seen in his dream. On the plains of Dura he erected an image 90 feet tall and nine feet wide and made entirely of gold. Then, on a special day of celebration, he required all his subjects to bow in honor to the image and recognize him as the sole ruler of the earth. Thousands of people were present for the ceremony, but of all present only three men refused to obey the order to worship the image. When they were brought before the king, he asked them a question that reminds us of one of the boasts of the giant Goliath. "And who is the god who will deliver you from my hands?" (Daniel 3:15).

The three young Hebrews were quick to answer, "Our God whom we serve is able to deliver us from the burning fiery furnace, and He will deliver us from your hand, O king. But if not, let it be known to you, O king, that we do not serve your gods, nor will we worship the gold image which you have set up" (Daniel 3:17, 18). The king was angry to start with, and now he became livid with fury. He commanded that the furnaces be heated seven times hotter than usual. This was probably not actually possible. Suffice it to say that they were as hot as they could be made. The three faithful Hebrews were bound hand and foot with all their clothes on and thrown into the fire. The fire was so hot that the men who threw them in were killed from the heat. And yet the only things that actually burned in the fire were the ropes that bound them. God's promise recorded in Isaiah 43:2 was literally fulfilled for them. "When you pass through the waters, I will be with you; and through the rivers, they shall not overflow you. When you walk through the fire, you shall not be burned, nor shall the flame scorch you."

The king was amazed at the sight in the fire. Instead of hearing the crackling of burning fat and the billowing smoke from burning clothes and flesh, the king saw four men walking around in the fire—and the fourth looked "like the Son of God." Every detail concerning this incident illustrates the awesome power of God. When the king called out the three young men, they didn't even have their hair singed or have any smell of smoke on their clothes! God had fulfilled a promise later recorded in Matthew 28:20 and other places in the Bible: "I will be with you wherever you go!" "As His witnesses were cast into the furnace, the Saviour revealed Himself to them in person, and together they walked in the midst of the fire. In the presence of the Lord of heat and cold, the flames lost their power to consume" *(Prophets and Kings, pp. 508, 509).*

These young men didn't have any trouble believing that the God they served was the Almighty God. This event proved their confidence in His power. If you were to ask them anything about the power of God they would have said, "He is able!" But why should we concern ourselves with the stories of the past that we learned as children? Because, "Important are the lessons to be learned from the experience of the Hebrew youth on the plain of Dura. In this our day, many of God's servants, though innocent of wrong-doing, will be given over to suffer humiliation and abuse at the hands of those who, inspired by Satan, are filled with envy and religious bigotry. **Especially will the wrath of man be aroused against those who hallow the Sabbath of the fourth commandment; and at last a universal decree will denounce them as deserving of death.**

"The season of distress before God's people will call for a faith that will not falter. His children must make it manifest that He is the only object of their worship, and that no consideration, not even that of life itself, can induce them to make the least concession to false worship. To the loyal heart the commands of sinful, finite men will sink into insignificance beside the word of the eternal God. Truth will be obeyed though the result be imprisonment or exile or death.

"As in the days of Shadrach, Meshach, and Abednego, so in the closing period of earth's history the Lord will work mightily in behalf of those who stand steadfastly for the right. He who walked with the Hebrew worthies in the fiery furnace will be with His followers wherever they are. His abiding presence will comfort and sustain. In the midst of the time of trouble—trouble such as has not been since there was a nation—His chosen ones will stand unmoved. . . . **Angels that excel in strength will protect them,** and in their behalf Jehovah will reveal Himself as a 'God of gods,' able to save to the uttermost those who have put their trust in Him" *(ibid., pp. 512, 513).*

Our great God will prepare us for that day and protect and provide for us if we now learn to trust Him and are willing to obey His commandments. But we will never trust God with our very lives if we don't trust Him enough to be faithful with our tithes now.

In the Lions' Den

When Darius the Mede conquered Babylon, he immediately entered upon a total reorganization of the government. He set up over the kingdom 120 princes and over these three presidents or governors. Then, because Daniel distinguished himself with an excellent spirit, the king gave him the overall leadership. This made the others jealous, and they conspired to find some occasion or reason to discredit him. But they could find nothing because he was faithful and they could find no error or fault. It is obvious to anyone tuned to current events in U.S. politics that very few on Capitol Hill could boast of such a record—no errors and no faults. These jealous colleagues of Daniel conspired to devise a scheme to bring about his death. Their plan was to trick the king into thinking he was being honored by a law that would limit honor to anyone but him for a period of 30 days. Darius' pride got the best of him and he signed their decree.

Daniel's enemies counted on his faithfulness to God and principle for the success of their plan. And they had not underestimated Daniel as to his character. Though now an old man, he quickly read their scheme, but he did not change his course in any way. Why should he stop praying now, when he needed to pray the most? He calmly performed his duties as the chief of princes. Then at the hour of prayer he went to his quarters and, following his usual custom, opened his windows toward Jerusalem and prayed. Thus he did three times a day. Have you ever wondered what Daniel found to pray about three times a day? The Bible says he was without fault. When you study his prayers he prayed for strength to be faithful, and he prayed for his people, because, "We have sinned and committed iniquity, we have done wickedly and rebelled, even by departing from Your precepts and Your judgments" (Daniel 9:5).

Informed of Daniel's failure to honor the decree, the king was stunned and greatly displeased with himself for signing the decree. He spent the rest of the day trying to figure out a way for Daniel to be made an exception. But at the end of the day the "princes" came again and reminded him that the law could not be changed.

In the evening, Daniel was called before the king and informed that he was to thrown into the den of lions. Then, before the decree was carried out, the king said to Daniel, "Your God, whom you serve continually, He will deliver you" (Daniel 6:16). Whereupon, Daniel was thrown to the lions.

The king was so distressed that he skipped his evening meal, canceled the music concert, and did not sleep at all. Very early in the morning he hurried to the lions' den and shouted down to its depths: "Daniel, servant of the living God, has your God, whom you serve continually, been able to deliver you from the lions?" (Daniel 6:20). What do think Daniel said? He shouted back, "HE IS ABLE! God has sent His angel and shut the lions' mouths, so that they have not hurt me." He was not mauled, scratched, or eaten upon. He was unharmed.

The king was overjoyed to have his trusted servant restored to him, and he commanded that the conspirators be cast to the lions, along with their wives and children. It wasn't a pretty sight. The Bible says the lions broke "all their bones in pieces before they ever came to the bottom of the den" (Daniel 6:24). Finally the king made a decree honoring Daniel's God and had it circulated throughout the realm.

But why would God allow an old man to be thrown to the lions? I can think of two reasons. First, "The experience of Daniel as a statesman in the kingdoms of Babylon and Medo-Persia reveals the truth that a businessman is not necessarily a designing, policy man, but that he may be a man instructed by God at every step. Daniel, the prime minister of the greatest of earthly kingdoms, was at the same time a prophet of God, receiving the light of heavenly inspiration. A man of like passions as ourselves, the pen of inspiration describes him as without fault. His business transactions, when subjected to the closest scrutiny of his enemies, were found to be without one flaw. He was an example of what every businessman may become when his heart is converted and consecrated, and when his motives are right in the sight of God" *(Prophets and Kings,* p. 546).

The second reason involves the true value of things in the light of eternity and the necessity of preparing for it now. "A careful study of the working out of God's purpose in the history of nations and in the revelation of things to come, will help us to estimate at their true value things seen and things unseen, and to learn what is the true aim of life. Thus, viewing the things of time in the light of eternity, we may, like Daniel and his fellows, live for that which is true and noble and enduring. And learning in this life the principles of the kingdom of our Lord and Saviour, that blessed kingdom which is to endure for ever and ever, we may be prepared at His coming to enter with Him into its possession" *(ibid.,* p. 548).

There is much evidence in the New Testament of similar acts of deliverance granted by God's power: Peter's deliverance from prison; the protection of Paul in shipwrecks and other trials. However, God's power to save eternally is perhaps the most significant evidence of His ability.

Jesus was entreated by two blind men that He heal them. They followed Him into a house and Jesus asked them, "Do you believe that I am able to do this?" and they said, "Yes, Lord." And He touched their eyes and said, "According to your faith let it be done to you." And their eyes were opened! Many such accounts in the ministry of Jesus and in the New Testament church show us that God is able.

"But as many as received Him, to them He gave power to become the sons of God" (John 1:12).

"I am not ashamed of the gospel of Christ, for it is the power of God to salvation for everyone who believes" (Romans 1:16).

"And my God shall supply all your need according to His riches in glory by Christ Jesus" (Philippians 4:19).

"Now to Him who is able to do exceedingly abundantly above all that we ask or think, according to the power that works in us" (Ephesians 3:20).

"For when we were still without strength, in due time Christ died for the ungodly" (Romans 5:6).

"And He said to me, 'My grace is sufficient for you, for My strength is made perfect in weakness'" (2 Corinthians 12:9).

I Believe He Is Able

It is quite exciting to review the story of the Bible; especially those where miracles were performed. We know that He was able to dispose of Goliath; save the three young men in the fiery furnace; and save Daniel from the lions, but is He able to solve my problems and yours?

If Jesus is able to create the world, He is able to create a new heart in me. He is able!

If Jesus is able to kill a giant who is a trained man of war by using a shepherd boy, He is able to take care of the giants in my life. He is able!

If Jesus can heal a demoniac and restore him to society as His representative, He is able to heal me of my inherited and cultivated tendencies to evil. He is able!

If Jesus can save to the uttermost, He is able to save me. He is able!

If Jesus is able to walk in the fire with His faithful followers, I know He is able to go with me wherever I go. He is able!

If Jesus can deliver Daniel from the lions, He can deliver us. Is He able to do what He says He will do? He is able!

If Jesus is able to open the eyes of the blind, He can open my eyes to the truths of His Word. He is able! Thank God, He is able!

In his final Epistle Paul tells young Timothy of the hope that he has in Jesus and the gospel. After recounting the sufferings he had endured because of his work as a preacher, an apostle, and a teacher he states, "Nevertheless, I am not ashamed, for I know whom I have believed and am persuaded that **He is able** to keep what I have committed to Him until that Day." And he concludes this final Epistle with words of confidence and hope: "For I am already being poured out as a drink offering, and the time of my departure is at hand. I have fought the good fight, I have finished the race, I have kept the faith. Finally, there is laid up for me the crown of righteousness, which the Lord, the righteous Judge, will give me on that Day, and not to me only but also to all who have loved His appearing" (2 Timothy 1:12; 4:6-8).

He is able!

CHAPTER 15

Unity Versus Compromise

Unity is a high priority with Jesus. It was painful to Him that the disciples were still arguing over who would be the greatest among them—even after He had told them that He would soon die for them. Comforting the disciples before the Crucifixion and after participating with them in the Last Supper, Jesus took them once again to the Garden of Gethsemane. We are told that the Passover moon, broad and full, shone from a cloudless sky. The city of Jerusalem was full of the tents of pilgrims who had come for the great feast. But now the city was sleeping as Jesus led His remaining 11 disciples toward the garden. They noticed that a marked change had come over Him. He became sad and silent as He thought on what was ahead of Him. It is in this setting that John records for us the prayer of Jesus. It is the longest recorded prayer of Jesus. He prayed for Himself, His disciples, and then for all the believers.

In His prayer, "Christ, amid His sufferings, and being daily rejected of men, looks down the lines two thousand years to His church which would be in existence in the last days, before the close of this earth's history" (Review and Herald, November 8, 1856). And He prayed for unity! He also prayed for unity among His disciples. After they had come into full unity the Holy Spirit was poured out upon them.

Jesus promised that when He went back to heaven He would send the Spirit with its general and special gifts. Ephesians 4 lets us know that the gifts were to bring about unity of faith and to solidify doctrines so that believers are not tossed on the waves of uncertainty.

What a wonderful change came over the disciples when they joined together in unity! Their ministry was filled with power and the gospel quickly spread abroad. "Unity is the strength of the church. Satan knows this, and he employs his whole force to bring in dissension. He desires to see a lack of harmony among the members of the church of God. <u>Greater attention should be given to the subject of unity</u>. What is the recipe for the cure of the leprosy of strife and dissension? Obedience to the commandments of God" *(Notebook Leaflets From the Elmshaven Library,* vol. 1, p. 22).

Unity does not come naturally from the unconverted heart. It takes the indwelling of God's Spirit to bring this about. "The Spirit of God alone can bring about this oneness. He who sanctified Himself, can sanctify His disciples. United with Him, they will be united with one another in the most holy faith. When we strive for this unity as God desires us to strive for it, it will come to us" *(The Southern Watchman,* February 2, 1904).

Truth is basic to real unity. In Jesus' "unity" prayer of John 17, He prayed, "Sanctify them by Your truth. Your word is truth" (John 17:17). "<u>God is leading out a people to stand in perfect unity upon the platform of truth</u>. Christ gave Himself to the world that He might 'purify unto Himself a peculiar people, zealous of good works.' This refining process is designed to purge the church from all unrighteousness and the spirit of discord and contention, <u>that they may build up instead of tear down, and concentrate their energies on the great work before them</u>. God designs that His people should all come into the unity of the faith. The prayer of Christ just prior to His crucifixion was that His disciples might be one, even as He was one with the Father, that the world might believe that the Father had sent Him. <u>This most touching and wonderful prayer reaches down the ages, even to our day; for His words were: 'Neither pray I for these alone, but for them also which shall believe on Me through their word</u>" *(Testimonies for the Church,* vol. 4, p. 17).

We are all as different as snowflakes. We have different backgrounds, different personality types, different ways of looking at things, yet, in Christ, we can be one in purpose. We can learn to love one another. The disciples were a very diverse group, yet in Christ, and by His Spirit, they formed a team that changed the world. It is important to note that not until they submitted to the infilling of the Spirit of Christ did they really become effective in their witnessing.

"It is the same today as it was in the days of Christ. As the disciples were brought together, each with different faults, some inherited or cultivated tendency to evil, so in our church relations we find men and women whose characters are defective; not one of us is perfect. <u>But in Christ, and through Christ, we are to dwell in the family of God, learning to become one in faith, in doctrine, in spirit</u>, that at last we may be received into our eternal habitation. We shall have our tests, our grievances, our differences of opinion; but if Christ is abiding in the heart of each, there can be no dissension. <u>The love of Christ will lead to love of one another, and the lessons of the Master will harmonize all differences, bring us into unity till we shall be of one mind and one judgment</u>. **Strife for supremacy will cease,** and no one will be disposed to glory over another, but we shall esteem others better than ourselves, and so be built up into a spiritual temple for the Lord" *(The Signs of the Times,* April 20, 1891).

We as church members today are all of different temperaments and dispositions. We have come together from different denominations and religious backgrounds. God's great cleaver of truth has cut us out of the world and placed us together in His church. By His power we learn to work together as we become one in faith, doctrine, and spirit.

Apparently, one of the reasons why there are different spiritual gifts and different personality types in the church is because there are different minds to be reached in the great harvest field. Some will reject the message when it is presented by one worker, only to open their hearts to the same message when presented in a different manner by another worker. Our different talents should all be under the control of the same Spirit. The world will then know that we are Christ's disciples. Christianity will make a man a gentleman and we can all be kind, courteous, and tenderhearted.

One very unique and distinguishing characteristic of God's true people at the end is the racial harmony among them. We must pray earnestly that our inherited and cultivated prejudice will be taken away so that the world will recognize our love and give God the glory.

One of the methods of ministry modeled in the New Testament and recommended in the Spirit of Prophecy is the formation of small groups or bands for encouragement and sharing. Obviously, these groups should not become cliques or closed social groups. They can be a benefit to the cause of unity if God's Spirit is present.

Regarding the purpose and results of forming small bands of workers Ellen White stated, "The formation of small companies as a basis of Christian effort is a plan that has been presented before me by One who can not err. If there are a large number in the church, let the members be formed into small companies, to work not only for the church members, but for unbelievers. If in one place there are only two or three who know the truth, let them form themselves into a band of workers. Let them keep their bond of union unbroken, pressing together in love and unity, encouraging one another to advance, each gaining encouragement and strength for the assistance of the other. . . . As they work and pray in Christ's name, their numbers will increase; for the Saviour declares: 'I say unto you, that if two of you shall agree on earth as touching anything that they shall ask, it shall be done for them of My Father which is in heaven" *(The Pacific Union Recorder,* October 9, 1902).

We know that there is a great work before us. When we are converted we will strengthen the brethren. With God's promised blessing mighty things will happen. The closer we come to Christ as individuals, the closer we will come to each other, and the more focused will be our ministry. "The secret of true unity in the church and in the family is not diplomacy, not management, not a superhuman effort to overcome difficulties—though there will be much of this to do—but union with Christ" *(Mind, Character, and Personality,* vol. 2, p. 501).

As we get closer to the end our friends in the church will be the closest people to us on earth. The bond between Christians will be cemented by the Spirit of God. Some will have left or have been abandoned by family members as a result of their Christian commitment. As Jesus said, they become our brothers and sisters. These people will love to gather together for Christian fellowship and in fact are encouraged to do so. "Not forsaking the assembling of ourselves together, as is the manner of some, but exhorting one another, and so much the more as you see the Day approaching" (Hebrews 10:25).

"The very first work we are to do is to unite in the bonds of Christian fellowship. Those who are working for God should put away all unkind criticism, and draw together in unity. Christ desires His soldiers to stand shoulder to shoulder, united in the work of fighting the battles of the cross. He desires the union between those who work for Him to be as close as the union between Him and His Father. Those who have felt the sanctifying power of the Holy Spirit will heed the lessons of the divine instructor, and will show their sincerity by doing all in their power to work in harmony with their brethren" *(Review and Herald,* October 29, 1901).

Each of us should show our interest in the prosperity of the church by identifying ourselves with it and working with our brethren in the completion of the work of the Great Commission. Precisely because unity is such a positive blessing to the church and a witness to the world, Satan works to bring about division. Why can't we learn by now that any thought that it is God's plan to separate from our brethren comes from the devil? There are those who have become so mad at the church for this reason or that—theological or social—that they absent themselves from church and will even pass by a local church to go and "fellowship" in a "home church." There is counsel for those thus inclined. "The Captain of our salvation leads His people on step by step, purifying and fitting them for translation, and <u>leaving in the rear those who are disposed to draw off from the body, who are not willing to be led, and are satisfied with their own righteousness.</u> 'If therefore the light that is in thee be darkness, how great is that darkness!' **<u>No greater delusion can deceive the human mind than that which leads men to indulge a self-confident spirit, to believe that they are right and in the light, when they are drawing away from God's people, and their cherished light is darkness</u>**" *(Testimonies for the Church,* vol. 1, p. 333).

A Positive Approach to Unity

What happens when we gather around our family altars? What do we say about God's church and its leaders? What kind of picture do our children see of the church—the one we paint with our words? What if every weakness spotted in the church were taken as an occasion to pray for the person or situation? We all know things would be a lot different if we practiced that.

"Make the home life as nearly as possible like heaven. Let the members of the family forget not, as they gather round the family altar, to pray for the men in positions of responsibility in God's work. The physicians in our sanitariums [the hospital system], the ministers of the gospel, those in charge of our publishing houses and schools, need your prayers. They are tempted and tried. <u>As you plead with God to</u>

bless them, your own hearts will be subdued and softened by His grace" *(In Heavenly Places,* p. 211).

We know that a house divided against itself cannot stand. How unbecoming and unfitting it is then for us to criticize and ridicule our own brethren, especially since there is still a great work for God's Holy Spirit to do for each of us. What benefit is there ever developed by criticism and ever-surmising. We should pray for those in error. Let us always present them before the throne of God. "Unity with Christ establishes a bond of unity with one another. This unity is the most convincing proof to the world of the majesty and virtue of Christ, and of His power to take away sin" *(Sons and Daughters of God,* p. 286).

Yes, unity is important. The unity that Christ spoke of was unity of faith and doctrine based on the platform of truth. True unity can never be at the expense of truth. Truth is more important than unity. It is the work of God's Spirit to bring unity. The Spirit also guides us into all truth. Accordingly, we can't have Spirit-inspired unity apart from truth.

There are many calls to us today to join with other churches in the great ecumenical movement or to drop our "denominational barriers" and become the type of one happy Christian family espoused by the Promise Keepers organization. Let us remember that God has called the remnant church to uphold unity on the platform of truth. The last message to the world and those in apostate religions is to "come out of her, My people" (Revelation 18:4). "God is leading **out** a people and fitting them for translation. Are we who are acting a part in this work standing as sentinels for God? Are we uniting our forces: Are we willing to become servants of all? Are we imitating the great Pattern?" *(Testimonies to Ministers,* p. 252). How can we call folks out of something if we ourselves are part of it?

"Jesus prayed that His followers might be one; but we are not to sacrifice the truth in order to secure this union, for we are to be sanctified through the truth. Here [on truth] is the foundation of all true peace. Human wisdom would change all this, pronouncing this basis too narrow. Men would try to effect unity through concession to popular opinion, through compromise with the world, a sacrifice of vital godliness. But truth is God's basis for the unity of His people" *(Our High Calling,* p. 329).

In February of 1996 nearly 40,000 ministers of most denominations met as part of the Promise Keepers organization in the Georgia

Dome in Atlanta. The theme for all the Promise Keeper rallies in 1996 was "Break Down the Walls." The walls referred to were the walls of racism and denominationalism. Promise Keepers' founder, Bill McCartney, called for cooperation among religious groups. "Contention between denominations has gone on long enough," he said. "If the church ever stood together, Almighty God would have His way" *(Christianity Today,* April 8, 1996). Many other presenters such as Max Lucado presented similar sentiments to the group.

A Catholic pastor, writing in a local newspaper, wrote the following: "Years ago a prominent church leader (Rev. Bernard Law) said: 'We can no longer afford the dubious luxury of a fragmented Christendom.' We all know that Christianity is sliced up into lots of denominations. Obviously, Jesus does not want this. All this division is contrary to His final prayer. But what can we do about it?

"We have to realize that we are on the threshold of a whole new era as far as the church and its mission to mankind is concerned. But at least a beginning has been made on every level. There is now a special responsibility upon every member of every church to work toward unity.

"The Catholic church is not alone in working toward oneness. Dr. Robert McAffe Brown, Presbyterian minister and professor at Stanford, years ago stated what is involved in Christian unity: 'The only condition under which Protestants and Catholics can take genuine "steps to Christian unity" is at some kind of real risk. The risk is that what will emerge at the end will not be simply the Catholic Church as it is now with all Protestants absorbed into it, nor will it be the Protestant Church as it is now with all Catholics absorbed into it. <u>What will emerge is something we do not really see. Unity will come only as both groups move out toward each other, recognizing that after their confrontation with each other, neither will be quite the same as it is before the encounter took place</u>'" (Rev. Roland Hautz, pastor, St. Francis of Assisi Catholic Church, *The Post Express,* West Jefferson, N.C., Tuesday, January 28, 1997).

Centuries ago when faithful Christians were faced with compromise in the church they had a decision to make. It was painful. It cost some their lives, but they felt they had no alternative. "After a long and severe conflict, the faithful few decided to dissolve all union with the apostate church if she still refused to free herself from falsehood and idolatry.

<u>They saw that separation was an absolute necessity if they would obey the word of God</u>. They dared not tolerate errors fatal to their own souls, and set an example which would imperil the faith of their children and children's children. <u>To secure peace and unity they were ready to make any concession consistent with fidelity to God</u>; **but they felt that even peace would be too dearly purchased at the sacrifice of principle.** <u>If unity could be secured only by the compromise of truth and righteousness, then let there be difference, and even war</u>" *(The Great Controversy,* p. 45).

This is not an easy issue to deal with and must be handled with great care. We do not want to appear aloof—however, when there are warning flags we cannot seek unity. In fact, we are told that the revival which precedes the latter rain will be so deceptive that the only major points of difference will be the teaching of the immortality of the soul and Sunday sacredness—both of which are taught by the Promise Keepers.

We have specific counsel in this delicate situation. "May the Lord bless His people with spiritual eyesight, to see that the children of God and the world can never be in copartnership. Whosoever will be the friend of the world is the enemy of God. <u>While every individual should work with Christ to transform the children of darkness by showing them the Lamb of God that taketh away the sins of the world, they cannot have overflowing sympathy with worldlings in such a degree that they lend them their influence to carry out their suggestions to weaken and do injustice to God's chosen ones</u>. God does not work in this way. In perfect and complete unity there is strength. Not in numbers, but in the perfect trust and unity with Christ, one can chase a thousand, and two put ten thousand to flight. <u>Let us not form unholy bonds of union with the friends of the world; for God has pronounced His curse upon all such unions</u>. Let the people of God take their stand firmly for truth and for righteousness. Already we see the terrible consequences of uniting believers with unbelievers. The result is, the unbelievers are given the confidence that belongs to those only who love and revere God" *(Testimonies to Ministers,* pp. 276, 277).

Let us pray for wisdom, kindness, and firmness as we deal with the implementation of Christ's prayer for unity. "Sanctify them by Your word. Your word is truth" (John 17:17).

CHAPTER 16

Love Me, Love My Church

With the enormous emphasis today on ecumenism and the push to break down denominational walls, much more study should be given to the topic of the church, to what scholars call ecclesiology. On what basis should one become a member of a church? Is it a compromise to be a member of a denomination or should I just be a part of the "church at large" and "fellowship" with some nondenominational group?

Apparently, church was God's idea. He organized it. The New Testament is full of the evidence—with apostles, elders, deacons, gifts, fellowship—the assembling together and more. The Lord blessed the efforts of the early church. "And the Lord added to the church daily, those who were being saved" (Acts 2:47). Barnabas, one of the early church leaders, went to Tarsus to find Paul. "And when he found him, he brought him to Antioch. So it was that for a whole year they assembled with the church and taught a great many people. And the disciples were first called Christians in Antioch" (Acts 11:26). The church was a close-knit and vibrant group.

When Peter was thrown in prison, "constant prayer was offered to God for him by the church." The church organized a prayer vigil. There was a prayer group in earnest prayer for his deliverance 24 hours a day. They were praying for one of their leaders! God gave the "gifts" to the church. He wanted the church to benefit. "And God has appointed these in the church: first apostles, second prophets, third teachers, after that miracles, then gifts of healings, helps, administrations, varieties of tongues" (1 Corinthians 12:28). The gifts were to be manifested to "edify" the church (see 1 Corinthians 14:12).

"Christ loved the church, and gave Himself for it" (Ephesians 5: 25). There is a very close connection between Christ and His church. He is the vine—the church members are the branches. He is the head—the church members with their various gifts are the body. He is the chief cornerstone—the church members are the living stones. He is the bridegroom—the church is the bride.

When counseling young people regarding their lifework, Ellen White encouraged, "Another obligation, too often lightly regarded,—one that to the youth awakened to the claims of Christ needs to be made plain,—is the obligation of church relationship.

"Very close and sacred is the relation between Christ and His church—He the bridegroom, and the church the bride; He the head, and the church the body. Connection with Christ, then, involves connection with His church.

"The church is organized for service; and in a life of service to Christ, connection with the church is one of the first steps. Loyalty to Christ demands the faithful performance of church duties" *(Education,* pp. 268, 269).

Many years ago a person with much experience shared with me his observation that everyone who was a church member of any church was involved with his particular church for one of three reasons. Over the years I have noted the truth of his observations. Here are the reasons:

1. The reason that most people are members of a particular church is that they were raised in that church. Their family have been members for years. They were born in that church. They were dedicated or baptized in that church. Perhaps they were married in that church. Almost all of their close friends are in that church.

2. The second reason, and a quite common one, is that people are members of a particular church out of convenience. For example, let's say that a Baptist and a Methodist get married. They are not going to be members of both churches or alternate between them on Sundays. Most of the time one will join the other's church out of convenience, and that is the end of the story. Another example of this convenience idea might be if a person who is a member of the Congregational church in New England moves to Alabama. He can't find a Congregational church near his home, so he becomes a Presbyterian.

3. The third and last reason for church membership is quite different from the first two. This reason involves personal belief. A person decides to study the Bible in an effort to determine what it says and means. This may be a private, personal study, or with a group, seminar, or evangelistic meeting. Once a basic knowledge of God and His will is discovered, the person seeks fellowship with those whom he feels are following what he believes the Scriptures teach. This reason for church membership involves theology— what a person understands about God and His will. In my personal judgment this is the only justifiable reason for being a church member. Membership that is based on an understanding of truth rather than heritage or convenience is the only biblical reason.

Church membership is very important for end-time Christians. However, as I have discovered and tried to convey in this book, church membership alone will not save anyone. There still must be a basic change of heart—the new birth and the worn wedding garment.

"All, high or low, if they are unconverted, are on one common platform. Men may turn from one doctrine to another. This is being done, and will be done. Papists may change from Catholicism to Protestantism; yet they may know nothing of the meaning of the words, 'A new heart also will I give you.' Accepting new theories, and uniting with a church, do not bring new life to anyone, even though the church with which he unites may be established on the true foundation. Connection with a church does not take the place of conversion. To subscribe the name to a church creed is not of the least value to anyone if the heart is not truly changed" *(Evangelism,* pp. 290, 291).

Another one of the great deceptions at the end is to repeat the devil's criticisms of the church. Through his influence, it is just about as popular to criticize the church as it is to criticize the government. As a result many congregations are trying to distance themselves from the conference. Some families are so disgruntled with God's bride that they won't have any fellowship at all with the church and choose to drive right past churches that are near them and attend "house" churches where they think there are no problems. What should be our attitude toward the church today?

The first chapter of *Acts of the Apostles* addresses the question of God's purpose for His church. It is very clear that God holds His church in high regard. "The church is God's appointed agency for the salvation of men. It was organized for service, and its mission is to carry the gospel to the world. <u>From the beginning it has been God's plan that through His church shall be reflected to the world His fullness and His sufficiency</u>. The members of the church, those whom He has called out of darkness into His marvelous light, are to show forth His glory. <u>The church is the repository of the riches of the grace of Christ; and through the church will eventually be made manifest</u>, even to 'the principalities and powers in heavenly places,' <u>the final and full display of the love of God</u>" *(Acts of the Apostles,* p. 9).

"The church is God's fortress. His city of refuge, which He holds in a revolted world. <u>Any betrayal of the church is treachery to Him who has bought mankind with the blood of His only-begotten Son</u>. From the beginning, faithful souls have constituted the church on earth. In every age the Lord has had His watchmen, who have borne a faithful testimony to the generation in which they lived. These sentinels gave the message of warning; and when they were called to lay off their armor, others took up the work. <u>God brought these witnesses into covenant relation with Himself, uniting the church on earth with the church in heaven. He has sent for His angels to minister to His church, and the gates of hell have not been able to prevail against His people</u>" *(ibid.,* p. 11).

But what about the problems in the church? An experience I had while I was in college in the middle 1960s helped me to understand the answer to this question. Like many of my theology classmates, I had the life-changing and character-building experience during two summers of selling books as a student literature evangelist. I learned a very important lesson one day while canvassing.

I had just finished my freshman year at Southern Missionary College. I was almost 18 years old, and I was very shy. But I was determined to be a successful minister, and I was told that canvassing was an excellent training on how to meet people and depend on the Lord. I was really too shy just to go cold turkey door-to-door. But they gave us lead cards filled out by people who had seen the books in doctors' offices. With the card in hand you at least had the name of someone in the house and knew that they had some interest in the books.

So I took my cards one morning, found their approximate location on the map, and started out. I found the first house quite easily. But then I got nervous and drove around the block and stopped and prayed. When I came back, I parked in the street in front of the house, got out, picked up my briefcase, and started toward the gate. Just then I spotted this old mangy dog coming down the street. It was awful looking. The hair was missing from parts of its body. It came right up to me and sat down and started scratching itself. It had this real raspy bark like it had bronchitis or something.

I tried to shoo it off, but it wouldn't leave. And when I opened the gate to the yard it ran in and right up on the porch ahead of me. You can imagine how I felt. Frankly, I was mortified. I was scared to start with and now I knew that whoever opened the door would see not only a salesman with a briefcase but also this mangy dog. For a moment I thought, *I ought to kick this crazy dog off the porch or my chances of getting into this house are zero.* But before I could do it the door opened and there stood the lady of the house behind the screen door.

But instead of saying, "I don't want any" or "What are you selling sonny?" she took one look at that dog and shouted, "O Julie Bell, where have you been, baby?" She then opened the door and scooped up the dog and held it to her breast and kissed it on the head and then she let the dog lick her on the cheek. Meanwhile, I was standing there with my mouth hanging open in disbelief! Since the door was already opened, she invited me in, and bought one of my books.

The lesson I learned that day was, "Love me, love my dog."

Have you ever learned that lesson? People have some of the most dreadful looking cats and dogs, but you don't dare criticize them or hurt them or you will be in big trouble. Love me, love my dog.

In a recent quarter's Sabbath School lesson we studied the topic of "God's Family—the Church." I have found the material to be very enlightening and highly recommend its study.

But if we are really honest with ourselves we must admit that sometimes we don't look too good. I mean, we sometimes see in the church such "mangy" characteristics as pride, greed, self-centeredness, dishonesty, egotism, and bigotry—to say nothing of materialism and immorality. We even hear some say that we are never going to get the work finished until we clean up the church. How can we expect to have people join us when we are such a motley group at times? Lest you get too discouraged here, let me interrupt myself and tell you that I believe that warts and all, the Seventh-day Adventist Church is still the remnant church of Bible prophecy and proclaims the truth of God's Word. And God **loves** this church.

If we criticize the church, we don't understand the great controversy and we are actually working for the devil. Don't ever forget that the devil knows that his time is short and he is determined to make war with the remnant—those who keep the commandments of God and have the gift of prophecy. As part of his warfare the enemy infiltrates the church. He plants tares among the wheat.

Ellen White knew this church like few others and yet she never left the church nor encouraged others to do so. And when you check out her counsel regarding the church (nearly 17,000 hits on the CD-ROM), WOW! what insights she gives. She knew what caused the problems and what we should do about them.

She stated in *The Great Controversy,* p. 396, that . . . "in every revival Satan is ready to bring into the church those who are unsanctified in heart and unbalanced in mind. Then he uses these people as his agents to cause problems in the church."

We have heard of the early church, the church in the wilderness, the Laodicean church, the militant church, and the triumphant church. Listen: "Has God no living church? He has a church, but it is the church militant, not the church triumphant. We are sorry that there are defective members. . . . While the Lord brings into the church those who are truly converted, Satan at the same time brings persons who are not converted into its fellowship. While Christ is sowing the good seed, Satan is sowing the tares" *(The Faith I Live By,* p. 305.).

Many join the church because they recognize truth. You can't argue with our message if you accept the Scriptures as the Word of God. But sometimes these same ones do not understand or experience the transforming and renewing power of the Holy Spirit and are not really born again.

However, in spite of all the devil's work, who else is holding up the banner of the Reformation? Where are all of the Protestants who stood up to the errors of Rome? I will tell you where they are. They are riding their tour buses on the highway back to Rome! As Jan Chenski, the Associated Press writer from Richmond who blasted our book *God's Answers to Your Questions,* has stated, "No one believes anything of what's written in that book anymore!"

So what is one to do—join the critics?

We are warned: "Let all be careful not to make an outcry against the only people who are fulfilling the description given of the remnant people, who keep the commandments of God and have the faith of Jesus. . . . God has a distinct people, a church on earth, second to none, but superior to all in their facilities to teach the truth, to vindicate the law of God. . . . My brother, if you are teaching that the Seventh-day Adventist Church is Babylon, you are wrong" *(Testimonies to Ministers,* p. 47; *Last Day Events,* p. 43).

Some folks have the mistaken idea that when they join the church and enter into fellowship they will meet only those who are pure and perfect. They are at a high point in their zeal and experience and when they see faults in other church members, they say, "We left the world to get away from the likes of this! What's the story here? Maybe this isn't the remnant church after all."

The servants in the parable of the wheat and the tares asked the same question. "We thought you planted wheat—but look at all the tares." But Jesus reminded them that the wheat and tares would grow together until the harvest. Apparently, only after the persecution in connection with the agitation for a Sunday law will the church be composed of only saints.

You realize, of course, that tares don't take too well to persecution, and when it begins, they leave the church like rats jumping off a sinking ship (parable of the sower, and the man who built his house on the sand); then the wheat types join together, put aside all differences, and work together in unity to "finish the work." It is then that the Holy Spirit will be poured out on them in such a way that it will eclipse the day of Pentecost. When this happens another amazing thing happens. We are told that "when the storm of persecution really breaks upon us . . . self-denying efforts will be put forth to save the lost, and many who have strayed from the fold will come back to follow the great Shepherd" *(Maranatha,* p. 194). That will be a happy day. It makes people happy to see their loved ones come back.

Not long ago I was having the evening meetings at a camp meeting. Early in the week a lady came up to me and introduced herself. She had purchased my book *Sunday's Coming!* at an earlier camp meeting that summer and after reading it she laid it on the coffee table without saying a word to her husband about it. As a former Adventist, who had been out of the church for many years, he had become very critical of the church. But one evening while she was away he picked up the book and started reading it. He told her he couldn't put it down. After he finished reading he apologized to her for the mean spirit that he had shown and asked for forgiveness. Then she told me, "He has been with me at church every Sabbath since then. He is even here with me now." She was beaming from ear to ear.

That Sabbath evening I made a call for commitment and recommitment to Christ and His church. The Spirit of God was present and it seemed that everyone was coming forward as we sang together "Shall We Gather at the River." The response was in the affirmative— Yes, we will be there! Later, as I was greeting people this lady came up to me again and joyfully stated, "He came forward." She was thrilled. This type of story will be repeated again and again when the church has that great manifestation of the love of God.

In an article that appeared in the *Review and Herald,* dated October 12, 1905, we read the following: "The work is soon to close. The members of the church militant who have proved faithful will become the church triumphant. In reviewing our past history, having traveled over every step of advance to our present standing, I can say, Praise God! As I see what God has wrought, I am thrilled with astonishment and with confidence in Christ as leader. We have nothing to fear for the future, except as we shall forget the way the Lord has led us, and his teaching in our past history."

So what are we to do about the bad guys and the problems in the church? What about church discipline? We all understand its proper place; but, look at this paradoxical situation: "Those who are carnally minded will be found in the church. They are to be pitied more than blamed. The church is not to be judged as sustaining these characters, though they be found within her borders. Should the church expel them, the very ones who found fault with their presence there, would blame the church for sending them adrift in the world; they would claim that they were treated unmercifully" *(Fundamentals of Christian Education,* p. 294).

Maybe we should live as Moses and Daniel did—identifying themselves with God's wayward people. Maybe we should pray diligently for the church rather than working with the devil against it.

I remember watching the inauguration of John F. Kennedy. He stood in his overcoat on the steps of the Capitol that cold January morning, the heat of his voice making steam in the air, as he stated so eloquently: "Ask not what your country can do for you but rather ask what you can do for your country." So instead of asking, "What has the church done for me lately," I should ask, "What have I done for God's church lately?"

"Church relationship is not a light matter. Every believer should be whole-hearted in his attachment to the church of God. <u>Its prosperity should be his first interest</u>. Unless he feels under sacred obligations to make his connection with the people of God a blessing to the church rather than to himself, the church can do far better without him" *(Signs of the Times,* September 1, 1888).

Forget about the scroungy old dog that you may want to kick and get away from. Think of the church as Jesus sees it. Remember that the Laodicean church becomes the church triumphant!

John, while writing his great revelation of Jesus Christ, saw the church at the very end and wrote, "And I heard, as it were, the voice of a great multitude, as the sound of many waters and as the sound of mighty thunderings, saying, 'Alleluia! For the Lord God Omnipotent reigns! Let us be glad and rejoice and give Him glory, for the marriage of the Lamb has come, <u>and His wife has made herself ready</u>.'

"And to her it was granted to be arrayed in fine linen, clean and bright, for the fine linen is the righteous acts of the saints. Then he said to me, 'Write: "Blessed are those who are called to the marriage supper of the Lamb!"'" (Revelation 19:6-9).

We are all invited! Aren't you getting excited?

Every year a day or two before the fourth Thursday in November our family takes its annual journey down to Tennessee for Thanksgiving. We take the 495 beltway around Washington, D.C., and then take I-66 west to I-81 and the Shenandoah Valley. We will stay on I-81 south all the way through Virginia and on into Tennessee. Then we pick up I-40 for the last few miles toward Knoxville. Grand mommy's exit is 402. It is usually close to midnight before we get there, if the traffic isn't too bad. But she leaves the light on for us. . . . You really haven't had Thanksgiving dinner till you've had it at Grand mommy's. I wouldn't miss it for anything, except for the marriage supper of the Lamb! Then the church will be clean and bright, a glorious church, not having spot or wrinkle—holy and without blemish" (Ephesians 5:25-27).

I plan to be a part of the church from now on and until that awsome day. We are headed to the great supper—the marriage supper of the Lamb! He has left the lights on for us. . . . We can almost see the lights of home!

Although there are evils existing in the church, and will be until the very end, it is still God's church and He has big plans for it. So let's not stand off to the side and take potshots at the church and criticize the preachers and withhold our tithes and indulge in all kinds of other craziness.

"The church, enfeebled and defective, needing to be reproved, warned, and counseled, is the only object upon the earth upon which Christ bestows His supreme regard" *(Testimonies to Ministers,* p. 46).

And so Jesus stands today holding the church close to His heart, like the old woman and her pitiful dog; and He says, "In spite of your fleas, your mange, your bad breath and all—I love you!"

And He says to the world and to all the skeptics out there, "LOVE ME, LOVE MY CHURCH!"

CHAPTER 17

The Overcomers

Heaven is an awesome place. I might try to describe it for you, but, of course it is not possible for human thoughts and realities to come close to its transcendence. The Bible says, "Eye has not seen, nor ear heard, nor have entered into the heart of man the things which God has prepared for those who love Him" (1 Corinthians 2:9). The capital city—now in heaven, and then of a recreated earth, the New Jerusalem—is also beyond adequate description, though we are given a pen picture of the city in Revelation 21.

In that same chapter Jesus describes who will enter heaven and have a home in the glorious city. "He who overcomes shall inherit all things, and I will be his God and he shall be My son" (Revelation 21:7). In addition to the beauty of that place, there is no pain, no death, no crying, no heartache, no separation from friends and loved ones, no stress, no debt, no "natural disasters," no wars, no suffering, no starvation, no heart attacks, no cancer. In short, all that troubles us here will pass away! None of it has a part in that new land. But best of all we will enjoy the companionship of Jesus and the angels. It will be an atmosphere of peace, joy, love, understanding, growing, and learning. All this and more is the promised inheritance of the overcomer.

Promises to the Overcomer

Later on we will examine the profile of an overcomer. We will look at the "how-to's" in becoming one of the exultant citizens of the New Jerusalem. Only overcomers will be translated to heaven. Accordingly, all of the rewards of the righteous will be theirs. The following verses paint a picture:

"To him who overcomes <u>I will give to eat of the tree of life,</u> which is in the midst of the Paradise of God" (Revelation 2:7).

"He who overcomes <u>shall not be hurt by the second death</u>" (Revelation 2:11).

"To him who overcomes <u>I will give some of the hidden manna to eat. And I will give him a white stone, and on the stone a new name written which no one knows except him who receives it</u>" (Revelation 2:17).

"He who overcomes <u>shall be clothed in white garments, and I will not blot out his name from the Book of Life; but I will confess his name before My Father and before His angels</u>" (Revelation 3:5).

"He who overcomes, <u>I will make him a pillar in the temple of My God, and he shall go out no more. And I will write on him the name of My God and the name of the city of My God, the New Jerusalem, which comes down out of heaven from My God. And I will write on him My new name</u>" (Revelation 3:12).

"To him who overcomes <u>I will grant to sit with Me on My throne, as I also overcame and sat down with My Father on His throne</u>" (Revelation 3:21).

These verses are all written in red in my Bible. They are promises from Jesus! There are also a number of statements from the Spirit of Prophecy that tell of the reward of the overcomers.

"<u>The glories that await the faithful overcomer are beyond any description</u>. The Lord will greatly honor and exalt His faithful ones. They shall grow like the cedar, and the comprehension will be certainly increasing. And at every advanced stage of knowledge <u>their anticipation will fall far beneath the reality</u>" *(The Upward Look,* p. 151).

Though it is impossible for us to fully comprehend the beauty and glory of heaven, we can by faith, at least partially visualize the reward of the faithful. " 'This is the victory that overcometh the world, even our faith' [1 John 5:4]. It is faith that enables us to look beyond the present, with its burdens and cares, to the great hereafter, where all that now perplexes us shall be made plain. Faith sees Jesus standing as our Mediator at the right hand of God. Faith beholds the mansions that Christ has gone to prepare for those who love Him. Faith sees the robe and crown prepared for the overcomer, and hears the song of the redeemed" *(Gospel Workers,* pp. 259, 260).

The overcomer's reward is not <u>just</u> eternal life. It is eternal life <u>with Jesus</u>. Eternal life with no devil to tempt us. It sounds almost too good to be true—eternal bliss. A life where we begin again living a new creation. When writing to the youth of the church, Ellen White stated, "An eternal weight of glory awaits the overcomer. <u>If we gain heaven, we gain everything</u>. Shall we not put away sin, and let Christ abide in our hearts by faith? Not until we have the mind of Christ shall we be like Him, and see Him as He is. <u>When the warfare is ended, and we have gained the crown of immortality, the harp of God, the palm branch of victory, and wear the white robe of Christ's righteousness, we shall say</u>, **Heaven is cheap enough**" *(The Youth's Instructor,* January 11, 1900).

Whose heart does not warm to such promises! Trials, heartache, and delay all seem less important as we read and think on them: "If you walk with Jesus here in humble obedience, you will share His triumph and His joy. The shades of darkness will soon pass away; the morning cometh; the conflict is well-nigh ended. <u>There is a crown of life laid up for every one who has been a partaker with Christ in His suffering. The imagination in its most exalted flight cannot picture the glorious destiny that awaits the overcomer</u>" *(Manuscript Releases,* vol. 14, p. 16).

The Struggle to Overcome

The expression used in many of the verses quoted above is "He who overcomes." This clearly indicates that there is something for us to overcome. "He that overcometh (<u>his own inherited and culti-vated tendencies</u>), [words in parenthesis supplied by Ellen White in the original] the same shall be clothed in white raiment; and I will not blot out his name out of the book of life; but I will confess his name before My Father, and before His angels" *(Manuscript Releases,* vol. 19, p. 384).

The inherited and cultivated tendencies to sin are so hard for us to conquer. Yes, some of our weaknesses come from inherited ten-dencies. And in other things we have consciously developed a habit or craving which has a hold on us. Both aspects are covered in the need to overcome. These things <u>must</u> be overcome. Satan opposes our efforts to advance in the Christian pathway—but we have the many promises of God's Word to encourage us and "the Lord has pledged His word that in every effort toward righteousness He will help us" *(The Youth's Instructor,* September 1, 1896).

"Each one will have a close struggle to overcome sin in his own heart. This is at times a very painful and discouraging work; because we see the deformities in our character, [and] we keep looking at them, when we should look to Jesus and put on the robe of righteousness. Everyone who enters the pearly gates of the city of God will enter there as a conqueror, and his greatest conquest will have been the conquest of self" *(Testimonies for the Church,* vol. 9, pp. 182, 183).

The answer to every problem is Jesus. He provides the power for victory. Accordingly, overcomers look to Jesus for strength. "We are to exert every energy of the soul in the work of overcoming, <u>and to look to Jesus for strength to do what we cannot do of ourselves.</u> No sin can be tolerated in those who shall walk with Christ in white. The filthy garments are to be removed, and Christ's robe of righteousness is to be placed upon us. <u>By repentance and faith we are enabled to render obedience to all the commandments of God</u>, and are found without blame before Him" *(ibid.,* vol. 5, p. 472).

The Hereditary and Cultivated Tendencies to Evil

When God's Spirit comes into our hearts we will naturally desire to overcome our most deep-seated sins. But so many try and try and seem to fail. Is there any hope for those with problems with alcohol, tobacco, drug dependency, dishonesty, debauchery, an appetite for too much or forbidden foods, homosexual inclinations? The answer is yes! Accordingly, "Never should we lower the standard of righteousness in order to accommodate inherited or cultivated tendencies to wrong-doing. We need to understand that imperfection of character is sin. <u>All righteous attributes of character dwell in God as a perfect, harmonious whole, and everyone who receives Christ as a personal Saviour is privileged to possess these attributes</u>" *(Christ's Object Lessons,* p. 330).

Let me be very plain. The way to deal with sin is not to make excuses for it but to overcome it by the power of God. Yes, many inherited and cultivated habits are well nigh impossible for us to overcome. But with God—all things are possible! Surely the Creator can recreate a clean heart and mind! (see Matthew 19:26). "<u>Those who put their trust in Christ are not to be enslaved by any hereditary or cultivated</u>

habit or tendency. Instead of being held in bondage to the lower nature, they are to rule every appetite and passion. God has not left us to battle with evil in our finite strength. **Whatever may be our inherited or cultivated tendencies to wrong, we can overcome through the power that He is ready to impart**" *(The Ministry of Healing, p. 175).* What a promise! And there are so many more like this one.

"We are on test and trial. Satan is playing the game of life for our soul. No matter what may be our inherited or cultivated tendencies to wrong, we can overcome through the power that God gives. The Holy Spirit is our helper" *(Manuscript Releases, vol. 18, p. 139).*

"Those who through an intelligent understanding of the Scriptures view the cross aright, those who truly believe in Jesus, have a sure foundation for their faith. They have that faith which works by love and purifies the soul from all its hereditary and cultivated imperfections" *(Testimonies for the Church, vol. 6, p. 238).*

Heaven Is Worth Dying For

What if I have such a terrible addiction to sin that when I decide to terminate this activity the stress on my body could actually kill me? For some alcoholics and other drug addicts, this can almost be the case—withdrawal itself seems life-threatening. I found a very interesting statement on this very question. "No amount of money can buy a single victory over the temptations of Satan. But that which money is valueless to obtain, which is integrity, determined effort, and moral power, will, through the name of Christ, obtain noble victories upon the point of appetite. What if the conflict should cost man even his life? What if the slaves to these vices do really die in the struggle to free themselves from the controlling power of appetite? They die in a good cause. And if the victory be gained at the cost of human life, it is not too dearly earned if the victor can come up in the first resurrection, and have the overcomer's reward" *(Review and Herald, March 18, 1975).*

Jesus works through the Holy Spirit to give us the victory over every sin. "In describing to His disciples the office work of the Holy Spirit, Jesus sought to inspire them with the joy and hope that inspired His own heart. He rejoiced because of the abundant help He had provided for His church. The Holy Spirit was the highest of all gifts that He could solicit from His Father for the exaltation of His people. The

Spirit was to be given as a regenerating agent, and <u>without this the sacrifice of Christ would have been of no avail</u>. The power of evil had been strengthening for centuries, and the submission of men to this satanic captivity was amazing. <u>Sin could be resisted and overcome only through the mighty agency of the Third Person of the Godhead, who would come with no modified energy, but in the fullness of divine power. It is the Spirit that makes effectual what has been wrought out by the world's Redeemer. It is by the Spirit that the heart is made pure. Through the Spirit the believer becomes a partaker of the divine nature</u>. **Christ has given His Spirit as a divine power to overcome all hereditary and cultivated tendencies to evil, and to impress His own character upon His church"** *(The Desire of Ages,* p. 671).

Amazing and visible changes in the life of the overcomer will give tangible evidence of the power of the Holy Spirit in the life of the believer. Those who are restored, restore God's law (Isaiah 58:12). "One of the strongest evidences that the new birth has taken place is that the new-born soul is not self-centered" *(Signs of the Times,* November 30, 1891). People notice a change in our words, actions, and interests. Men who were formerly rough and coarse become humble and teachable.

Yes, God's power is available, but we must seek for it. John and Judas represent the different reactions to contact with Jesus and truth. Both of these men had the same opportunities to study and follow the Divine Pattern. They both had serious defects of character when they first came to Jesus. And they both had access to the divine grace that transforms the heart. But while one in humility was learning from Jesus, the other showed that he was a hearer but not a doer. John died to self and overcame sin, and was sanctified through the truth. Judas resisted the transforming power of God and became trapped in bondage to Satan.

"There may be marked defects in the character; evil temper, irritable disposition, envy, and jealousy may bear sway; yet if the man becomes a true disciple of Jesus, the power of divine grace will make him a new creature. Christ's love transforms, sanctifies him. <u>But when persons profess to be Christians, and their religion does not make them better men and better women in all the relations of life,—living representatives of Christ in disposition and character,—they are none of His</u>" *(Review and Herald,* February 15, 1881).

Two particular areas in the life of the overcomer bear clear testimony to the power of God's transforming power. They are the removal of racial prejudice and the ability to get along with fellow members. These two areas trouble God's people today. A spirit of selfishness and pride perpetuates these tendencies—they can only change by the power of God. With regard to racial prejudice, which seems to just come "naturally" to many people—because of their hereditary and cultivated tendencies to evil—we are told: "As the truth is brought to bear upon the minds of both colored and white people, as souls are thoroughly converted, they will become new men and women in Christ Jesus. Christ says, 'A new heart also will I give you,' and that new heart bears the divine image. Those who are converted among the white people will experience a change in their sentiments. The prejudice which they have inherited and cultivated toward the colored race will die away. Those who are converted among the colored race will be cleansed from sin, [and] will wear the robe of Christ's righteousness, which has been woven in the loom of heaven. Both white and colored people must enter into the path of obedience through the same way" (The Southern Work, p. 22). So ingrained and subtle is prejudice that sometimes it is hard to tell superficially whether or not one has racial prejudice in his life. We should each pray that God will give us a loving, Christlike attitude toward all races and toward all who are "different" or differ from us.

The power and wisdom of God is so evident in the transformation of the disciples. They were a group of men whom most of us would not have chosen as leaders. Yet by their association with Jesus they were all, save one, transformed into dedicated and committed followers of Jesus. In discussing the differences and the transformation of the disciples in the chapter in Desire of Ages, on their ordination, Ellen White noted: "The apostles differed widely in habits and disposition. There were the publican, Levi-Matthew, and the fiery zealot Simon, the uncompromising hater of the authority of Rome; the generous, impulsive Peter, and the mean-spirited Judas; Thomas, truehearted, yet timid and fearful, Philip, slow of heart, and inclined to doubt, and the ambitious, outspoken sons of Zebedee, with their brethren. These were brought together, with their different faults, all with inherited and cultivated tendencies to evil; but in and through Christ they were to dwell in the family of God, learning to become one in faith, in doctrine, in spirit.

They would have their tests, their grievances, their differences of opinion; but while Christ was abiding in the heart, there could be no dissension. His love would lead to love for one another; the lessons of the Master would lead to the harmonizing of all differences, bringing the disciples into unity, till they would be of one mind and one judgment. Christ is the great center, and they would approach one another just in proportion as they approached the center" *(The Desire of Ages,* p. 296).

That same harmonizing power is available in God's church today. "As the disciples were brought together, each with different faults, some inherited or cultivated tendency to evil, so in our church relations we find men and women whose characters are defective; not one of us is perfect. But in Christ, and through Christ, we are to dwell in the family of God, learning to become one in faith, in doctrine, in spirit, that at last we may be received into our eternal habitation. We shall have our tests, our grievances, our differences of opinion; but if Christ is abiding in the heart of each, there can be no dissension. The love of Christ will lead to love of one another, and the lessons of the Master will harmonize all differences, bringing us into unity, till we shall be of one mind and one judgment. Strife for supremacy will cease, and no one will be disposed to glory over another, but we shall esteem others better than ourselves, and so be built up into a spiritual temple for the Lord" *(The Signs of the Times,* April 20, 1891). There is good evidence that God puts us together with others so that we can learn to practice our spiritual/social skills.

This is the "how-to" part of salvation. If our experience with God doesn't have practical results and benefits, what good is it? Jesus tells us clearly that "without Me you can do nothing." And Paul exalts that "I can do all things through Christ." But exactly how does the process work? Here are some inspired tips that will facilitate our experience of victory.

1. Make a decision. "By faith grasp God's promises and determine that you will be Christians here below while preparing for translation" *(Counsels to Teachers,* p. 548).

2. Make your preparation for heaven a matter of prayer. "Perseverance in prayer has been made a condition to receiving. We must pray always if we would grow in faith and experience" *(Steps to Christ,* p. 97).

3. Open your heart to God. "The work of your salvation and mine depends wholly upon ourselves, for it rests with us to accept the provision that has been made for us. God has done everything for us that a God can do. . . . When the heart is opened to Christ, the Holy Spirit will work in it with mighty, renewing power" *(The Upward Look,* p. 25).

4. Accept Christ as your Advocate and Intercessor. "We who have fallen through the transgression of the law of God have an Advocate with the Father, Jesus Christ the righteous. The way is open for everyone to prepare himself for the second appearing of Jesus Christ, that at His appearing we may be vindicated, having put away all evil, and having overcome through the cleansing blood of Christ. Through the intercession of Christ, the image of God is renewed in mind, and heart, and character" *(ibid.,* p. 64).

5. We must be born again. "Whatever his calling or profession, whatever his rank or station in life, that man must realize in himself the truth of the words spoken to Nicodemus: 'Verily, verily, I say unto you Ye must be born again.' 'Except a man be born again, he can not see the kingdom of God'" *(Signs of the Times,* March 11, 1897).

6. Take hold of God's love. "If man by faith takes hold of the divine love of God, he becomes a new creature through Christ Jesus. The world is overcome, human nature is subdued, and Satan is vanquished" *(ibid.,* November 15, 1883).

7. Be regular in Bible study. "The creative energy that called the worlds into existence is in the word of God. This word imparts power; it begets life. Every command is a promise; accepted by the will, received into the soul, it brings with it the life of the Infinite One. It transforms the nature and re-creates the soul in the image of God" *(Education,* p. 126). "Your word I have hidden in my heart, that I might not sin against You" (Psalm 119:11).

8. Follow the example of Jesus. "The holy life and character of Christ is a faithful example.

(1) His confidence in His heavenly Father was unlimited.

(2) His obedience and submission were unreserved and perfect.

(3) He came not to be ministered unto, but to minister to others.

(4) He came not to do His own will, but the will of Him that sent Him.

(5) In all things He submitted Himself to Him that judgeth righteously. From the lips of the Saviour of the world were heard these words: 'I can of Mine own self do nothing'" *(Testimonies for the Church,* vol. 3, p. 107).

9. Get involved in the work of God. "The only way to grow in grace is to be disinterestedly doing the very work which Christ has enjoined upon us—to engage, to the extent of our ability, in helping and blessing those who need the help we can give them. Strength comes by exercise; activity is the very condition of life" *(Steps to Christ,* p. 80).

10. Have regular morning worship. "Every morning dedicate yourself, soul, body, and spirit to God. Establish habits of devotion and trust more and more in your Saviour" *(In Heavenly Places,* p. 227).

11. Be prepared to fight. "Each one has a personal battle to fight. Each must win his own way through struggles and discouragements. Those who decline the struggle lose the strength and joy of victory. No one, not even God, can carry us to heaven unless we make the necessary effort on our part" *(Testimonies for the Church,* vol. 5, p. 345).

12. Get involved personally. Cooperate with God. "Let no man present the idea that man has little or nothing to do in the great work of overcoming; for God does nothing for man without his cooperation. Neither say that after you have done all you can on your part, Jesus will help you. Christ has said, 'Without Me ye can do nothing' (John 15:5). From first to last man is to be a laborer together with God. Unless the Holy Spirit works upon the human heart, at every step we shall stumble and fall. Man's efforts alone are nothing but worthlessness; but cooperation with Christ means a victory" *(Selected Messages,* vol. 1, p. 381).

13. Trust in God. "Genuine faith appropriates the righteousness of Christ, and the sinner is made an overcomer with Christ; for he is made a partaker of the divine nature, and thus divinity and humanity are combined" *(Review and Herald,* July 1, 1890).

14. Practice temperance. By God's grace, gain control of yourself. "All who would perfect holiness in the fear of God must learn the lessons of temperance and self-control. The appetites and passions must be held in subjection to the higher powers of the mind. This self-discipline is essential to that mental strength and spiritual insight which will enable us to understand and practice the sacred truths of God's word. <u>For this reason temperance finds its place in the work of preparation for Christ's second coming</u>" *(The Desire of Ages,* p. 101). "Christ fought the battle upon the point of appetite, and came off victorious; and <u>we also can conquer through strength derived from Him</u>. Who will enter in through the gates into the city?—Not those who declare that they cannot break the force of appetite" *(Counsels on Diet and Foods,* pp. 169, 170).

15. Link your humanity with Christ's divinity. "Humanity and divinity must be linked together in the experience of every overcomer. In our weakness we are to accept Christ's power" *(Signs of the Times,* August 14, 1901). "<u>It is by combining divine power with his human strength that man becomes an overcomer</u>" *(The Youth's Instructor,* December 28, 1899). "You must have the power of the Holy Spirit, else you cannot be an overcomer" *(This Day With God,* p. 11).

16. Separate from the world. "Here is a grand promise: 'Come out from among them and be ye separate.' Separate from what? The inclinations of the world, their tastes, their habits; the fashions, the pride, and the customs of the world. 'Come out from among them, and be ye separate, and touch not the unclean, <u>and I will receive you</u>.' In making this move, in showing that we are not in harmony with the world, the promise of God is ours. <u>He does not say perhaps I will receive you, but 'I will receive you</u>.' It is a positive promise. You have a surety that you will be accepted of God. Then in separating from the world you will be accepted of God" *(Signs of the Times,* January 31, 1878).

17. Don't wait. Decide today to be an overcomer. Great and significant events are already taking place in the world. God is at work preparing the way for Christ's return. "The third angel's message is swelling into a loud cry, and you must not feel at liberty to neglect the present duty, and still entertain the idea that at some future time you will be the recipients of great blessings, when without any effort on your part a wonderful revival will take place. **Today** you are to give yourselves to God that He may make you vessels unto honor, and meet for His service. **Today** you are to give yourself to God, that you may be emptied of self, emptied of envy, jealousy, evil surmising, strife, everything that shall be dishonoring to God. **Today** you are to have your vessel purified that it may be ready for the heavenly due, ready for the showers of the latter rain; <u>for the latter rain will come, and the blessing of God will fill every soul that is purified from every defilement</u>. **It is our work today** to yield our souls to Christ, that we may be fitted for the time of refreshing from the presence of the Lord—fitted for the baptism of the Holy Spirit" *(God's Amazing Grace,* p. 205).

18. Pray for the latter rain. The latter rain will be given to those who are seeking to be overcomers and it will put the finishing touches on the preparation for translation. "Those who come up to every point, and stand every test, and overcome, be the price what it may, have heeded the counsel of the true Witness, and <u>they will be fitted for translation by the latter rain</u>" *(Spiritual Gifts,* vol. 4B, p. 34).

19. Don't be discouraged. "Whatever may come to tempt you, bear in mind the fact that with every temptation, Christ has made a way of escape. You should not give up to discouragement. Bear in mind the fact that Jesus is at your right hand, and that He helps you. You may trust Him implicitly, irrespective of what others may think of you or how others may treat you. <u>You will become an overcomer through the blood of the Lamb and the word of your testimony</u>" *(Manuscript Releases,* vol. 19, p. 203).

20. Remember that you have supernatural help. "The <u>angels</u> of God will be around the tempted soul who is striving for the victory. His determination, his importunity, will bring to him the necessary strength and grace" *(Signs of the Times,* July 18, 1895). "Seek to reach a high standard. . . . <u>Heavenly angels will help you, and more than that, Christ will help you</u>. The Prince of life is more interested than anyone else in your salvation. . . . <u>Be determined that opposite your names in the books of heaven shall be written</u> the word 'Overcomer'" *(The Upward Look,* p. 47).

The following statement is in essence a short summary of the tips for the overcomer. Above all it should help us realize the greatness and goodness of God.

"<u>When you have done all that you can on your part, you may in faith ask help of the Captain of your salvation, and **He will bring divine aid to be combined with human effort;** and He will bind on your brow the laurels of the conqueror, just as though you had yourself wrought out the victory.</u>** And remember, it is the overcomer that enters the portals of the kingdom of glory; it is the overcomer that wears the crown of life, and stands with the blood-washed throng around the great white throne" *(Signs of the Times,* October 22, 1885). Did you note that phrase "just as though you had yourself wrought out the victory"? Another gift from Jesus! Let me diagram this concept along with the justification model.

Justification model:

"The gift of God is eternal life in Christ Jesus our Lord" (Romans 6:23).

The result of justification is—Just as if you had never sinned!

Sanctification model:

"But thanks be to God, who gives us the victory through our Lord Jesus Christ" (1 Corinthians 15:57). He **gives** us the victory.

The result of sanctification is—Just as though you had yourself wrought out the victory!

The bottom line is that both justification and sanctification are gifts from God, but He gives us the credit! Praise the Lord!

The Close of Probation

Probation means "the act of proving." It is used in this sense when referring to the initial period of employment, for example, during which a new, transferred, or promoted employee must prove or show that he is capable of performing the required duties of the job or position before he will be considered as permanently employed in that position. Sometimes students with less than good grades are accepted into college on "scholastic probation." Under this arrangement they are allowed to prove themselves during a school term.

From the standpoint of our criminal justice system, probation is the status of a convicted person who is allowed his freedom after a conviction subject to the condition that for a stipulated period he shall conduct himself in a manner approved by a special officer to whom he must make periodic reports. Probation is considered an act of grace and clemency which may be granted by the trial court to a seemingly deserving defendant whereby such defendant may escape the extreme rigors of the penalty imposed by law for the offense of which he stands convicted.

J. N. Andrews, that well-known Seventh-day Adventist pioneer, was a leading scholar, administrator, and missionary. He described the probation of mankind in the realm of the great controversy this way: "When God created man, He placed him upon probation as He had previously placed the angels. After a brief period, man sinned against God, and brought upon himself the sentence of death. But because there were some mitigating circumstances in the case of Adam, for he did not sin against so great light as did the angels, God saw fit to give to man a second probation,—a mercy which was not extended to the angels.

"We know that this second probation of the human race will end at the day of Judgment, so that man will be judged at the time originally appointed for the judgment of the angels [see Jude 6; 2 Peter 2:4]. And we have reason to believe that if the human race had not sinned against God, the probation under which man was first placed would have terminated at the same time that his second probation will terminate; namely, at the day of Judgment. His first probation was to determine the question of whether he would be faithful to God in preserving his innocence; **his second probation is under circumstances much more difficult, for he must recover his lost innocence, and in the same trial must prove his fidelity**" (J. N. Andrews, *The Review and Herald,* July 17, 1883).

In every type of probation there is a stipulated period or term. For example, a new employee may be "on probation" for 90 days. A student may be on probation for one academic quarter. In all types of probation, if the one on probation has successfully completed the requirements, the close or end of probation is good news. In the case of a convicted criminal he is set free. On the other hand, if he has violated the terms of his probation he will likely go back to jail and "serve" his sentence.

From the perspective of the scope of this book and our understanding of the great controversy, for the born-again Christian, who has accepted the substitutionary death of Christ on his behalf and has been transformed by the Holy Spirit, the close of probation is good news indeed. He has been sealed for eternal life! The unrepentant and unregenerated person must serve his own sentence—and the wages of sin is and always has been death. Accordingly, for the unsaved person, the close of probation is quite frightful.

Though the concept is evident in Scripture, the word "probation" does not occur in the King James Version of the Bible. We do know, however, from the Bible outline of events that the years of probation are closing fast. The time of testing is almost over.

Ellen White describes the probationary state in the following manner. "Those who transgress the law of God must suffer the penalty of transgression; but by repentance of sin, by faith in Christ, who, innocent, suffered the punishment for the guilty, the sinner may be pardoned, and through the merit of Christ, may have another probation in which he may have opportunity to form a character like Christ's character. No one will enter the abodes of bliss who has not been tested and proved; for it must be demonstrated that those who enter heaven will be obedient to its laws, and in harmony with its government. If through the merits of Christ, we develop a character in submission to the will and way of God in this world, our names will stand registered in the Lamb's book of life. Every soul is now deciding his own destiny, proving whether he will be worthy to unite with the saints in light, or unworthy of an entrance into the city of God—fit only to remain with the wicked and to perish with them" (The Youth's Instructor, January 19, 1893).

The probationary period demonstrates both the justice and mercy of God. In fact, "The more we study the attributes of the character of God as revealed in Christ, the more we see that justice has been sustained in the sacrifice that met the penalty of the law, and that mercy has been provided in the only begotten Son, who bore the penalty of the law in the sinner's place, in order that man might have another probation, another opportunity to be obedient to the law of God's government, that it might be made manifest who could be trusted to become members of the Lord's family, children of the heavenly king. Those who are obedient to the law of the government of God while in this brief probation, amid all the counter-influences of Satanic agencies, will be pronounced in heaven loyal children of the Lord of Hosts" (Review and Herald, March 9, 1897).

When God set the probationary period before the Flood, He said,

"My Spirit shall not strive with man forever, for he is indeed flesh; yet his days shall be one hundred and twenty years" (Genesis 6:3). And at the end of the probationary period for the final generation God says, "He who is unjust, let him be unjust still; he who is filthy, let him be filthy still; he who is righteous, let him be righteous still; he who is holy, let him be holy still. And behold, I am coming quickly, and My reward is with Me, to give every one according to his work" (Revelation 22:11, 12). After quoting this verse Ellen White adds, "The destiny of all will be decided. A few, yes, only a few, of the vast number who people the earth will be saved unto life eternal, while the masses who have not perfected their souls in obeying the truth will be appointed to the second death" *(Testimonies for the Church,* vol. 2, p. 401).

Satan knows that time is short. He sees that the period of probation is almost ended. His strategy for many is to keep us occupied with the cares of this life, entranced with the things of the world. Thus deceived and deluded, the close of probation will catch many people unready.

Now Is the Time to Prepare

"Behold, now is the accepted time; behold, now is the day of salvation" (2 Corinthians 6:2). "There will be no future probation in which to prepare for eternity. It is in this life that we are to put on the robe of Christ's righteousness. This is our only opportunity to form characters for the home which Christ has made ready for those who obey His commandments" *(Christ's Object Lessons,* p. 319).

"Now is our day of probation, and we are now to perfect characters that will stand the test of the judgment. When Christ comes, there is to be no change of character; this mortal shall put on immortality, and this corruption shall put on incorruption; and those who are alive and remain upon the earth will be caught up to meet the Lord in the air, if their characters are blameless and pure. Transformation of character must take place during the precious hours of probation" *(The Signs of the Times,* August 29, 1892).

The devil deceives men into comforting themselves that there will be another time of probation after the second coming of Christ during an age of peace when all the world will be converted. This, of course, is a dangerous error, and many will be lost as a result. It is obvious to students of Scripture that probation must close before the Second Coming, because when Jesus returns "His reward is with Him." Before His coming, then, the character of every person's work will have been determined.

Study the great preponderance of the evidence on this topic of readiness and one point keeps coming up. Those who are ready for heaven will be different from those who are not planning to go there. By their fruits you will know them is not just a cliché, but a defining criteria for the overcomer. If we are Christians, indeed, then we will act Christlike. A good way for a self-test is to ask ourselves "How do we treat our family members? What do those who know us best see in our lives?" If we find ourselves deficient in the area of family relations, then God is telling us we need to depend on Him for more love in our lives.

"Our words and actions in the home bear testimony to our true character, and they are recorded in the books of heaven. The daily acts of life tell the measure and mold of our disposition and character. Where there is a lack of home religion, a profession of faith is valueless. Then let no unkind words fall from those who compose the home circle. Make the atmosphere fragrant with tender thoughtfulness of others. Only those will enter heaven who in probationary time have formed a character that breathes a heavenly influence. The saint in heaven must first be a saint on earth" *(The Signs of the Times,* November 14, 1892).

The Unspeakable Gift

Much more wonderful than a miracle of physical healing is the miracle wrought when a person becomes a child of God—an overcomer. We are told that there is joy in heaven over one sinner that repents! Jesus tackled the human problem—He was tempted on every point that we are tempted on. And for power to resist He spent whole nights in prayer and communion with His Father. He did this for us! He didn't leave this earth until He had both forged the way by example and then promised Power to make it possible for every person to live a life of faith and obedience—to develop a Christlike character.

We all know that Jesus is coming soon. Time to act, to prepare, is short. The hours of probation are almost over. Let's determine that we will get ready for the Lord's return. "Seek the Lord while He may be found, call upon Him while He is near. Let the wicked forsake his way, and the unrighteous man his thoughts; let him return to the Lord, and

He will have mercy on him; and to our God, for He will abundantly pardon" (Isaiah 55:6, 7).

The Overcomer's Motto

This is something to write in your Bible and in your day planner. Read it out loud every morning:

"God helping me, I am determined to be an overcomer. Through Christ I shall obtain the victory. Then His joy will remain in me, and my joy [will] be full. I will talk of His goodness; I will tell of His power. Through a dependence upon the divinity of Christ, I may overcome as He overcame" *(Sermons and Talks,* vol. 2, p. 294).

Our conversion is a powerful testimony. A transformed life is a positive testimony that the conversion is more than profession—it is the indication of God's power to save. "If our profession of faith is sustained by heartfelt piety, it will be a means of good; for thereby souls will be influenced to comply with the terms of salvation. God designs that His grace should be manifest in the believer, that through the Christlike character of individual members, the church may become the light of the world" *(Fundamentals of Christian Education,* p. 202).

We are given a pen picture of the work of God as it circles the earth. The message of victory in Christ is the good news that will appeal to mankind. "The message of the renewing power of God's grace will be carried to every country and clime, until the truth shall belt the world. Of the number of them that shall be sealed will be those who have come from every nation and kindred and tongue and people" *(Maranatha,* p. 261).

We are now a part of the church militant. True, we are facing a world that is almost totally given over to Satan. But the day is coming when the battle will have been fought and the victory won. Then the will of God will be done on earth as it is in heaven. All the creation of God will be a happy, united family. All will be clothed in the garments of praise and thanksgiving—the robe of Christ's righteousness. All nature, as well, in its unsurpassed beauty, will be a constant praise to God. The world will be covered with the light of heaven. And the years will move on, not in sadness, but in gladness!

So let's grow in the grace and knowledge of our Lord and Saviour Jesus Christ. To Him be the glory both now and forever!

CHAPTER 18

The Enoch Factor

To our knowledge, only two people born on this earth have left this planet alive—being translated without seeing death. They are the Old Testament era heroes of faith—Enoch and Elijah. The Bible records, "And Enoch walked with God; and he was not, for God took him." "By faith Enoch was translated so that he did not see death, 'and was not found, because God had translated him'; for before he was taken he had this testimony, that he pleased God" (Genesis 5:24; Hebrews 11:5). And regarding Elijah we have an eyewitness. "Then it happened, as they [Elijah and Elisha] continued on and talked, that suddenly a chariot of fire appeared with horses of fire, and separated the two of them; and Elijah went up by a whirlwind into heaven. Now Elisha saw it, and he cried out, 'My father, my father, the chariot of Israel and its horsemen!' So he saw him no more. And he took hold of his own clothes and tore them in two pieces" (2 Kings 2:11, 12). Enoch and Elijah are the firstfruits—the proof that translation is a reality.

Enoch looked down through time and saw and then predicted the Second Coming as recorded in Jude 14. At that time, at the end of the world, a large number will be translated—alive from earth to heaven.

The translation of the two Old Testament characters is corroborated by the New Testament. Enoch's translation is mentioned by Paul in the faith chapter—Hebrews 11. And Elijah's translation is verified by his presence at the transfiguration recorded in Matthew 17:3 and Mark 9:4. At that time the disciples reported that they saw Moses and Elijah talking with Jesus.

Many today, even in the remnant church, give only lip service to this idea of leaving earth alive—of being translated. They really do not think that it is possible they will actually see or participate in the event. Many think it would be exciting but actually too good to be true.

This state of mind reminds me of many families I encounter while teaching the biblical Principles of Money Management seminar. I meet many families who are so far in debt with student loans, credit card debt, home mortgages, business debt, back taxes, and the like that they despair of ever getting out of debt. But I am happy to report that many of these families do indeed get out of debt. They do so by following a very simple process: making a decision to become debt-free, and then taking the necessary steps to do so. Obviously, this includes asking for God's promised wisdom and blessing.

In like manner, many of earth's inhabitants will realize by study-ing the Bible's end-time prophecies and comparing them to current events that the end is near. They will make a decision that, whatever it takes, they want to be ready for that great event. They want to be trans-lated from earth to heaven. And the Bible clearly lays out the steps for sanctification and renewal which are the prerequisite for translation.

Learning From Enoch

For nearly 1,000 years Adam lived among men, witnessing all the while the terrible results of sin. He faithfully tried to stem the tide of evil and instruct his descendants in the way of the Lord. Yet there were very few who listened to his counsel. Adam had learned from the Creator the history of Creation, and he himself observed world events for nine centuries. For in those preflood times there were as many as seven generations alive upon the earth at the same time. Accordingly, these had the opportunity of learning from Adam, the first man, of the kindness and love of God and His plan for their redemption. Enoch was one of the few who heeded the counsel of Adam.

"Of Enoch it is written that he lived sixty-five years, and begat a son. After that he walked with God three hundred years. During these earlier years Enoch had loved and feared God and had kept His com-mandments. He was one of the holy line, the preservers of the true faith, the progenitors of the promised seed. From the lips of Adam he had learned the dark story of the Fall, and the cheering one of God's grace as seen in the promise; and he relied upon the Redeemer to come. But after the birth of his son, Enoch reached a higher experience; he was drawn into a closer relationship with God. He realized more fully his own obligations and responsibility as a son of God. And as he saw the child's love for its father, its simple trust in his protection; as he felt the deep, yearning tenderness of his own heart for that first-born son, he learned a precious lesson of that wonderful love of God to men in the gift of His Son, and the confidence which the children of God may repose in their heavenly Father. . . .

"Enoch's walk with God was not in a trance or vision, but in all the duties of his daily life. He did not become a hermit, shutting himself entirely from the world; for he had a work to do for God in the world. In the family and in his intercourse with men, as a husband and father, a friend, a citizen, he was the steadfast, unwavering servant of the Lord" *(Patriarchs and Prophets,* pp. 84, 85).

It seems that it is just human nature for us to get excited about the Second Coming because we realize that it is almost here. But Enoch's faith in God grew stronger and his love for God grew deeper with the passing of centuries!

So what was it about Enoch that fitted him for translation? The Bible tells us. Let's look at the text again. "<u>By faith Enoch was translated</u> so that he did not see death, 'and was not found because God had translated him'; <u>for</u> [because] before his translation he had this testimony, **that <u>he pleased God</u>**" (Hebrews 11:5). So he was translated because he pleased God. What does it mean to please God? The next verse tells us. "But without faith it is impossible to please Him, for he who comes to God must believe that He is, and that He is a rewarder of those who diligently seek Him" (Hebrews 11:6). True faith in God—saving faith—not only believes in God, but believes that <u>He is able</u> to do what He says He will do. Enoch had that kind of faith in God.

But how did Enoch develop the kind of faith to not only believe in God but to believe that God could do what He said He would do? The following quotations give us the answer in no uncertain terms. "Enoch walked with God three hundred years previous to his translation to heaven, and the state of the world was not then more favorable for the perfection of Christian character than it is today. <u>And how did Enoch walk with God?</u> He educated his mind and heart to ever feel that he was in the presence of God, and when in perplexity his prayers would ascend to God to keep him. He refused to take any course that would offend his God. He kept the Lord continually before him. He would pray, 'Teach me Thy way, that I may not err. What is thy pleasure concerning me? What shall I do to honor Thee, my God?' Thus he was constantly shaping his way and course in accordance with God's commandments, and **he had perfect confidence and trust in his heavenly Father, that He would help him.** He had no thought or will of his own; it was all submerged in the will of his Father" *(Sermons and Talks,* vol. 1, p. 32).

A later more concise statement again points to Enoch's devotional life. "It is our privilege today to stand with the light of heaven upon us. It was thus that Enoch walked with God. It was not easier for Enoch to live a righteous life in his day than it is for us at the present time. The world at that time was no more favorable to growth in grace and holiness than it is now, but Enoch devoted time to prayer and communion with God, and this enabled him to escape the corruption that is in the world through lust. **It was his devotion to God that fitted him for translation**" *(Review and Herald,* April 15, 1909).

In closing this section on Enoch, I want to refer to the summation of the story of Enoch in *Patriarchs and Prophets.* The insights and ramifications are awesome.

"By the translation of Enoch the Lord designed to teach an important lesson. There was a danger that men would yield to discouragement, because of the fearful results of Adam's sin. Many were ready to exclaim, 'What profit is it that we have feared the Lord and have kept His ordinances, since a heavy curse is resting upon the race, and death is the portion of us all?' But the instructions which God gave to Adam, and which were repeated by Seth, and exemplified by Enoch, swept away the gloom and darkness, and gave hope to man, that as through Adam came death, so through the promised Redeemer would come life and immortality. Satan was urging upon men the belief that there was no reward for the righteous or punishment for the wicked, and that it was impossible for men to obey the divine statutes. **But in the case of Enoch, God declares 'that He is, and that He is a rewarder of them that diligently seek Him.' Hebrews 11:6. He shows what He will do for those who keep His commandments.** Men were taught that it is possible to obey the law of God; that even while living in the midst of the sinful and corrupt, they were able, by the grace of

God, to resist temptation, and become pure and holy. They saw in his example the blessedness of such a life; and his translation was an evidence of the truth of his prophecy concerning the hereafter, with its reward of joy and glory and immortal life to the obedient, and of condemnation, woe, and death to the transgressor" *(Patriarchs and Prophets,* p. 88). This single paragraph contains the most profound concepts in this entire book.

Our whole discussion of overcoming, preparing for translation, raises many practical questions for the application to our life today in a corrupt and busy world. Here in this next passage, Ellen White underscores the parallel between Enoch's experience and ours if we expect to live to see Christ's return.

"In the midst of a world by its iniquity doomed to destruction, Enoch lived a life of such close communion with God that he was not permitted to fall under the power of death. **The godly character of this prophet represents the state of holiness which must be attained by those who shall be 'redeemed from the earth' (Revelation 14:3) at the time of Christ's second advent.** Then, as in the world before the Flood, iniquity will prevail. Following the promptings of their corrupt hearts and the teachings of a deceptive philosophy, men will rebel against the authority of Heaven. But like Enoch, God's people will seek for purity of heart and conformity to His will, until they shall reflect the likeness of Christ. **Like Enoch, they will warn the world of the Lord's second coming and of the judgments to be visited upon transgression,** and by their holy conversation and example they will condemn the sins of the ungodly. As Enoch was translated to heaven before the destruction of the world by water, so the living righteous will be translated from the earth before its destruction by fire. Says the apostle: 'We shall not all sleep, but we shall be changed, in a moment, in the twinkling of an eye, at the last trump.' 'For the Lord Himself shall descend from heaven with a shout, with the voice of the Archangel, and with the trump of God;' 'the trumpet shall sound, and the dead shall be raised incorruptible, and we shall be changed.' 'The dead in Christ shall rise first: then we which are alive and remain shall be caught up together with them in the clouds, to meet the Lord in the air: and so shall we ever be with the Lord. Wherefore comfort one another with these words.' 1 Corinthians 15:51, 52; 1 Thessalonians 4:16-18" *(ibid.,* pp. 88, 89).

Here we have the basic message of this book and the lessons from the life of Enoch portrayed in just two paragraphs. Consider these points:

Satan is the great deceiver.

He wants us to be lost.

He says there is no reward or punishment and that no one can keep God's law.

The life of Enoch demonstrates that there is a reward and that man can keep God's law in this life while living in a sinful world with the grace and power of God.

There is a preparation necessary before translation.

This can be accomplished by prayer and communion with God in His Word.

There is a job for us in the world.

We have a message of warning regarding the coming judgments and the Second Coming.

We will be leaving here before the final destruction by fire!

Enoch was "the man." The man who believed in God. The man who trusted God. The man who obeyed God. The man who walked with God through a daily devotional life. The man who was not, for God took him.

One additional and very interesting insight regarding preparation for translation becomes evident in the last part of Elijah's ministry. He moved around a lot. Apparently, God did not want him to settle down and become comfortable in this world. Every time Elijah moved again, he asked Elisha to stay behind, but Elisha had been told that if he saw the translation of Elijah he would receive a double portion of his spirit. Accordingly, every time Elijah moved, he gave Elisha the opportunity to stay or turn back. He never did. "As time passed, and Elijah was prepared for translation, so Elisha was prepared to become his successor. And again his faith and resolution were tested. Accompanying Elijah in his round of service, knowing the change soon to come, he was at each place invited by the prophet to turn back. 'Tarry here, I pray thee.' Elijah said: 'for the Lord hath sent me to Bethel.' . . . [But] as often as the invitation to turn back was given, his answer was, 'As the Lord liveth, and as my soul liveth, I will not leave thee.' 2 Kings 2:2" *(Education, p. 59)*.

Why was Elijah moving around a lot just before he was translated? Was it because he was making his farewell visits? Apparently, only

Elisha knew of his impending translation. Here is an interesting insight. "A life of monotony is not the most conducive to spiritual growth. Some can reach the highest standard of spirituality only through a change in the regular order of things. When in His providence God sees that changes are essential for the success of the character building, He disturbs the smooth current of life. He sees that a worker needs to be more closely associated with Him; and to bring this about, He separates him from friends and acquaintances. When He was preparing Elijah for translation, God moved him from place to place, that the prophet might not settle down at ease, and thus fail of gaining spiritual power. And it was God's design that Elijah's influence should be a power to help many souls to gain a wider, more helpful experience" *(Gospel Workers,* pp. 269, 270).

Have we "settled in down here"? Have we become a part of a large "Adventist ghetto"—living close to the Adventist Book Center and the health food store? Maybe God has a move planned so that we can see all the "stuff" we have accumulated—stuff that we don't need. And so we can find the place that He has designated where we are to work for Him. (See *Christ's Object Lessons,* p. 327.)

Elijah was also a man of prayer and devotion to God. (The chapter "The Revival Is Coming" in my book *Sunday's Coming!,* looked at Elijah in some detail.) His experience on Mount Carmel was a high point in the history of Israel. James mentions his power in prayer. "Elijah was a man with a nature like ours, and he prayed earnestly that it would not rain; and it did not rain on the land for three years and six months. And he prayed again, and the heaven gave rain, and the earth produced its fruit" (James 5:17, 18).

Elijah had the same trust and confidence in God as did Enoch. He had developed a Christ-like character by his submission to the will of God. His experience of moving a lot near the end of his life on earth is a unique aspect of his life that is appropriate for us today.

Preparing Children for Translation

We have been counseled to live in the country. Studying that counsel you will very quickly get the picture that we do not leave the cities to "hide." It is largely for the benefit of our families. It is so that we can raise our children away from the noise, the pollution, the violence, and the evil influences of the city. It is so that we can breath fresh air, be in contact with nature, and raise our children in the nurture and admonition of the Lord.

"Let children no longer be exposed to the temptations of the cities that are ripe for destruction. <u>The Lord has sent us warning and counsel to get out of the cities</u>. Then let us make no more investments in the cities. <u>Fathers and mothers, how do you regard the souls of your children? Are you preparing the members of your families for translation into the heavenly courts</u>? Are you preparing them to become members of the royal family? children of the heavenly King? 'What shall it profit a man, if he shall gain the whole world, and lose his own soul?' (Mark 8:36). <u>How will ease, comfort, convenience, compare with the value of the souls of your children</u>?" *(Selected Messages,* vol. 2, p. 355).

Jesus' allusion to the perils of city living is recorded in Luke 17. Discussing the necessary preparation for the Second Coming, He gave a profound warning in just three words: "Remember Lot's wife" (Luke 17:32). Leaving the secure but rugged highlands to his uncle Abraham, Lot decided to "pitch his tent toward Sodom." A big mistake. Living in Sodom, his family became attached to the ways of the world. As a result, he lost his wife and most of his children; and even the two who escaped became the mothers of two idolatrous nations. "How terrible were the results that followed one unwise step! . . . When Lot entered Sodom he fully intended to keep himself free from iniquity and to command his household after him. But he signally failed. The corrupting influences about him had an effect upon his own faith, and his children's connection with the inhabitants of Sodom bound up his interest in a measure with theirs. <u>The result is before us</u>.

"Many are still making a similar mistake. In selecting a home they look more to the temporal advantages they may gain than to the moral and social influences that will surround themselves and their families. They choose a beautiful and fertile country, or remove to some flourishing city, in the hope of securing greater prosperity; <u>but their children are surrounded by temptation</u>, and too often they form associations that are unfavorable to the development of piety and the formation of a right character. <u>The atmosphere of lax morality, of unbelief, of indifference to religious things, has a tendency to counteract the influence of the parents</u>. Examples of rebellion against parental and divine authority are ever before the youth; many form attachments for infidels and unbelievers, and cast in their lot with the enemies of God.

"In choosing a home, God would have us consider, first of all, the moral and religious influences that will surround us and our families. . . . When we voluntarily place ourselves in an atmosphere of worldliness and unbelief, we displease God and drive holy angels from our homes.

"Those who secure for their children worldly wealth and honor at the expense of their eternal interests, will find in the end that these advantages are a terrible loss. Like Lot, many see their children ruined, and barely save their own souls. Their lifework is lost; their life is a sad failure. Had they exercised true wisdom, their children might have had less of worldly prosperity, but they would have made sure of a title to the immortal inheritance" *(Patriarchs and Prophets,* pp. 168, 169). Let's not neglect our children. They are our first responsibility.

The Health Connection

The whole plan of salvation is designed to restore us to the condition of Adam before he sinned. The advertising expression "You've come a long way, baby!" was used to note the modern liberation of women which should allow them to smoke like men. And indeed we all have come a long way—a long way from God's original plan. We are so far removed that Adam would be shocked to see what people eat today. In different parts of the world the diet includes such things as dogs, cats, mice, rats, snakes, possum, pigs, snails, bugs—and the list could go on and on. Of course none of the items just listed were part of man's original diet and will not be eaten in heaven or in the new earth. "But," some say, "what difference does it make what I eat or do with my body anyway? And besides, whose business is it but mine?"

Just two weeks after the Seventh-day Adventist Church was organized in May of 1863, Ellen White was given her first major health vision on June 6. The stated purpose of the "health reform" was twofold. First, to provide the optimum health for God's people so they would have clear minds and enjoy "life more abundantly." This first reason also recognized that our bodies are the temple of God and we need to keep our bodies as a fit dwelling for God's Holy Spirit, the active agent in our restoration and sanctification. The second reason is to prepare our tastes to enjoy the food of heaven.

We have learned that "the body is the only medium through which the mind and the soul are developed for the upbuilding of character. Hence it is that the adversary of souls directs his temptations to the enfeebling and degrading of the physical powers" *(Ministry of Healing,* p. 130). How important then that we learn how our bodies function and what is best for them. In this way we will have clear minds and healthy bodies with which to battle with temptation.

So what can we do to preserve our health in the best possible condition? Realizing that an ounce of prevention is worth a pound of cure, we will really want a lifestyle that will help us stay healthy or restore health and prevent disease. Most of us have heard of the eight natural remedies. The more we include them in our lifestyle, the healthier we will be and the more prepared we will be to live in the atmosphere of heaven!

Here now is the prescription of the Great Physician: "Pure air, sunlight, abstemiousness [temperance], rest, exercise, proper diet, the use of water, trust in divine power—these are the true remedies. Every person should have a knowledge of nature's remedial agencies and how to apply them. . . . The use of natural remedies requires an amount of care and effort that many are not willing to give. . . . The surrender of hurtful indulgences requires sacrifice. But in the end it will be found that nature, untrammeled, does her work wisely and well. Those who persevere in obedience to her laws will reap the reward in health of body and health of mind" *(Ministry of Healing,* p. 127).

Man's Original Diet

The Creator gave Adam and Eve the ideal diet: "I give you every seed-bearing plant on the face of the whole earth and every tree that has fruit with seed in it. They will be yours for food" (Genesis 1:29, NIV). After the Fall, God added to their diet "the plants of the fields" (Genesis 3:18, NIV).

"Today's health problems tend to center on the degenerative type of diseases that are directly traceable to diet and lifestyle. The diet God planned, consisting of grains, fruits, nuts, and vegetables, offers the right nutritional ingredients to support optimum health. The Bible does not condemn the eating of clean animals. But God's original diet for man did not include flesh foods because He did not envision the taking of any animal's life and because a balanced vegetarian diet is the best for health—a fact for which science offers mounting evidence.

"Furthermore, studies conducted in recent years indicate that increased meat consumption can cause an increase of atherosclerosis, cancer, kidney disorders, osteoporosis, and trichinosis, and can decrease life expectancy.

"The diet God ordained in the Garden of Eden—the vegetarian diet—is the ideal, but sometimes we cannot have the ideal. In those circumstances, in any given situation or locale, those who wish to stay in optimum health will eat the best food that they can obtain" *(Seventh-day Adventists Believe,* pp. 284, 285).

The indulgence of appetite was the factor that caused Adam and Eve to sin. It was this very temptation that Satan first presented to Christ in the wilderness. Christ was successful on this point where Adam failed, and He offers us the power to have His victory. "Because man fallen could not overcome Satan with his human strength, Christ came from the royal courts of heaven to help him with His human and divine strength combined. . . . He obtained for the fallen sons and daughters of Adam that strength which it is impossible for them to gain for themselves, that in His name they might overcome the temptations of Satan" *(Confrontation,* p. 45).

By studying the Creation story, we can better understand the ideal diet for man. It stands to reason that the closer we get to that ideal the better off we will be. There is nothing legalistic about "health reform." It was given in the mercy of the Almighty—in an act of love. Now that we are in the end-times the need for better health and preparation for the ideal Creation diet in heaven finds us eager to learn about healthful living. "If ever there was a time when the diet should be of the most simple kind, it is now. . . . <u>Grains and fruits prepared free from grease, and in as natural a condition as possible, should be the food for the tables of all who claim to be preparing for translation to heaven.</u> . . . Gratification of taste should not be consulted irrespective of physical, intellectual, or moral health" *(Testimonies,* vol. 2, p. 352).

But what about eating clean meat? Doesn't the Bible make the distinction between clean and unclean so we will know which to eat and which to discard? Yes, it does. But those of us who have chosen the vegetarian diet have done so for the two reasons previously stated. We enjoy better health now and are preparing our taste buds to enjoy the food in heaven. If my idea of a banquet feast is a big steak with trimmings, I will surely be disappointed in heaven. McDonald's, Burger King, Wendy's, Arby's, and all their equivalents—if such could exist in heaven—will all be selling Garden Burgers exclusively! (Financial tip: buy stock in Garden Burgers now!) Seriously, we do have some very balanced counsel in this regard. It is simply to make it a goal for you and your family to move from flesh eating to vegetarianism.

"Among those who are waiting for the coming of the Lord, meat eating will eventually be done away; flesh will cease to form a part of their diet. We should ever keep this end in view, and endeavor to work steadily toward it. I cannot think that in the practice of flesh eating we are in harmony with the light which God has been pleased to give us. All who are connected with our health institutions especially should be educating themselves to subsist on fruits, grains, and vegetables. If we move from principle in these things, if we as Christian reformers educate our taste, and bring our diet to God's plan, then we may exert an influence upon others in this matter, **which will be pleasing to God**" *(Christian Temperance and Bible Hygiene,* p. 119).

It has been said that the children of Israel could have gone from Egypt to Canaan in about two weeks, but it took them 40 years. Why? Because they were walking backwards. They kept their eyes on the fleshpots of Egypt and disdained the angels' food God provided for them. (See Exodus 16:3 and Psalm 78:22-31.) It will be a real problem for many in the final days who have not made that gradual change to vegetarianism. "The reason why many of us will fall in the time of trouble is because of laxity in temperance and indulgence of appetite. Moses preached a great deal on this subject, and the reason the people did not go through to the promised land was because of repeated indulgence of appetite. Nine tenths of the wickedness among the children of today is caused by intemperance in eating and drinking. Adam and Eve lost Eden through the indulgence of appetite, and we can only regain it by the denial of the same" *(Temperance,* p. 150). Let's turn our backs on Egypt and keep our eyes on the banquet table in heaven.

"The controlling power of appetite will prove the ruin of thousands, when, if they had conquered on this point, they would have had moral power to gain the victory over every other temptation of Satan. But those who are slaves to appetite will fail in perfecting Christian character" *(Testimonies,* vol. 3, p. 492).

As folks prepare for translation, a change will be seen in their demeanor and attitudes. Of course, it will not be something that they boast about. In fact, they may not even feel that they are making any progress at all. But others will notice. Jesus said, "By this all will know that you are My disciples, if you have love for one another" (John 13:35). And John adds this insight, "If we love one another, God abides in us, and His love has been perfected in us" (1 John 4:12). Being loving and kind is not something that comes naturally to the unconverted person. When this characteristic is evident in the life of an individual, it is an indication to others of God's transforming power.

"Those who are sanctified through the truth will show that the truth has worked a reformation in their lives, that it is preparing them for translation into the heavenly world. . . . In the lives of those who are partakers of the divine nature there is a crucifixion of the haughty, self-sufficient spirit that leads to self-exaltation. In its place the Spirit of Christ abides, and in the life the fruits of the Spirit appear. Having the mind of Christ, His followers reveal the graces of His character" *(Lift Him Up,* p. 301).

Translation Preparation Is Not a Holy Flesh Movement

It seems that whenever God has outlined His plan for something in the future, the devil produces a counterfeit just beforehand. In early Adventism the devil tried to invade the church with fanaticism. It was called the holy flesh movement.

In 1898 and 1899 Elder S. S. Davis, conference evangelist in Indiana, developed and promulgated teachings that led to this movement. The basic features of this strange doctrine, which was called "the cleansing message," were that when Jesus passed through the Garden of Gethsemane He had an experience that all who follow Him must have. It was taught that Jesus had holy flesh, and that those who followed Him through this Garden experience would likewise have holy flesh. They were the "born" sons of God and they had "translation" faith. Having holy flesh like Christ, they could not experience corruption any more than He did; thus they would live to see Him come. This faith, it was claimed, was similar to that which led to the translation of Enoch and Elijah. Those who did not have this experience were "adopted" sons. They did not have translation faith; they must pass through the grave and thus go to heaven by "the underground railway."

Many members were eager to obtain the Garden experience, and strange things were happening in church meetings. "Attempting to gain this Garden experience that would give them holy flesh, the people gathered in meetings in which there were long prayers, strange, loud instrumental music, and excited, extended, hysterical preaching. Bass drums and tambourines aided in this. It was expected that one, possibly more, of their number would fall prostrate to the floor. He would then be carried to the platform, where a dozen or more people would gather around and shout, 'Glory to God!' while others prayed or sang. When this person regained consciousness, it was declared that he had passed through the Garden experience—he had holy flesh, he had translation faith" (Arthur L. White, *Ellen G. White Biography,* vol. 5, p. 101).

In late 1899 this movement swept through the Indiana Conference. The conference president, Elder R. S. Donnell, a major proponent of the movement, was joined by most of the ministers in Indiana. In their summer, 1900, camp meeting there were two visiting ministers from the General Conference, Elders S. N. Haskell and A. J. Breed. However, the conference president did not give these two General Conference brethren much opportunity to speak. He had warned his ministers that since these men had not had "this experience" they should not be allowed to be influenced by them. After Haskell's visit to this camp meeting he wrote the following to Ellen White in a letter dated September 25, 1900, giving his impressions of the camp meeting.

"To describe it, I hardly know what to say. It is beyond all description. I have never seen any company held with a firmer grasp by a certain number of leading ministers, than they are held in Indiana. Brother R. S. Donnell is president [Ellen White would have normally known who the conference presidents were, but she was just returning to the United States after having been gone for nearly 10 years to Australia], and they have an experience in getting the people ready for translation. They call it the 'cleansing message.' Others call it the 'holy flesh'; and when I say the 'cleansing message' and the 'holy flesh,' no doubt these terms will bring to your mind experiences that illustrate what we saw. . . .

"There is a great power that goes with the movement that is on foot there. It would almost bring anybody within its scope, if they are at all conscientious, and sit and listen with the least degree of favor, because of the music that is brought to play in the ceremony. They have an organ, one bass viol, three fiddles, two flutes, three tambourines, three horns, and a big bass drum, and perhaps other instruments which I have not mentioned. They are as much trained in their musical line as any Salvation Army choir that you have ever heard. In fact, their revival effort is simply a complete copy of the Salvation Army method, and when they get on a high key, you cannot hear a word from the congregation in their singing, nor hear anything, unless it be shrieks of those who are half insane. I do not think I overdraw it at all" *(ibid.,* p. 102).

This fanaticism had to be met head-on at the General Conference session of 1901. Ellen White chose to address it at the 5:30 a.m. worker's meeting on Wednesday, April 17. In the audience that morning were the Indiana Conference president, R. S. Donnell, and S. S. Davis, the minister who had led out in this teaching. In addition, due to the close proximity of Indiana to Battle Creek, many of the Indiana ministers were also present. Here are a few from the remarks that she read to the ministers:

"Instruction has been given me in regard to the late experience of brethren in Indiana and the teaching that they have given to the churches. Through this experience and teaching the enemy has been working to lead souls astray.

"The teaching given in regard to what is termed 'holy flesh' is an error. . . .

"I have been instructed to say to those in Indiana who are advocating strange doctrines, you are giving a wrong mold to the precious and important work of God. Keep within the bounds of the Bible. Take Christ's lessons, and repeat them again and again again. . . .

"Those who meet Christ in peace at His coming must in this life walk before Him in humility, meekness, and lowliness of mind. It becomes every human being to walk modestly and circumspectly before God, in harmony with the great testing truths He has given to the world.

"But the late experience of brethren in Indiana has not been in accordance with the Lord's instruction. . . .

"Again and again in the progress of our work, fanatical movements have arisen, and when the matter was presented before me,

I have had to bear a message similar to the message I am bearing to my brethren from Indiana. I have been instructed by the Lord that this movement in Indiana is of the same character as have been the movements in years past . . .

"The manner in which the meetings in Indiana have been carried on, with noise and confusion, does not commend them to thoughtful, intelligent minds. There is nothing in these demonstrations which will convince the world that we have the truth. Mere noise and shouting are no evidence of sanctification, or the descent of the Holy Spirit. Your wild demonstrations create only disgust in the minds of unbelievers" *(ibid.,* pp. 104-106).

Of course no one knew how the ministers from Indiana would respond to the direct testimony of Ellen White, but the very next day at the early morning workers' meeting, Elder Donnell stood to his feet and asked whether he might make a statement. It appears in the *General Conference Bulletin* for the 1901 session, p. 422:

"I feel unworthy to stand before this large assembly of my brethren this morning. Very early in life I was taught to reverence and to love the Word of God; and when reading in it how God used to talk to His people, correcting their wrongs, and guiding them in all their ways, when a mere boy I used to say: 'Why don't we have a prophet? Why doesn't God talk to us now as He used to do?'

"When I found this people, I was more than glad to know that there was a prophet among them, and from the first I have been a firm believer in, and a warm advocate of, the *Testimonies* and the Spirit of Prophecy. It has been suggested to me at times in the past, that the test on this point of faith comes when the testimony comes directly to us.

"Nearly all of you know, in the testimony of yesterday morning, the test came to me. But, brethren, I can thank God this morning that my faith in the Spirit of Prophecy remains unshaken. God has spoken. He says I was wrong, and I answer, God is right, and I am wrong. . . .

"I am very, very sorry that I have done that which would mar the cause of God, and lead anyone in the wrong way. I have asked God to forgive me, and I know that He has done it. As delegates and representatives of the cause of God in the earth, I now ask you to forgive me my sins, and I ask your prayers for strength and wisdom to walk aright in the future. It is my determination, by the help of God, to join hands with you in the kingdom of God."

And with this confession the holy flesh fanaticism was broken. Many said that the General Conference session was among our best meetings.

But now we are beginning to see similar things creeping into the evangelical circles and we have at times a desire to follow them. There has been the "Toronto Blessing" movement that sprang from the Vineyard movement. Now there has also been the "Pensacola [Florida] Blessing." In both cases physical manifestations of the spirit are expected and praised. In fact, they are encouraged and expected as a "genuine experience." And so as not to come behind, even some of our churches have attempted to manufacture a similar experience by loud music and singing, etc. One does not have to travel very far to find the same musical instruments described by Elder Haskell in his letter to Ellen White. Let us remember that God spoke to Elijah, who was later translated, in a still small voice and through his daily communion in prayer.

It should be very obvious to the reader that my research in preparation for this book did not uncover any of this "excitement and noise" business as part of the preparation for translation. In fact, just the opposite is true. Though as we near the end of time God's people will get together often to pray and study, the work of preparation is largely an individual matter. It involves time alone with God in the study of His Word and in earnest prayer. It involves joyfully obeying all the commandments of God and sharing the good news of the gospel with others. It is true that God's faithful will be leaving for their heavenly home soon, but not by following a misguided guru. Those who enter heaven will follow Jesus, the way, the truth and the life.

"We are pilgrims seeking a better country, a city whose Builder and Maker is God. Is our conversation in heaven? Are we preparing to receive the Majesty of heaven when He shall come with all His holy angels to raise the righteous dead and translate the righteous living to heaven? Satan will try to becloud our minds on this important subject. But we must so live that we can say as did Paul, 'I have fought a good fight, I have finished my course, I have kept the faith.' 2 Timothy 4:7" *(Manuscript Releases,* vol. 3, p. 92).

CHAPTER 19

All on the Altar

There are so many problems in the world—wars, bloodshed, crime, violence, natural disasters, uncertain economy, political corruption, and more. No wonder many individuals and families have come to the conclusion that it is imperative to look after number one. Many today take the position that you have to look out for yourself because no one else will.

So much thought and effort is expended in seeking security in these uncertain times. The toils of life do take a great amount of our time. With debts to pay, kids to raise, property to maintain, it just takes time. And of course we do need clothes to wear, food to eat, and a place to live. In His sermon on the mount Jesus addressed these very basic needs: clothing, food, and shelter. And then He says, "Your heavenly Father knows that you need all these things. But seek ye first the kingdom of God and His righteousness, and all these things shall be added to you" (Matthew 6:32, 33).

There's no place for our number one selfishness with Jesus—He demands the number one place in our lives. Jesus has asked us to put Him first, not because He is selfish, but for our own good. He knows that if we fail to trust Him at the basic levels of life, we can become distracted and eventually lost. In the parable of the soils, Jesus gives the reaction to the gospel seed by the different types of soil—wayside, rocky, thorny, and good ground. When the seed falls into the thorny ground the seeds are choked by the cares, riches, and pleasures of life and the seed cannot mature (see Luke 8:4-15). And when pointing out the need to prepare for His second coming, Jesus stated, "But take heed to yourselves, lest your hearts be weighed down with carousing, drunk-

242

enness, <u>and cares of this life</u>, and that Day come on you unexpectedly" (Luke 21:34).

No Halfway Christians

The parables and teachings of Jesus, the stories of Bible characters, and the counsel of the Spirit of Prophecy all indicate that there is no halfway commitment to Christ. You either are or you are not on the Lord's side. Just before his death, Joshua gathered the leaders of the tribes of Israel together and asked them to renew the covenant with God. After recounting the wonderful blessings of God and the many times He had delivered them, Joshua stated, "If it seems evil to you to serve the Lord, choose for yourselves this day whom you will serve, whether the gods which your fathers served that were on the other side of the River, or the gods of the Amorites, in whose land you dwell. <u>But as for me and my house, we will serve the Lord</u>" (Joshua 24:15).

We are part of the great controversy struggle. Spiritual warfare is a part of the Christian life. We are asked to put on the whole armor of God in Ephesians 6:10-17; and to fight the good fight of faith. When one is in an army he can be on only one side or the other. Being on two sides at once or pretending to be on one side and helping the other side is considered treason. Battles are lost that way and traitors are universally distrusted and subject to the maximum punishment.

Remember that little parable of the yeast or leaven. One either has the yeast in the heart or he doesn't. No one is halfway leavened. And the enmity factor is equally exclusive. We simply can't serve two masters. Either we will love the one and hate the other, or we will be loyal to one and despise the other. Jesus didn't say it was difficult to serve two masters. He said it couldn't be done—impossible.

One is either saved or lost depending on his response to the appeals of God. In the story of the wedding garment, one either has the garment on or he doesn't. There was no such thing as having it partway on, or just carrying it over the arm. It had to be worn. Just so with the robe of righteousness. It does not cost the wearer anything but the willingness to wear it. But it must be on! It is not given to cover evil but rather to replace it.

All on the Altar

When asked by a scribe which commandment was the greatest, Jesus answered, "You shall love the Lord your God with <u>all your heart</u>, with <u>all your soul</u>, with <u>all your mind</u>, and with <u>all your strength</u>" (Mark 12:30). When we give <u>all</u> to Christ, there is nothing left for another master. That's the way it is. That is the way it must be!

In the book *Early Writings,* Ellen White tells of being shown a view of the glories of heaven and the reward of the faithful. "Then my eyes," she said, "were taken from the glory, and I was pointed to the remnant on the earth. <u>The angel said to them,</u> 'Will you shun the seven last plagues? Will you go to glory and enjoy all that God has prepared for those who love Him and are willing to suffer for His sake? If so, ye must die that ye may live. <u>Get ready, get ready, get ready</u>. Ye must have a greater preparation than ye now have. For the day of the Lord cometh, cruel both with wrath and fierce anger, to lay the land desolate and to destroy the sinners thereof out of it. <u>Sacrifice all to God. Lay all upon His altar—self, property, and all, a living sacrifice</u>. **It will take all to enter glory.** Lay up for yourselves treasure in heaven, where no thief can approach or rust corrupt. Ye must be partakers of Christ's sufferings here if ye would be partakers with Him of His glory hereafter' " *(Early Writings, pp. 66, 67).*

Christ is ready to receive all who come to Him with a sincere heart. But we must make a full commitment. He is our only hope! He is our wisdom, our justification, our sanctification—our righteousness. The big question for each of us is: **"Are we willing to pay the price for eternal life?** <u>Are we ready to sit down and count the cost, whether heaven is worth such a sacrifice as to die to self and let our will be bent and fashioned into perfect conformity to the will of God</u>? Until this shall be, the transforming grace of God will not be experienced by us" *(In Heavenly Places, p. 155).*

Sometimes we may be tempted to ask, "Why is the way so narrow? Why do I have to give up so much?" But we just need to ask ourselves, "What did Christ give up for me?" This question puts everything that we might call self-denial in the shade. Nothing on this earth can be compared with what God has prepared for those who love Him. This will become ever more apparent as we study God's Word and read of His great sacrifice for us, and as we meditate on the descriptions of heaven and the new earth. Let us always remember that as Christians our citizenship is in heaven.

A Great Promise to All Who Make the Commitment

The devil would like us to believe that the sacrifice in becoming a Christian is too great. But the fact is "The way of the transgressor is hard. And the wages of sin is death."

One of the ways to spiritual growth is by sharing with others. When we unselfishly give of our time and resources to advance the kingdom of God many amazing promises of God will be fulfilled to us.

The following is one of my favorites: "Heavenly intelligences are waiting to co-operate with human instrumentalities, that they may reveal to the world what human beings may become, and what, through union with the Divine, may be accomplished for the saving of souls that are ready to perish. There is no limit to the usefulness of one who, putting self aside, makes room for the working of the Holy Spirit upon his heart and lives a life wholly consecrated to God. **All who consecrate body, soul, and spirit to His service will be constantly receiving a new endowment of physical, mental, and spiritual power.** The inexhaustible supplies of heaven are at their command. Christ gives them the breath of His own Spirit, the life of His own life. The Holy Spirit puts forth its highest energies to work in mind and heart. **Through the grace given us we may achieve victories that because of our own erroneous and preconceived opinions, our defects of character, our smallness of faith, have seemed impossible"** *(The Ministry of Healing,* p. 159).

Every promise in the Bible provides us with subject matter for prayer. We can claim these promises if we are willing to meet the conditions. Here is another simple and great promise: "If you are willing and obedient, you shall eat the good of the land" (Isaiah 1:19). It's time to settle our commitment to God. We know that's what we want. We now know that He will give us strength to endure and power for transformation.

I found an interesting statement that describes what happens to a person who is transformed by the power of God

"The transforming power of Christ's grace molds the one who gives himself to God's service. Imbued with the Spirit of the Redeemer,

[1] he is ready to deny self,

[2] ready to take up the cross,

[3] ready to make any sacrifice for the Master.

[4] No longer can he be indifferent to the souls perishing around him.

[5] He is lifted above self-serving.

[6] He has been created anew in Christ, and self-serving has no place in his life.

[7] He realizes that every part of his being belongs to Christ, who has redeemed him from the slavery of sin;

[8] [He realizes] that every moment of his future has been bought with the precious lifeblood of God's only-begotten Son" (*God's Amazing Grace,* p. 236).

All on the Altar Includes Our Treasures

When we put all on the altar it will necessarily include our possessions. The converted person loves to spend time studying God's Word. It will soon become very clear to that person that this earth is not our final home. Our citizenship is in heaven. In addition, we soon recognize that all our possessions really belong to God. "The earth is the Lord's and all its fullness, the world and those who dwell therein" (Psalm 24:1)

When King David had selected all the materials for the building of the Temple, he gathered the leaders of Israel together and had a praise service to God. The king and the people had worked together to provide all the materials necessary to build that magnificent building. But David didn't take any credit for this great effort. In his public prayer of thanksgiving David said, "Now therefore, our God, we thank You and praise Your glorious name. But who am I, and who are my people, that we should be able to offer so willingly as this? For all things come from You, and of Your own we have given You. For we are aliens and pilgrims before You, as were all our fathers; our days on earth are as a shadow, and without hope. O Lord our God, all this abundance that we have prepared to build You a house for Your holy name is from Your hand, and is all Your own" (1 Chronicles 29:13-16).

"Some think that only a portion of their means is the Lord's. When they have set apart a portion for religious and charitable purposes, they regard the remainder as their own, to be used as they see fit. But in this they mistake. All we possess is the Lord's, and we are accountable to Him for the use we make of it" *(Christ's Object Lessons,* p. 351). Does this mean that we must spend all our money and give all our possessions to forward the work of God? Not necessarily, but it does mean that we recognize who owns it and that after our needs are met we will give liberally to help others and to advance the cause of God. Frequently when individuals heard Ellen White speak on the topic of full surrender and faithful stewardship they would ask, "Just how much should we give to God?" Here is her general answer: "Some may inquire, 'Must we actually dispossess ourselves of everything which we call our own?' We may not be required to do this now; but we must be willing to do so for Christ's sake. We must acknowledge that our possessions are absolutely His, by using of them freely whenever means is needed to advance His cause" *(Testimonies for the Church,* vol. 4, p. 479).

What would happen if we actually practiced the principle of God's ownership? Well, first of all there would be plenty of money to carry on the work of God. But even beyond that the testimony of our lives would tell the world that we are really serious about our commitment to God. "The church is asleep as to the work it might do if it would give up all for Christ. **A true spirit of self-sacrifice would be an argument for the reality and power of the gospel which the world could not misunderstand or gainsay, and abundant blessings would be poured upon the church"** *(ibid.,* p. 484).

As the signs of the end continue to multiply, a change needs to take possession of God's true people. Instead of thinking only of ourselves, we will recognize that we can't take it with us; and so before the point where we can't buy or sell we should give all to advance the cause of God so that our possessions do not fall into the hands of those who are serving Satan.

"If we have given our hearts to Jesus, we also shall bring our gifts to Him. Our gold and silver, our most precious earthly possessions, our highest mental and spiritual endowments, will be freely devoted to Him who loved us, and gave Himself for us" *(The Desire of Ages,* p. 65).

The picture of liberality to God's cause at the end is amazing, but it must happen so that not much of our "stuff" gets burned up at the end. "In the last extremity, before this work shall close, thousands will be cheerfully laid upon the altar. Men and women will feel it a blessed privilege to share in the work of preparing souls to stand in the great day of God, <u>and they will give hundreds as readily as dollars are given now</u>" *(Counsels on Stewardship,* p. 40).

The devil recognizes that where our treasure is there will our heart be also. He uses two motivations to encourage us to spend our money on ourselves: selfishness and fear of the future. And, of course, he has been quite successful with his plan. But in the end the selfish and the fearful will not only lose their money but also their eternal life. "As the people of God approach the perils of the last days, Satan holds earnest consultation with his angels as to the most successful plan of over-throwing their faith. . . . Says the great deceiver: . . . 'Go, make the pos-sessors of lands and money drunk with the cares of this life. Present the world before them in its most attractive light, that they may lay up their treasure here and fix their affections upon earthly things. . . . Make them care more for money than for the upbuilding of Christ's kingdom and the spread of the truths we hate, and we need not fear their influ-ence; <u>for we know that every selfish, covetous person will fall under our power, and will finally be separated from God's people</u>'" *(Testimonies to Ministers,* pp. 472-474).

Nothing on this earth is worth trading for eternal life. Let's make a commitment to be faithful with our tithes and generous offerings so that our affections will be on things above.

A Personal Appeal

What should be our response if we see someone we love drifting away from Christ through attention to the cares of this life, some mis-understanding at church, or some other problem? Shouldn't we feel some concern? We are in fact our brother's keeper. The story of Frank Belden demonstrates the concern we should have for others. Frank Belden, a nephew of Ellen White's, was a worker at the publishing house and a songwriter. He was one of the musical editors of the early Adventist hymnal, *Hymns and Tunes,* that was published in 1886. Later he was a superintendent at the Review and Herald publishing house. He wrote hundreds of Sabbath school songs and hymns; in most cases both the words and music. Many of his songs have been in sub-sequent Adventist hymnals.

Near the turn of the century Frank Belden entered into certain business dealings relating to the publication of his music. Though from what I have gleaned from church history and Ellen White's letter which follows, he was treated fairly but felt somehow that he was not. This supposed grievance led to his separation from the church about 1907. He lived until 1945. Apparently, Ellen White perceived that he was losing his way spiritually long before the business grievance and his separation from the church, because she wrote to him and his wife in 1893 from New Zealand. It was quite a lengthy letter. I will just quote some key sentences. I quote:

B-9-1893

Banks Terrace, Wellington, New Zealand

Mr. and Mrs. Frank Belden,

Dear Nephew and Niece,

I have read your letter with deep interest hoping to catch the vibration of the right ring in it; but if it is there I do not discern it. I am concerned in regard to your spiritual condition. For several years you have not been walking in the light. I have had much concern for you, but when I learned by experience my words had not much weight with you I felt sorry indeed, but could do nothing to change the course of things. . . .

Our God will not be trifled with. I entreat of you for your souls' sake to waste no time. You have been lukewarm long enough. . . .

If you will resolve now to be wholehearted and unselfish, and persevering in your Lord's service, and will act with an eye single to His glory, discharging every duty, and improving every gracious opportunity then you will unlearn some lessons you have been learning the past few years, and will come into the school of Christ and learn of Jesus, and will if a diligent student realize a transformation of character, and receive Christ's mold upon you, and become complete in Christ Jesus. You will be a partaker of the divine nature, having escaped the corruption that is in the world through lust.

Should accidental death surprise you I fear greatly for your future. I could not say it is well with Frank for he sleeps in Jesus; but I should greatly fear that you would in that great day be weighed in the balance and found wanting. <u>You had better lose everything on earth than heaven</u>. . . . Be ready to sacrifice anything and everything rather than the favor of God. Cultivate love and affection for religious devotion. Better far give up earth than heaven. . . .

You must be renewed, transformed, converted, and your whole life should be ordered and fashioned after the likeness of Christ. God has given you capabilities, and talents to use wholly to His glory. God will not accept a divided half and half service. . . .

I press it home to your soul; you have no time to lose. It is life or death with you. Your Aunt Ellen loves your soul too well to gloss over your present condition. God has a work for you to do, and you can do it if you are truly and genuinely converted. . . .

God help you and Hattie that you will not turn away as you have done from His testimony given to you; but walk in the light. Put on the robe of Christ's righteousness. Prepare for heaven by yielding your soul, body and spirit to God. Jesus has bought you with a price, God loves you both, and I am constrained by the love I have for Jesus and your souls to warn you to make no delay. Seek God day and night till you find Him to the joy of your souls. . . . [She closed the letter with this appeal.]

And when He came near He beheld the city and wept over it, saying, 'O that thou hadst known even thou in this thy day, the things that belong unto thy peace! But now they are hid from thine eyes.' Why did not that guilty nation know? Because they could not? No! Because ye would not. 'O Jerusalem, Jerusalem, which killest the prophets, and stonest them that are sent unto thee; how often would I have gathered thy children together, as a hen gathers her brood under her wings, (and ye could not, no,) and ye would not!

In much love, Aunt Ellen G. White

Christian Commitment

Within the past few months the following statement of commitment has come across my desk from two different sources. Neither knew the name of the author. Whether he wrote them or not, these had become the sentiments of a brave young Christian pastor who was martyred for his faith in Zimbabwe, Africa. It summarizes well for all of us what it means to lay all on the altar.

"I am a part of the fellowship of the unashamed. I have the Holy Spirit power. The die has been cast. I have stepped over the line. The decision has been made. I'm a disciple of His. I won't look back, let up, slow down, back away, or be still.

"My past is redeemed, my presence makes sense, my future is secure. I'm finished with low living, sight walking, small planning, smooth knees, colorless dreams, tamed visions, worldly talking, cheap giving and dwarfed goals.

"I no longer need preeminence, prosperity, position, promotions, plaudits or popularity. I don't have to be right, first, tops, recognized, praised, regarded or rewarded. I now live by faith, lean on His presence, walk by patience, am uplifted by prayer, and I labor with power.

"My face is set, my gait is fast, my goal is heaven, my road is narrow, my way rough, my companions few, my guide reliable, my mission clear. I cannot be bought, compromised, detoured, lured away, turned back, deluded or delayed. I will not flinch in the face of sacrifice, hesitate in the presence of the adversary, negotiate at the table of the enemy, ponder at the pool of popularity, or meander in the maze of mediocrity.

"I won't give up, shut up or let up, until I have stayed up, stored up, prayed up, paid up and preached up for the cause of Christ. I am a disciple of Jesus. I must go till He comes, give till I drop, preach till all know, and work till He stops me.

"And when He comes for His own, He will have no problem recognizing me—my banner will be clear!"

Paul expressed similar sentiments to the Philippians: "But one thing I do, forgetting those things which are behind and reaching forward to those things which are ahead, I press toward the goal for the prize of the upward call of God in Christ Jesus" (Philippians 3:13, 14).

Our Certain Future

When Jesus left this earth after His earthly ministry the Bible says, "While they watched, He was taken up, and a cloud received Him out of their sight. And while they looked steadfastly toward heaven as He went up, behold, two men stood by them in white apparel, who also said, 'Men of Galilee, why do you stand gazing up into heaven? This same Jesus, who was taken up from you into heaven, will so come in like manner as you saw Him go into heaven'" (Acts 1:10, 11).

Yes, "Christ is coming with clouds and with great glory. A multitude of shining angels will attend Him. He will come to raise the dead, and to change the living saints from glory to glory. He will come to honor those who have loved Him, and kept His commandments, and to take them to Himself. He has not forgotten them nor His promise. There will be a relinking of the family chain. When we look upon our dead, we may think of the morning when the trump of God shall sound, when 'the dead shall be raised incorruptible, and we shall be changed.' 1 Corinthians 15:52. A little longer, and we shall see the King in His beauty. A little longer, and He will wipe all tears from our eyes. A little longer, and He will present us 'faultless before the presence of His glory with exceeding joy.' Jude 24. Wherefore, when He gave the signs of His coming He said, 'When these things begin to come to pass, then look up, and lift up your heads; for your redemption draweth nigh'" *(The Desire of Ages,* p. 632).